Centering the Margin

Asian Anthropologies
General Editors:
Shinji Yamashita, The University of Tokyo
J.S. Eades, Ritsumeikan Asia Pacific University

CENTERING THE MARGIN

Agency and Narrative in Southeast Asian Borderlands

Edited by
Alexander Horstmann and Reed L. Wadley

Berghahn Books
New York • Oxford

First published in 2006 by
Berghahn Books
www.berghahnbooks.com

©2006, 2009 Alexander Horstmann and Reed L. Wadley
First paperback edition published in 2009

Library of Congress Cataloging-in-Publication Data
Centering the margin : agency and narrative in Southeast Asian borderlands /
edited by Alexander Horstmann and Reed L. Wadley
p. cm.—(Asian anthropologies ; v. 5)
Chiefly papers presented in a two-session panel organized for the Third
International Convention for Asian Scholars (ICAS) in Singapore, Aug.
19-22, 2003.
Includes bibliographical references and index.
ISBN 978-1-84545-019-9 hardback -- ISBN 978-1-84545-591-0 paperback
1. Nomads—Southeast Asia. 2. Ethnicity—Southeast Asia. 3. Minorities—
Southeast Asia. 4. Demographic anthropology—Southeast Asia.
5. Transnationalism. 6. Ethnic barrier—Southeast Asia. 7. Southeast
Asi—Boundaries. 8. Southeast Asia—Ethnic relations. 9. Southeast
Asia—Emigration and immigration. I. Horstmann, Alexander. II.
Wadley, Reed L. III. International Convention for Asian Scholars (3rd:
2003: Singapore) IV. Series.

GN635.S58C46 2006
305.9'069180959—dc22   2006040107

British Library Cataloguing in Publication Data

A catalogue record for this book is available from the British Library
Printed in the United States on acid-free paper

ISBN 978-1-84545-019-9 hardback
ISBN 978-1-84545-591-0 paperback

CONTENTS

Preface

ALTHOUGH THE CONCEPTS OF BORDERLANDS and border crossing have grown in popularity in recent years, the contributors to this volume feel that many of the borderlands in Southeast Asia remain virtually unknown. We thus set out in the footsteps of Edmund Leach, Gehan Wijeyewardene, and Thongchai Winichakul—scholars who have paved the way for a renewed focus on the nation-state from the perspective of the border. This focus is less on the international border per se, than on the people who live in the borderland, negotiate border crossings in their local activities, and extend the borderland into central spaces through their movements. The chapters here explore how people at the border form translocal and transnational spaces and moral communities, sometimes bleeding through violence and exploitation, sometimes putting international frontiers to their advantage.

This volume brings together anthropologists and historians from the U.S.A., Europe, Australia, Thailand, and Indonesia who work on the borderlands of Southeast Asia. Most of the papers were presented in a two-session panel organized by Alexander Horstmann for the Third International Convention for Asian Scholars (ICAS) in Singapore, 19–22 August 2003. As part of a wider academic network, we hope to promote further initiatives on Southeast Asian borderlands through this volume.

Since the beginning of this endeavor, the vocabulary of borders and borderlands has continued to penetrate conferences and workshops around the world. We hope that these too will encourage sound, empirical work on borderlands, which may help us recognize the crucial depth that the borderland concept lends to our questioning of cultural baggage in Southeast Asian area studies: We have perhaps been too accustomed to think in terms of the nation-state and lately transnationalism, to the exclusion of the spaces created by the borders.

As it has wound its way to publication, the volume has benefited from the help of a number of people as have its editors. Hearty thanks are due to the Asian Anthropologies series editors, Shinji Yamaschita (Tokyo) and especially Jeremy Eades (Kent, UK/Beppo, Japan), for accepting the volume in their series and for encouraging us throughout. Thanks are also extended to Marion Berghahn for her personal and perceptive support, and to Christopher Duncan for the use of his excellent map of Southeast Asia.

FIGURES AND TABLES

Figures

Tables

INTRODUCTION:
CENTERING THE MARGIN IN SOUTHEAST ASIA

Alexander Horstmann and Reed L. Wadley

New Horizons in Southeast Asian Anthropology

ALTHOUGH BORDERS AND BORDER CROSSING are by now familiar terms in anthropology, few ethnographic projects take up the crucial development of research questions. This volume on agency and narrative in the borderlands of Southeast Asia is a first attempt in doing just that, by bringing together the imminent work of borderland studies through a comparative framework. In a reversal of perspective, the focus of this collection is on the experiences of border people with the state, at the local level of state borders (e.g., Tokoro 1999). Borders are matrixes of social and cultural change, dynamic in identity and space, in contrast to essentialized tradition and community on the state border. This collection aims to illuminate some of this agency and challenge the peripheral identities that are assumed in the national community.

Although it is a relatively recent focus of study, anthropologists increasingly recognize the national border region as an arena of social and cultural change. There is no place where the contradictions inherent in bounded collectivities and their representations could be more pronounced. In fact, the very notion of the state border or boundary has historically been a driver of ethnogenesis—the production and invention of ethnic groups and minorities (e.g., Nugent and Asiwaju 1996).

While permeable and ambiguous national borders can be said to play a crucial role in Anderson's (1983) work on the imagined community of the modern nation, as well as in Thongchai's (1994) groundbreaking study on the emergence of a hierarchical ethnogeography of modern Siam, it is astonishing how little attention has been given so far to the agency of bor-

Endnotes for this chapter begin on page 21.

der people in Southeast Asia. There are thus good reasons why the study of borders in Southeast Asia and their borderlands is timely. For example, Thongchai shows that the formation of the territorial Thai geo-body implies, from the very beginning, a hierarchical relationship of the national center and the Other, not only in terms of class and status, but in terms of an ethnogeography as well (see Vandergeest and Peluso 1995).

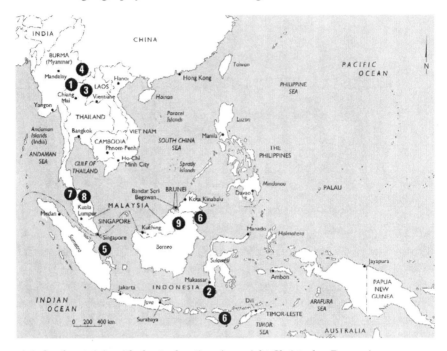

A.1. Southeast Asia with chapter locations (copyright Christopher Duncan).

To be sure, many scholars have written ethnographies on the transformation of ethnic minorities' livelihoods on the borders. No ethnographic collection can afford to ignore the pioneering role of Edmund Ronald Leach in deconstructing the notion of national borders and in his seminal emphasis on the dynamism of social space through group exchange (Leach 1954, 1960). This collection comes very much in the spirit of Leach, in that it highlights the reconceptualization of communities at the border through movement and identification.

On the one hand, as Tapp (2000) remarks (not without self-criticism), scholars of ethnic minorities tend to essentialize the identities of "their" study populations and underplay the relationships with powerful ethnic majorities. Yet, on the other hand, anthropologists and geographers have increasingly challenged the way we view the state's political organization and its compartmentalization of the world. Newman and Paasi (1998) argue, for example, that boundaries and their meanings are historically contingent, that they are part of the production and institutionalization of territories. Study of borderlands should thus pay attention to boundary-producing practices and to narratives of inclusion and exclusion.

These ideas about boundaries and territoriality are particularly important in the contemporary world, where social groups aim continually to define and redefine the relations between social and physical space. People on the fringe of the nation-state—by their very existence—question its monopoly of identification and help to transform concepts of nationalism that are otherwise taken for granted. Their routine practices of crossing international borders have important implications for our understanding of spatial and social organization of society and culture. In this way, the everyday life of borderland communities shakes some of our basic assumptions in social-cultural anthropology that are unconsciously bound to a spatial system characterized by more or less exclusive state boundaries. In particular, a focus on the intensification of border crossing practices overcomes the conceptual straightjacket of the nation-state. But we must be cautious in proclaiming, not without some satisfaction, that borderlander agency necessarily undermines and undercuts the state and its attempts at spatial hegemony (e.g., Adler 2004: 73). Agency moves equally between "resistance" and accommodation, and it may just as easily reaffirm and strengthen state legitimacy (Wadley 2003).

In this review essay, we aim to discuss a coherent concept of border, borderlands, and frontier, and to identify what it is that the research questions and agendas of separate border studies have in common. We review studies of border crossings in Southeast Asia in a comparative scheme, offering a more systematic approach to what are now individual and scattered studies in the region. We aim to decipher common research questions and emerging paradigms on which middle range theoretical structures can be built, thereby justifying an anthropology of borders in Southeast Asia.[1] Finally, we propose a research agenda with profound implications for the study of social and cultural change in Southeast Asia, such that border crossings may bring us more dynamic concepts of nation-state, identity, and community. We argue that future research lies in a project of marginal history, centered on the agency of transnational communities and on the ways in which these communities give meaning and shape to marginal spaces and effect their transformations. This necessarily implicates the historical dimension, especially that of oral history, in the study of border people as borders undergo proliferation, decline, and renewal.

Frontiers of Nation and State

Newman and Paasi argue, in their persuasive survey of boundary narratives in political geography, that boundaries and borders were initially conceived as being no more than lines separating sovereign territories, while frontiers were assumed to constitute the area in proximity to the border, the internal development of which was effected by the line's existence (Newman and Paasi 1998). Borderlands represent the state margin, magnifying both interethnic relations and the explosion of identity politics in Southeast Asian countries. For example, Rajah (1990) discusses definitions of the state, invented identity, and imagined community in relation to national boundaries in mainland Southeast Asia. He argues that precolonial and postcolonial states may coexist at the Thai-Burmese border, and that Karen separatists, in controlling the means of ethnic identification (i.e., the schools), form their own imagined, postcolonial state along the Burmese frontier.

On the basis of his material, Rajah (1990) argues that there are clearly important issues in the study of ethnogenesis across national boundaries, but their substance is obscured by the fact that we, as Wijeyewardene (1989) has cautioned, tend to think in nation-state terms. Rajah develops a framework in which anthropology is to devote more attention than hitherto to the relationship between ethnic boundaries, national boundaries, and the state. In Rajah's opinion, it may be more appropriate to say that there exist both a Thai border and a Burmese-Karen frontier region, and that the Karen separatist movement—and even the Burmese state—may be viewed as a kind of traditional state (Rajah ibid.: 122).

The unquestioned and unquestionable nature of the nation-state has come to dominate much contemporary thinking and social science discourse (see Benjamin, 1988, and Rajah, ibid.), provokes fundamental debates on the use of colonial knowledge: Western anthropological discourse (and, indeed, the discourse of the state) on ethnic minorities as primitive, tribal, or stateless should be abandoned. Moving the frontier to the center stage, the state can be liberated from its mystical or quasisacred character and, in a postcolonial perspective, be deconstructed into its various parts. For example, the Karen nationalist movement in Burma is a political organization, controlling the hilly area along the border (territory), the illegal border trade (economy), and the means of identification (education) with the Karen "nation-state" (military headquarters). The Karen movement in Burma operates from the Thai-Burmese border because of the border, which offers retreat for bases and refugees. Rajah (122) writes: "the notion of a border between existing states is intrinsic to the application of ideas about a common culture, language, and social and political organization, and their associated discontinuities." The incapacity of the modern state to maintain its boundaries provides an excellent reason to question the bases of the ideological baggage on which the modern nation-state is based—land, population, and the means of identification. Yet, paradoxically, the ability of borderlanders to shift from one side to the other—to accommodate the demands of one state and/or the other—reinforces the legitimacy of the state.

Active Borderlands

It is not surprising that the concept of transnationalism, currently a central element in many interpretations of global society, looks to the international border as one of its principal referents. But relatively little attention has been paid to the agent's negotiation of border crossing and the power of the state on the physical geography of borderlands. The concept of transnational social spaces suggests that the durable and regular networks of international migrants bring about a transnationalization of time and space (Pries 2000). Here, the nation-state seems to impinge less and less on the lives of international migrants. This perspective is belied, however, by the evidence that migrants are being subjected to tighter immigration laws and suppression that push a great number of them into illegal status, undermining their exercise of basic human rights and political participation.

The negotiations between populations and state are particularly intense in the borderlands of Southeast Asia, and thus we argue that this interaction should be an important focus of research. Following Donnan and Wilson (1998, 1999), not only are the borderlands symbols and locations of social and cultural change in Southeast Asia, they may often be their agents as well. Border crossing populations lie at the heart of current transformations in sovereignty, national identity, and citizenship. Indeed, we contend that anthropology of borderlands in Southeast Asia may serve in reexamining some of our key vocabulary in social sciences.

While many studies propagate this trend, few are grounded in solid empirical fieldwork. This may be because research on ethnic minorities in Southeast Asia tends not take the border and its conceptual impact into full account. In the same vein, most studies limit themselves to one country, largely ignoring the practice of border crossing and the transnationalization of social space that may involve two or more countries and may, through multiple networks and cultural contact over wide geographical distances, extend to pluri-local spaces, sometimes spanning continents. It is crucial to note that there are two sorts of narratives of the borders—one by the state, and one by the populations that inhabit the borders. The anthropology of borders is interested, by and large, in the narrative of borderlanders, though that of the state must necessarily inform our study as it impinges on borderlander narratives.

As Baud and van Schendel (1997) indicate in their review of the history of borderlands, while much has been written on how states deal with their borderlands, historians have paid much less attention to how borderlands have dealt with their states. We follow them in eschewing the view from the (state) center in favor of a new perspective from the borders and their populations themselves (Baud and van Schendel 1997: 212). Such efforts seek to redress the imbalance of state-centered studies, to discover which social forces originate in borderlands and what effects these have had, both locally and beyond. Borderlands in recent scholarship are at the center of study; such a focus is a productive way to generate meaningful comparisons with other borders and states, in an effort to develop equivalent descriptive categories and workable theories.

Thus, Baud and van Schendel (1997) suggest that we should view borderlands as social and cultural systems that transcend state boundaries (also Alvarez 1995), and play an active role in the construction of their states. We must thus place borderlands in their spatial and temporal contexts in order to investigate the relations between territory, identity, and sovereignty. The impact of a particular transformative moment in world history ("world time") on borderland social change must be related to the development of the states concerned ("state time"), as well as to the life cycle stages in which individual borderlands find themselves ("borderland time") (see, e.g., Martinez 1994).

While the supposed unity of community and nationhood assumes shared bonds in time and space, those assumptions, supported by law as well as convention, are out of touch in a setting of multiple disjunctions and disunities—the separate spaces and times that structure experience in border crossing networks (Shapiro and Hayward 1996). Modern communication technologies may overwhelm the (imagined) stable time and space to which nation-centered citizenship has been attached, and the lives of people's borderland may thus be freed from the imagined unities of national solidarity through an increasing attachment to global culture.

Reproduction and the Myth of Nationalism

The hegemonic national cultures of the postcolonial state in Southeast Asia have been experienced as a nightmare by the borderland ethnic minorities who have been doubly marginalized or "folklorized" in the space of the nation-state and constructed as inferior races. Yet, for both borderlanders and the hegemons, the border becomes a central place where land, population, and identification are most contested. As Donnan and Wilson (1999) caution, now that "border" concepts are in danger of being everywhere and in everything (Alvarez 1995), we must be careful not to unduly privilege state borders to the exclusion of equally important and often overlapping internal boundaries and marginalities (Cummings, this volume). But nonetheless the border plays a special role in the origin and development of states precisely because of its geographical location, setting border zones apart from the often more homogenous, developed, and powerful zones in the center. Borders are markers of statehood—the political membranes through which people, goods, wealth, and information must pass in order for the state to deem them legitimate or illegitimate. Yet, as we are beginning to see, borderlands reach into central state space.

As argued at the beginning of this essay, frontiers and borderlands are complex social systems that question the nature of the state. In Southeast Asia, perhaps with the exception of Singapore, the state's sovereignty in border regions may be marginal and sometimes even abandoned. In fact, the border is not definitive, and cultural borders between communities reach much further into the "geo-body" of the nation, or beyond its territorial limitations.

The special character of local borderland cultures deserves elaboration in our research. In Southeast Asia, often the most vulnerable local minorities are found in border regions, and in those remote corners the politics of homogenization play out in terms of language, religion, and way of life. Border regions have developed highly specific cultures, with things as they are *because of the border*. Thus, for example, in the context of economic expansion, border towns boom and grow rapidly. In addition to local fare, one finds the goods of border trade (e.g., gems, drugs, and teak from Burma; consumer items from Thailand). Huge sums of money are created in illegal trade at the borders, and political forces (e.g., the Thai military) benefit from the border and its political ecology. The economic sectors of border regions (e.g., fisheries and plantations) greatly depend on migrant labor from neighboring countries.

Donnan and Wilson (1998, 1999) conceptualize borders in relation to the nation, including the ways in which borders are enhanced or diminish. Going further, we suggest that border peoples have their own local perceptions of the border, and that at the beginning of the twenty-first century, the borderlands are not limited to the state borderline but reach into its central spaces. Thus, migrants who arrive in Ranong, a province at the southern end of the Thai-Burmese border, continue to look for jobs in Songkhla, Bangkok, and Malaysia, and thereby extend the borderland to the center, often to multiple centers.

Rather than assigning a definitive character to border landscapes in Southeast Asia, the empirical assumption underlying our research is the border's inherent ambiguity. Many borders exist only on the map. For example, traders in Borneo upset the authorities by dismantling border markers, thereby underscoring the fuzziness and ambiguity at the edge of the postcolonial nation. Likewise, border identities in southern Thailand have entered a stage in which the boundaries between Thai and Malay identity are increasingly blurred. In these places, where identity and culture are vague and shifting, local powers and social forces negotiate national intimacy, which may either fragment or become reinforced.

In a transnational world, border crossing affects the everyday lives of border people as they shuttle between two or more countries. On such a global stage, border crossing and its manifold networks engender numerous encounters and affiliations that cannot be grasped within the framework of the nation-state. Even in Singapore, though it tries hard, the state is unable to control ethnic and religious networks that reach beyond its shores. National identity, however, does not become meaningless.

Horstmann (2004, chap. 7) shows how transnational Buddhist networks and pilgrimage routes that link Thailand with Kedah (Malaysia) are reviving "blood ties" between the Thai "heartland" and the Thai partitioned minority in Malaysia, thereby strengthening Thai nationalism in daily practice. Conversely, in the proliferation of durable and regular transnational social spaces tying Malaysia, Indonesia, and the Middle East together, Pattani Muslims of southern Thailand are creating their own moral communities, effectively crosscutting the political and cultural boundaries of the nation.

Reducing the analysis of borders to nation and state borders risks overlooking other worlds of reference apart from the state. In his *The Peasant Robbers of Kedah 1900–1929,* Cheah Boon Kheng (1988) shows that rural crime in Kedah, while of much concern to the colonial state, operated largely outside of it. Many of the most notorious gang leaders were so-called Sam-Sam (meaning half-blood), Thai-speaking Muslims who played on, and made use of, the ambiguity of their identity between the Thai and Malay worlds. Clearly, the colonial and postcolonial state, mistrusting the loyalty of ethnic minorities on the edge of the state, has been involved in gigantic operations of development, and sometimes state terrorism, in order to transform uncertain borderlands into national landscapes. Most of these projects have failed. Following Herzfeld (1997) as scholars of borderlands, we are interested in exploring just how new national emotions are constructed in the growing encounters with alien worlds, as they increasingly intrude upon state hegemonic landscapes.

The Social and Spatial Organization of Ethnic Minorities

The border subjects partitioned ethnic minorities to varying levels of incorporation into the state. Southeast Asia holds manifold stories of state formation and expansion, nationalism and cultural imperialism, so a study of its borderlands concerns various geographies of incorporation. Local, national, and international levels merge and intersect at the frontier (see Bryant 1997), rendering marginal ethnic minorities in the border areas increasingly vulnerable to manipulation and exploitation by central authorities. Tapp (2000: 351ff.) draws our attention to the discourse of the state that classifies much of human movement and trade as "illicit": trade becomes "smuggling," and human mobility, "illegal immigration" and "refugee movement." From another viewpoint, Horstmann (2001, 2002) contends that the state produces certain categories of people—citizens and noncitizens. At the same time, ethnic minorities partitioned by borders are constructed as peripheral identities trapped in the space of the nation-state. Over the course of the eighteenth and nineteenth centuries, colonial interests shifted from maintenance of favorable trade zones along the coasts and rivers to an increasing control of territory and its human populations. During this time, many territorial boundaries were established as European colonial powers vied among themselves for influence. The formation of the border is a crucial step of the colonial state's ambition to establish control over people and territory in the occupied land and force them to produce revenues for the colonial masters. Meanwhile, the local perception of the border bears little resemblance to the vision of the colonial state.

Wadley (2000a, 2001, 2003, 2004) and Ishikawa (2001) make use of colonial archives to highlight the interaction of local people and colonial powers on the island of Borneo. Wadley (2001) shows how the Iban in the West Borneo borderlands frustrated many of the efforts by the British Brooke regime and the Dutch colonial state to define and demarcate state borders. The Iban defied both colonial powers in their refusal to end their headhunting practices, pay imposed taxes, or seek permission to move across the border. From the colonial perspective, the border was designed to restrict trade and movement of people across the intercolonial border and to promote legitimate activities like taxation, road construction, and resource extraction. The efforts to extend the colonial influence over the border culminated in numerous punitive expeditions against the Iban living on both sides of the border (Wadley 2004). The Iban for their part made regular use of the border to evade taxes, escape punishment from one state or the other, and headhunt. Evasion and flight were among the most efficient strategies of everyday resistance used by the Iban to counter colonial claims over their lives.

Likewise, Ishikawa (2001) focuses on border controls and other disciplinary mechanisms that aimed to incorporate local people in southwestern Sarawak, adjacent to Dutch Borneo, into nation-state space. The Brooke regime sought to control movements of mobile people across the border. Further, the government defined the national affiliation of colonial subjects through naturalization and regulation of marriage. Local people thwarted the ambitions of the Brooke regime via smuggling, migration, "transnational bigamy," and strategic naturalization. Perhaps it is possible to go even further than Ishikawa does: As the manifold disciplinary mechanisms were defied by local people, the vision of the colonial regime could not be realized, and the colonial government did not have the means to enforce its borders in time and in space. But lest we become too overjoyed with the frustration of the colonial powers, it is instructive to consider that resistance is only one side of the coin in dealing with imposed government. The other side is accommodation (Wadley 2003). Indeed, for every tax evader, smuggler, and outlaw, there are numerous others who pay their taxes and perform as good subjects should. A good deal of the time, the good citizen and the outlaw are one and the same, sometimes at different times, sometimes simultaneously.

Border Crossing and Migration

Migration has played a decisive role in shaping society and culture in Southeast Asia. Migration arrests our attention because it puts the border into question and challenges the nature of a seemingly established system (i.e., the nation). Migrants play a decisive role in the construction of communities, states, and their boundaries. In the era of the passport, island "hopping" among seafaring communities becomes illicit movement, and the politics of citizenship and identity come full circle. Traditional boat nomadism is everywhere disappearing from maritime Southeast Asia, but Sather (1997) reports that it has taken on a new meaning for the Sama refugees from Sibutu and Tawittawi in the southern Philippines, and for the dispossessed of Sulu. Most have returned to their boats in order to escape civil war, violence, declining fish stocks, and the destruction of coral.[2]

Horstmann (2001, chap. 7) looks at the social networks that are emerging in the context of intensified border crossings at the Thai-Malaysian border. One of his most significant findings is that borderland ethnic minorities are reworking centrist state concepts to their own advantage. The local reworking of citizenship is part of the struggle that ensures when the state sets important constraints on human movement. For example, the state issues border passes to the inhabitants of its border provinces in order to control movement, but Muslims in southern Thailand make use of kinship relations and religious networks to get citizenship rights in Malaysia. Thus, multiple citizenships and the organization of everyday life, work, and Islamic education in Thailand and Malaysia are part of the response to the tightening immigration regime in Malaysia and to the restrictions implemented by both the Thai and Malaysian governments.

Ishikawa (2001) details similar local resistance to restrictions implemented by the colonial regime in Sarawak. The Brooke government introduced various methods to control cross-border movements of migrants from Dutch Borneo to Sawarak, among them indentured Chinese laborers, maritime Malays, and Dayak swidden cultivators. The government further sought to define the national affiliation of its subjects through naturalization and marriage regulations. Local people responded through such activities as commodity smuggling and strategic naturalization.

Border crossing has led to new geographies of social and economic inequality. Brokers emerge in the border areas to profit the very precarious status of illegal migrants. Sather (1997) and Horstmann (2001) describe how brokers in Sabah and Langkawi recruit "kin" from neighboring Sulu and southern Thailand and establish relationships of bonded labor. In these exploitative relations, the refugees or illegal immigrants are expected to provide unpaid labor to their patrons or to pay them in kind. This illustrates how much state borders can affect the lives of ethnic minorities on the margins of the state. It also shows that the nature of kinship relations has changed. In fact, borders may have fundamentally altered cultures of relatedness, a topic that deserves much more attention. In the context of exploitative relations, kin can be invented and documents falsified. Illegal migrants from southern Thailand or the Sulu Sea may depend on traditional kin obligations for help, but less recent migrants with citizenship may distinguish themselves from new migrants without citizenship, suggesting limits to moral claims.

This negotiation between established residents and outsiders, between citizens and immigrants in border provinces, highlights the border crossing and migration that are rapidly changing the landscapes of Southeast Asia, with Thailand and Malaysia having emerged as the main migrant-receiving countries. In an age of rapidly intensifying migration, border crossing emerges as one of the major forces of social transformation, posing fundamental questions on the boundedness of nations and furthering the inevitable dilemma of differentiating citizens from noncitizens.

Borderland scholars are interested in the relationships between established people and immigrants, in the networks of partitioned ethnic minorities "trapped" in different nations but reviving their cultural ties, and in the everyday diversity in border provinces and towns. In short, we study how borders are set up, how the growing flow of people and the trafficking of human flesh are regulated, and how immigrants cope with the legal and material realities of the recipient countries. An additional sphere of interest concerns the phenomenon, spurred by huge economic differences between nations, of people moving across the border to benefit from the growing demand for cheap labor in the factories, construction, and fisheries of Thailand, Malaysia, Brunei, and Singapore.

For example, Horstmann (2002) and Wadley (2000b) write about transnational circular labor migration and transnational migrant circuits. In Ban Sarai, the Satun Malay from Thailand fish illegally in Langkawi, Malaysia, with every household having members working in Langkawi, and Satun Muslim women increasingly marry Langkawi Malaysians. Illegal men are subject to arrest, and women, to unequal gender relationships. For their part, West Kalimantan Iban men spend most of their time in East Malaysia and Brunei working as unskilled wage laborers, sometimes in possession of Malaysian identity cards and sometimes not, thus risking harassment by police. The Satun Malays and the West Kalimantan Iban are attracted by higher wages, resulting from large currency disparities. But unlike long distance migrants, such as Bosnian and Nigerian Muslims in the US and Europe, they mingle easily in local society, assimilating the local culture and language and relying on cross-border kin ties.

At the same time, although they share the same "roots," former Indonesian immigrants who have become fully "Malay" now seek to distinguish themselves from Indonesian newcomers (Miyazaki 2000). On the Thai-Burmese border, forced migration subjects laborers from Burma to the most severe exploitation, such as physical and sexual abuse (Koetsawang 2001). In these ways, socioeconomic differences stimulate circular labor migration, while moral and kin obligations, and status politics, motivate the return home. In the meantime, states try to regulate the flow of peoples and commodities across the border by issuing border passes, establishing fines, arresting migrants, and confining them in refugee camps.

Yet because the state consists of multiple, conflicting agencies and agendas, borderland scholars are also interested in the relations of power on a local level. On the Thai-Burmese border, Thailand's National Security Council, the Ministry of Labor and Social Welfare, the Immigration Bureau, and Royal Thai Police are all involved, in various ways, in the regulation and surveillance of illegal migrant workers. Yet the 2,400 km-long border between Thailand and Burma which stretches from the Golden Triangle in the north to Kawthaung in the south is generally very porous and not rigidly monitored by either country (Chantavanich, Bessey, and Paul 2000). Burgeoning in the flood of millions of migrants over the past decade, trafficking of women and children has become big business for well-established networks, some connected to local and regional government officials. In addition, in Ranong province alone, over 100,000 Burmese work in fishing and fish-related industries, constituting long-term Burmese immigrant communities.

Transnationalism, Moral Communities, and Globalization

We see borderlands as unique forms of peripheries, as zones between often competing or unequal states. This *inter-national* character increases the peripherality and ambiguity of the borderland as inhabitants seek benefits from both sides of the border, and as the states try to control their activities. This model outlines some important aspects of borderlands, but it risks oversimplifying the complexities of the border experience. A more comprehensive model welds the center-periphery together with the now ubiquitous concept of globalization. Globalization here is taken to mean the social-cultural, economic, political, and demographic processes occurring within and transcending nations; it represents an intensification of human relations around the world, linking and shaping events in widely separated localities (Kearney 1995; Giddens 1990). Although globalization is a process that has been ongoing for hundreds, if not thousands, of years (Cleveland 2000), modern communication systems allow information to be transmitted rapidly across national boundaries, creating the potential for economic power on a truly global scale. The globalization concept is well suited to the border context for it is conceived as being a multicentered and flexible phenomenon, with connectedness and transnationalism at its core. Social, economic, and political relations thus are not dichotomized as center-peripheries but are seen as complex, overlapping, and regional, with borderlanders as active participants in global process-es mediated through local and regional relations (e.g., Walker 1999).

The activities of crossriver boat operators, long-distance truck operators, and women involved in long-distance trade show that members of frontier communities are active participants in the creation and maintenance of bor-ders, and that traders are eager to benefit from the resources that borders create (Walker 1999). The role of women traders in the transformation of border economies cannot be overestimated: they may supply borderlan-ders with the bulk of commodities and the latest information (see Taglia-cozzo 1999 for a historical study). The intensification of border crossing is reliant on well-established kinship, trading, cultural, and religious net-works. Yet at the same time, the invention of borders and their regulation thereof are crucial factors in the marginalization of ethnic minorities in the space of the nation-state, where ethnic and religious minorities are some-times subjected to the brutality of state terror and even genocide. For exam-ple, from the 1950s until the 1970s in Sipsongpanna, century-old temples were destroyed, Buddhist images publicly burned, Thai monks forced to unfrock, and Thai elites sent to reeducation camps. This suppression of eth-nic and religious identity forced Buddhist activities underground and has created a shared oppressed identity. In Burma, too, the Thai alphabet was banned, and local religion repressed (Evans, Hutton, and Eng 2000).

However, more recently in Sipsongpanna, Buddhist monks are the key cultural agents in the revival of "precolonial" moral communities in China, Burma, Thailand, and Laos (Davis, 2003). Davis describes the joy and enchantment of postmodern reconstructions of Buddhist and ethnic identity in Sipsongpanna, where border crossing moral communities operate through a large network of minority Buddhist temples, which function as schools, sub-radar political centers, and inns for traveling monks. This horizontal temple network is held together by networks of mobile intellectuals and by flows of audio- and videotapes across the bor-der. Davis argues that postmodern flows of people and commodities build on premodern concepts of political and religious organization in Sipsong-panna, and that global forces have crisscrossed political boundaries and reintroduce ethnic consciousness, the Thai alphabet, and Buddhist educa-tion to the Thai Lue of Sipsongpanna. Through the networks of monks, traders, and artisans, Buddhist scriptures have been developed, musical instruments exchanged, and mural painting taught in temples.

Globalization sparks the revival of religious and ethnic identity in South-east Asia in many ways and presents the borderlands in a new spotlight. The flow of people, commodities, and ideas is not arbitrary, but is driven by historical ethnic and religious ties in local spaces. Partitioned ethnic minori-ties, trapped in marginal spaces of the nation-state, are especially using the new spaces to reconstruct transnational ethnic and religious communities. Tapp (1989, 2001) reports that since the 1980s there has been an upswing in return visits to Thailand and Laos by nostalgia-driven Hmong, who hope to find sources of cultural heritage and visit ancestral homelands. He shows that the remittances and folkloric projections of the returning Hmong diaspora are changing the culture of local action. The quest for authenticity has led the Hmong diaspora to use the space of the Internet to reinvent Hmong identity and to forge new global community links. Tapp describes how Hmong migrants return to refugee camps on the Thai-Lao border at the Hmong New Year in search of their roots. In the refugee process, whole families were divided, and reunions of family members in Lao villages are joyous and emotional, leading to regular remittances back to families in Laos. Remittances and images of the Hmong in the U.S. are thus reshaping the local economy and culture, and the studies on the Thai Lue and the Hmong show that the new space of communication, travel, and encounter reconstructs long-distance nationalism (Anderson 1998).

The Political Economy of Borderlands

The project of marginal history explores the entrenchment of the border in the local imagination. The idea is not that people somehow acquire a new identity; rather, the authors in this volume explore the ways in which local identities become increasingly tied to the state and to state definitions of ethnicity. In other words, the authors here are concerned with illustrating the relations of power as they manifest themselves along the border. In the process, the anthropology of borders informs the way in which borders are constructed and in which personal identities are subordinated to the master-narratives of national identities. States exercise considerable influence on the borders through border police and through customs regimes, and some states engage in illegal practices or collaborate quite closely with criminals (Heyman 1999). As Kearney (2004: 132) hypothesizes, "significant borders effect certain unequal exchanges of economic [and, we would argue, cultural] value between types of persons and regions defined by the boundaries in question."

The influence of states can also transcend borders: on the Kalimantan border in the Kelabit Highlands, labor migrants and raw timber move to the Malaysian side of the border, and goods to the Indonesian side (Amster, chap 9). Identification of oneself as Malaysian or Indonesian is fairly new, but Kelabit do divide each other into those categories. For example, a highlander recalls how he fought against the Indonesians as a scout of the new-formed Malaysian nation, thereby constructing the Indonesian nation discursively as an enemy. In addition, the large flow of Indonesian workers to Malaysia contributes to the Malaysian perception of Indonesians as economically deprived workers and foreigners, and the economic gap fuels marriage migration, with Indonesian women marrying Malaysian men in the Highlands.

Carsten (1998) describes the way in which foreigners have been integrated into Langkawi local systems of kinship and relatedness. This points to the border becoming increasingly entrenched in the ideas of the people, dissolving traditional structures of relatedness and introducing new, hierarchical forms of social relations. Indeed, marriage across borders itself yields topics for further research, such as whether women are forced into marriage, or whether they assertively pursue higher-status males. In addition, the tricking of local women into prostitution and slavery is typical of border zones in Southeast Asia. Askew (chap. 8) scrutinizes sex tourism and pilgrimage as two forms of border crossing that characterize the landscape of the Thai-Malaysian borderland. His findings show that we must move away from the nostalgic view of cultural communities toward new perspectives on the highly modern mobility of sex and spirituality. His case study illustrates that the border is a risk and a barrier, but also provides special resources for local agency.

Marriage migration is also a salient phenomenon in the Thai-Malaysian border area (Horstmann, chap. 7). Aspiring to better lives, Muslim women from the border province of Satun often marry Malaysian men. Though they cross the border frequently for reasons of kinship obligations, visa regulations, and friendship networks, they do not want to return to the hardships in Thailand. In order to assimilate, they stop conversing in Thai and adjust themselves and the education of their children to the Malay-Muslim way of life. The unequal status of women and men in the borderland is a strong signifier of the gendering of the border.

Although extensive kinship networks reach across borders, estrangement on both sides influences the way people conceptualize their cross-border neighbors and cousins. Thus, Malaysians in Langkawi call Thai Muslim men from the coastal province of Satun "Orang Siam" and not "Orang Muslim," thus emphasizing difference rather than similarity and brotherhood. Malaysians in Langkawi also distance themselves from Thai Muslim men who try to draw on kinship obligations. In this way, migrants are conceptualized as strangers. Strangers are not trusted and are perceived as dangerous, bringing in disease, criminality, and other antisocial influences. Similarly, Thai women migrants are blamed for undermining the positions of married women given perceptions of their greater liberty. Even women in cross-border marriages have problems integrating, as they may not be accepted by their Malaysian mothers-in-law or may have to submit themselves to the authority of their husbands. Moreover, they lack the security of Malaysian wives, having no regular visas or means to escape from official marriages across the border.

As Anzaldua (1987: 3) states, Mexicans and Chicanos "meet the border and bleed." It is this confrontation of people at the border of the state that is also of concern to border scholars. Indeed, the precarious status of migrants is underscored at the border, where migrants and refugees often become the victims of exploitation and human rights abuses. They are dependent on brokers, who constitute a ubiquitous force in borderlands, benefiting from economic gaps between nations. However, as Riwanto (chap. 6) shows, border people such as the Catholic Florenese can turn marginalization around and use their minority status as "cultural capital," enabling them to occupy a special niche and use their spiritual ties to form close-knit networks. In the case of the Florenese, Christianity is a vehicle for weaving social networks on both sides of the Malaysian-Indonesian border. Sara Davis (chap. 4) also takes up the theme of marginal history. She points out that the Buddhist revivalist movement in Sipsongpanna, Burma, Laos, and Thailand has roots in the network of Buddhist monasteries that was destroyed during the Chinese Cultural Revolution. The author thus provides a corrective to Appadurai (2001) and other cultural theorists, in that the social imagination of transnationalism is seen to have a much older history. She questions the newness of border crossing , even as the exchange of messages via palm leaf is replaced by walkie-talkies and e-mail.

The Border Zone

The state border and its special political ecology must necessarily remain central to the anthropology of borders, and we maintain that the border concept risks of becoming meaningless if the term is used too loosely, if "borders" are seen in everything humans might do. Most of the contributors to this volume focus on proximity to the state border: the border town differs from any other town in the center, because of the border zone. However, this does not mean that border scholars have to stop at the border. The state border is a mere political line, and the large variety of state borders in Southeast Asia ranges from porous borders in Thailand to heavily regulated borders in Singapore. Moreover, where does the border begin, and where does it end? For after all, borderlanders themselves may penetrate the heart of the state through labor or residential migration.

Having said this, the border concept can be productively applied to internal boundaries and marginalities within states (Alvarez 1995). As Cummings (chap. 2) shows, "border regions may be found throughout the geographical space of the nation." Precisely because the border concept harnesses some of our most familiar concepts (e.g., country, society, and culture), we can usefully apply it in dealing with unequal relations, such as between majorities and minorities, citizen and the stateless (i.e., migrants and refugees), and indigenous peoples and foreigners. Border zones may thus constitute third cultural spaces in between two mainstream cultures. The border concept serves to question the very notion of a bounded culture because it puts ruptures along the border into relief.

Postcolonialism has challenged the power and meaning of boundaries as they relate to our understanding of insiders and outsiders. Most of the contributions here highlight the relationships of the transnational center-periphery from the perspective of the margin. Not strictly about the material border, Cummings' Chapter 2 concerns the incorporation of Makassar into Indonesia, the making of a periphery, and the revalorization of Makassar as part of the nation-state. The Rmeet of mountainous northern Laos, on the other hand, are considered "backward" in terms of their rituals and their economy (Sprenger, chap. 3). In the creation myths of the Rmeet, this marginalization is at once taken into account and overcome: many of the lowland Laotion cultural markers are said to originate in Rmeet society—a nice and nonconfrontational way of centering the margin. Both case studies show how local actors in the so-called periphery re-center their specific location in the nation by reevaluating their local history.

Ethnic Minorities and the State

The essays in this volume focus on some of the responses of borderlanders as they face the mighty nation-state and its key symbol—the border. Most contributors feel that this interaction between border people and the nation-state must be reframed: translocal communities that cross political boundaries were formed the very moment these borders were established, yet past scholars failed to address this issue. Many of the contributions here take a particularistic and localized view of the border, to show how local people manipulate it (Amster, chap. 9; Askew, chap 8; Chou, chap. 5). Instead of celebrating the "weapons of the weak," the authors of this volume aim to provide a realistic account of how the original meaning of the border is transformed in the negotiation between states and local populations. For example, Horstmann (chap. 7) shows the vulnerability of illegal migrants for whom border crossing is a crucial source of social reproduction.

Interestingly, as noted by Donnan and Wilson (1999: 91), borders have created their own kinds of opportunities for informal commerce and illicit economic dealing. This is well illustrated by the paradox facing by the Orang Suku Laut (Chou, chap. 5): on the one hand, they consider themselves as owners of the vast maritime world, but on the other hand they are confronted with borders in their daily life. Chou shows that whereas the Orang Suku Laut must purchase permits to trade in Singapore, even the permit does not protect them from arrest and harassment, whereupon they must buy their way out through bribery, the usual route to obtain permits and identity cards.

The Project of Marginal History

The study of borderlands gives new impetus to the margin. At the same time, a focus on the everyday lives and struggles of borderlanders gives impetus to forgotten or suppressed histories. Thongchai (2002) has recently called for a project on marginal history from the interstices in Southeast

Asia. This follows from Tsing's (1993: 14–15) definition of "the margin" as conceptual sites from which to explore the imaginative qualities and specificities of local and global cultural formations.[3] Studies from the margin have a huge potential for circulating stories from particular locations—an imagined end of the nation-state and the beginning of autonomous histories. At those interstices, it is possible to discern the discursive regime of a national history, its logics, conditions, constitutions, mechanisms, and reproductions: "This is what I call history at the interstices, that is, the history of the locations and moments between being and not being a nation, becoming and not becoming a nation" (Thongchai 2002: 5).

Marginal history is thus local history of national minorities that have been forgotten or suppressed by national history. From a spatial perspective, marginal history lies at the extremity where the nation-state ends. As such, it is politically, economically, and culturally peripheral and subordinate to the center. But whose history is to be told? Thongchai pleads for the rediscovery of local stories that focus on the interaction of the local with the global and the processes by which global forces are localized and changed. Obviously, this project requires a new approach to the writing of history. Thongchai (1994) himself follows the path of the center and the elitist view in order to deconstruct the myth of the nation-state, and his work has pointed to the ambiguity of the margin that has been harnessed by the technologies of administration, infrastructure, and mapping.

But does not the writing of history from the interstices require a rethinking of methodology as well? The local stories of national history require a particular sensitivity to everyday life, and to the resistance prompted by state-building efforts to simplify and normalize.[4] Picking the example of a small border town, Niti (chap. 1) sketches the transformation of a borderland, focusing on the replacement of local oral memory by national history and the success of the official narrative in replacing all other narratives. Producing a genealogy of the borderland that traces the history of a border in order to deconstruct the nation from the margins, he recounts stories of resistance against the poll taxes, disputes over land, and the Thai administration's ban on males wearing long hair. Focusing on the myths of origin, Niti showcases the oral history approach, as a means of highlighting the process by which one narrative is deliberately replaced by another (rather than merely taking the domination of the prevailing identity for granted).

Common Agendas

Given that nationalism and national identity exert great pressure on transnational communities, borderlands in Southeast Asia are active arenas of social and cultural change. This introductory essay has identified some common agendas among a variety of existing studies. In order to advance the field, we need to center what has been historically regarded as marginal and peripheral (much as Rosaldo 2003 advocates for studies of citizenship), and to connect local studies to border studies throughout the world—in Africa, Latin America, Europe, and along the US-Mexico border. Clearly, most borderland studies of Southeast Asia at this stage are lacking in comparative depth.

One central question is how ethnic minorities give meaning and shape to marginal local space. What quickly emerges from borderland studies in Southeast Asia is the importance of the multiple and decentered ties of often partitioned ethnic minorities that have been incorporated into the space of the nation-state. The Thai Lue Buddhist networks in mainland Southeast Asia, the Muslim networks in mainland and insular Southeast Asia, and the traversing of vast maritime spaces from the Sulu Sea to the Mergui Archipelago by the Sama-Bajau and the Moken illustrate how indigenous cultures have been forced to drastically change their modes of living as the borders and hegemonic scripts of the colonial and postcolonial state are imposed on them. In addition, studies of the Thai-Burmese border and the Malaysian-Indonesian border show that migrants make great efforts to cross porous borders in hopes of escaping human rights abuses, the destruction of natural resources, and poverty. Transnational migrant circuits on the border, and the multiple ethnic and religious networks across borders, challenge the exclusive nature of the nation-state, its management of culture and people, and the exclusive character of state concepts. Yet the same citizenship that guarantees and protects the rights of some can become an instrument of control that increasingly distinguishes between citizen and noncitizen. Scholars of Southeast Asia cannot reduce their analyses to the state border and its surroundings, for migrants, refugees, and tourists do not restrict themselves to local spaces but have a presence even in the metropolis, though this existence may be low-profile and marginal.

One of the major conclusions here is that scholars of Southeast Asian borderlands should concentrate more on the cultural complexity of the borderland communities themselves, on their transnational networks and spaces, and less on the invented entities of the nation-states. In a framework of the study of world-society, scholars of borderlands can re-center the margin by documenting the life worlds of people, languages, and cultures that have been created by, and yet transcend, national borders.

The current revival of old ties, along with the globalization of ethnic and religious codes, is a particularly promising field for borderland scholars, marking a shift of emphasis to the concrete interaction of partitioned minorities and the state on the ground, and to the local reworkings and filters of national and global scripts in local contexts. The ethnography of this interface appears crucial to the social transformation of Southeast Asia. The upsurge in transnational, border-crossing lives and livelihoods challenges much of our intellectual baggage of static concepts. Identities are not just multifaceted; they are prone to change, and the fluidity and ambiguity of identities is a central feature of borderlands.

Written from the interstices (Thongchai 2000), border studies of state-building, globalization, and resistance in local spaces must take a perspective of the *longue durée,* even if territorial boundaries, passports, and visas are comparatively new phenomena. There is no doubt that the bounding of Southeast Asia has affected the lives of border people on a vast scale, yet the imagined communities of the postcolonial state are not always experienced as a promise, but often rather as a dangerous nightmare for indigenous people upon whom the state's program for development and civilization is imposed. In other instances, although state borders have been set up by nation-states as markers of statehood, basic state concepts (such as sovereignty and citizenship) exist more on paper than in reality. Far from the national center, the states' control of the transformation of borderlands may be limited; and many scholars of borders have shown that local people constantly defy the efforts of the state to control them but yet, at the same time, try to accommodate state power. Communities at the border play a very significant role in making and transforming identity via their negotiations of the highly ambiguous space of the frontier. In the marginal spaces where nation-states begin and end, and other histories begin and end, local communities routinely subvert national identities.

With social life being typically storied, the construction of an identity narrative is itself political action and is part of the distribution of social power in society.[5] In the study of state boundaries, it is important to know whose plots or turfs dominate these identity narratives, what is excluded or included by them, and how the representations of "us" and "them" are produced and reproduced in various social practices, such as media, education, and the like. Newman and Paasi (1998) remind us that the border is not a fixed entity, but is always constructed (and reconstructed) at various levels of the social order, historically contested and paradoxically renewed. And the marginal history project of Thongchai challenges us to explore the ways in which borders between ethnic groups —majorities and minorities—are dissolved or enhanced. One of the central interests of borderland scholars concerns the ethnography of local agency in border crossings, and the ways in which this agency influences the dissolution of borders and globalization, or their reinforcement as a basic structure of state formation. While every borderland is worthy of study in its own right, the question of just how border people are situated in a broader, comparative history may be an approach that is viable for all borderlands.

Notes

1. We do not intend, however, to review comprehensively the anthropology of borderlands, as this has been more than adequately dealt with elsewhere (e.g., Asiwaju 1983, 1985; Alvarez 1995; Martinez 1996; Donnan and Wilson 1998, 1999; Wendl and Rösler 1999; Wadley 2002).
2. Miyazaki (2000) puts it very aptly when he writes that people who have habitually moved as part of their life worlds are now settling, while hitherto sedentary people have begun to move, though we would note that those newly settled remain highly mobile nonetheless.
3. Margins here are not geographical, descriptive locations; rather, they are analytical categories that make evident both the constraining, oppressive quality of cultural exclusion, and its creative potential.
4. Oral history seems to be a very apt vantage point from which to critique colonial and national documents. For example, confronting oral and colonial histories of rebellion and pacification, Wadley (2004) shows how colonial and Iban narratives provide both converging and conflicting accounts of historical events, with different moral orders and interpretations.
5. Newman and Paasi (1998) note that boundaries are part of the discursive landscape of social power, control, and governance, which extends itself into the whole society and is produced and reproduced in various social and cultural practices.

References

Adler, Rachel H. 2004. *Yucatecans in Dallas, Texas: Breaching the Border, Bridging the Distance*. Boston: Pearson.

Alvarez, Robert R., Jr. 1995. "The Mexican-US Border: The Making of an Anthropology of Borderlands." *Annual Review of Anthropology* 24, 447–70.

Anderson, Benedict. 1983. *Imagined Communities: Reflections on the Origin and Spread of Nationalism*. London: Verso.

———.1998. *The Spectre of Comparisons: Nationalism, Southeast Asia and the World*. London and New York: Verso.

Anzaldúa, Gloria. 1987. *Borderlands: The New Mestiza = La Frontera*. San Francisco: Aunt Lute.

Appadurai, Arjun, ed. 2001. *Globalization*. Durham, N.C.: Duke University Press.

Asiwaju, A. I. 1983. *Borderlands Research: A Comparative Perspective*. Border Perspectives Paper No. 6. El Paso, Tex: Center for Inter-American and Border Studies, University of Texas.

———.1985. "The Conceptual Framework." In A. I. Asiwaju, ed., *Partitioned Africans: Ethnic Relations Across Africa's International Boundaries, 1884–1984*. London: Hurst.

Baud, Michiel, and Willem van Schendel. 1997. "Towards a Comparative History of Borderlands." *Journal of World History* 8, no. 2: 211–42.

Benjamin, Geoffrey. 1988. *The Unseen Presence: A Theory of the Nation-State and Its Mystifications*. Singapore: National University of Singapore.

Bryant, Raymond. 1997. *The Political Ecology of Forestry in Burma, 1824–1994.* London: Hurst.

Carsten, Janet. 1998. "Borders, Boundaries, Tradition and State on the Malaysian Periphery." In Hastings Donnan and Thomas M. Wilson, eds, *Border Identities: Nation and State at International Frontiers.* Cambridge: Cambridge University Press.

Chantavanich, Supang, Allen Bessey, and Shakti Paul. 2000. *Mobility and HIV/AIDS in the Greater Mekong Subregion.* Report of the Asian Research Center of Migration for the Asian Development Bank.

Cheah Boon Kheng. 1988. *The Peasant Robbers of Kedah, 1900–1929: Historical and Folk Perceptions.* Singapore: Oxford University Press.

Cleveland, David A. 2000. "Globalization and Anthropology." *Human Organization* 53, 370–4.

Davis, Sara. 2003. "Premodern Flows in Postmodern China: Globalization and the Sipsongpanna Tai Lue." *Modern China* 29, 176–203.

Donnan, Hastings, and Thomas M. Wilson, eds. 1998. *Border Identities: Nation and State at International Frontiers.* Cambridge: Cambridge University Press.

———. 1999. *Borders: Frontiers of Identity, Nation and State.* Oxford and New York: Berg.

Evans, Grant, Christopher Hutton, and Kuah Khun Eng, eds. 2000. *Where China Meets Southeast Asia: Social and Cultural Change in the Border Regions.* Singapore: Institute of Southeast Asian Studies.

Giddens, Anthony. 1990. *The Consequences of Modernity.* Stanford: Stanford University Press.

Herzfeld, Michael. 1997. *Cultural Intimacy: Social Poetics in the Nation-State.* NewYork and London: Routledge.

Heyman, Josiah M. 1999. *States and Illegal Practices.* Oxford and New York: Berg.

Horstmann, Alexander. 2001. "Trapped Ethnic Minorities and the Local Reworking of Citizenship at the Thailand-Malaysian Border." Paper presented at the Centre of Southeast Asian Studies (CSEAS), Kyoto University, 12 November 2001.

———. 2002. "Rethinking Citizenship in Thailand: Identities at the Fringe of the Nation-state in National and Post-National Times." Paper presented at the Eighth International Conference of Thai Studies, Nakhon Phanom, Thailand, 9–12 January 2002.

———. 2004. "Ethnohistorical Perspectives on Buddhist-Muslim Relations and Coexistence in Southern Thailand: From Shared Cosmos to the Emergence of Hatred?" *SOJOURN. Journal of Social Issues in Southeast Asia* 19, 1, 76–99.

Ishikawa, Noburu. 2001. "Genesis of Nation Space: A Case from the Borderland of Southwestern Sawarak, 1871–1941." Paper presented at the Conference on Globalization and Local Culture: A Dialectic toward New Indonesia, Padang, Indonesia, 18–21 July 2001.

Kearney, Michael. 1995. "The Local and the Global: The Anthropology of Globalization and Transnationalism." *Annual Review of Anthropology* 24, 547–65.

———. 2004. "The Classifying and Value-Filtering Missions of Borders." *Anthropological Theory* 4, 131–56.

Koetsawang, Pim. 2001. *In Search of Sunlight: Burmese Migrant Workers in Thailand*. Bangkok: Orchid Press.

Leach, Edmund R. 1954. *Political Systems of Highland Burma: A Study of Kachin Social Structure*. Boston: Beacon Press.

———.1960. "The Frontiers of Burma." *Comparative Studies in Society and History* 3, no. 1: 49–68.

Martinez, Oscar J. 1994. *Border People: Life and Society in the U.S.-Mexico Borderlands*. Tucson: University of Arizona Press.

Miyazaki, Koji. 2000. "Javanese-Malay: Between Adaptation and Alienation." *Sojourn* 15, no. 1: 76–99.

Newman, David, and Anssi Paasi. 1998. "Fences and Neighbours in the Postmodern World: Boundary Narratives in Political Geography." *Progress in Human Geography* 22, no. 2: 186–207.

Nugent, Paul, and A. I. Asiwaju, eds. 1996. *African Boundaries: Barriers, Conduits and Opportunities*. London and New York: Pinter.

Pries, Ludger. 2000. "Transnational Social Space: Do We Need a New Approach in Response to New Phenomena?" In Ludger Pries, ed., *New Transnational Social Spaces: International Migration and Transnational Companies*. London: Routledge.

Rajah, Ananda. 1990. "Ethnicity, Nationalism, and the Nation-State: The Karen in Burma and Thailand." In Gehan Wijeyewardene, ed., *Ethnic Groups across National Boundaries in Mainland Southeast Asia*. Singapore: Institute of Southeast Asian Studies.

Rosaldo, Renato, ed. 2003. *Cultural Citizenship in Island Southeast Asia: Nation and Belonging in the Hinterlands*. Berkeley: University of California Press.

Sather, Clifford. 1997. *The Bajau Laut: Adaptation, History and Fate in a Maritime Fishing Society of South-Eastern Sabah*. Oxford: Oxford University Press.

Shapiro, Michael J., and Hayward R. Alker. 1996. *Challenging Boundaries: Global Flows, Territorial Identities*. Minneapolis: University of Minnesota Press.

Tagliacozzo, Eric. 1999. *Secret Trades of the Straits: Smuggling and State-Formation along a Southeast Asian Frontier, 1870–1910*. Ph.D. dissertation, Yale University.

Tapp, Nicholas. 1989. *Sovereignty and Rebellion: The White Hmong of Southern Thailand*. Singapore: Oxford University Press.

——. 2000. "A New Stage in Thai Regional Studies: The Challenge of Local Histories." In Andrew Turton, ed., *Civility and Savagery: Social Identity in Tai States*. Richmond: Curzon.

——. 2001. "Diasporic Returns: The Sociology of a Globalised Rapprochement." Unpublished manuscript.

Thongchai Winichakul. 1994. *Siam Mapped: A History of the Geo-body of a Nation*. Honolulu: University of Hawaii Press.

——. 2000. "The Others Within: Travel and Ethno-Spatial Differentiation of Siamese Subjects 1885–1910." In Andrew Turton, ed., *Civility and Savagery: Social Identity in Tai States*. Richmond: Curzon.

Tokoro, Ikuya. 1999. *Border Crossings: From the Sulu Sea*. Tokyo: Iwanamishoten.

Tsing, Anna Lowenhaupt. 1993. *In the Realm of the Diamond Queen: Marginality in an Out-of-the-Way Place*. Princeton: Princeton University Press.

Vandergeest, Peter, and Nancy Lee Peluso. 1995. "Territorialization and State Power in Thailand." *Theory and Society* 24, 385–426.

Wadley, Reed L. 2000a. "Warfare, Pacification, and Environment: Population Dynamics in the West Borneo Borderlands (1823–1934)." *Moussons* 1, 41–66.

——. 2000b. "Transnational Circular Labour Migration in Northwestern Borneo." *Revue Europeene des Migrations Internationales* 16, no. 1: 127–49.

——. 2001. "Trouble on the Frontier: Dutch-Brooke relations and Iban Rebellion in theWest Borneo Borderlands (1841–1886)." *Modern Asian Studies* 35, no. 3: 623–44.

——. 2002. "Border Studies beyond Indonesia: A Comparative Perspective." *Antropologi Indonesia* 67, 1–11.

——. 2003. "Lines in the Forest: Internal Territorialization and Local Accommodation in West Kalimantan, Indonesia (1865–1979)." *South East Asia Research* 11, no. 1: 91–112.

——. 2004. "Punitive Expeditions and Divine Revenge: Oral and Colonial Histories of Rebellion and Pacification in Western Borneo, 1886–1902." *Ethnohistory* 51, no. 3: 609–36.

Walker, Andrew. 1999. *The Legend of the Golden Boat: Regulation, Trade and Traders in the Borderlands of Laos, Thailand, China and Burma*. Richmond: Curzon.

Wendl, Tobias, and Michael Rösler. 1999. "Frontiers and Borderlands: The Rise and Relevance of an Anthropological Research Genre." In Tobias Wendl and Michael Rösler, eds., *Frontiers and Borderlands: Anthropological Perspectives*. Frankfurt am Main: Peter Lang.

Wijeyewardene, Gehan. 1989. "Majorities, Minorities and National Boundaries." *Thai-Yunnan Project Newsletter* 4, 1–2.

Centering the Margin I:
Center and Periphery in
Southeast Asian Borderlands

1

"Once Were Burmese Shans": Reinventing Ethnic Identity in Northwestern Thailand

Niti Pawakapan

THIS IS AN ESSAY ON A SMALL TOWN in Thailand named Khun Yuam, which was established by migrants from Burma's southern Shan States in the nineteenth century. It focuses on the political economic developments in recent years that have led to changes in local culture and self-awareness. It is also about the narratives contested within a nation-local memories versus national history and the success of the official narrative in overcoming all other narratives. The prevalence of the Thai nation, however, is not solely based on the creation of a consensual belief that the people in this remote northwestern corner are living in the same "imagined" community with the majority Thai, especially those who live in the central region, but also on legends from the distant past in which they are related as "brothers." Such a belief is supported by an oral tradition of the past relationships between the Thaj Jaj and the Thaj Nauj that has been told for generations (see Srisakr and Suchitt 1991). British colonial officers working in Burma and historians in the nineteenth century also believed that the Shan and the Siamese were related (Milne 1970: 24).[1]

Being "Tai"[2]

I should note that the title of this paper is somewhat inaccurate. The word "Burmese Shan" is used to distinguish the majority "Thai" in central Thailand from the local people mentioned here. The town residents of Khun Yuam have never referred to themselves as "Shan," an English word borrowed from Burmese. Nor have they ever seen themselves as "Burmese." Like all the so-called "Shan" people living in Thailand and the Shan States, their self-designation is "Tai" or, in some places, "Tai Long" (meaning, Great Tai). They of course have a long history of economic and cul-

---

Endnotes for this chapter begin on page 45.

tural relations with Burma's Shan States. Elderly townspeople tell stories of their adventures to the Shan States—some even went as far as Moulmein. They enjoyed their trips to Burma, the food, entertainment and modernization. But all this is about to change.

Diller (1994: 15) estimates that some three million people speak various dialects of "Shan." He states that the language of "Southern Shan is traditionally written with a distinctive Burmese-like orthography which distinguishes neither tone nor certain vowel contrasts." The people in the central region, who referred to themselves in the past as "Thaj Nauj"[3](Thai Noi—literally, Lesser Thai), have called them "Thaj Jaj" (Thai Yai—Greater Thai) or "Ngiaw."[4] Some Thai academics remark that the "Thaj Jaj" included those who settled on the Salween and Mao (or Shwe) Deltas; on the other hand, the "Thaj Nauj" were the people who dwelt to the east, in the valley of the Mekong River, including the territories of Thailand, Laos and Vietnam (Srisakr and Suchitt 1991: 89). Similar comments appear in Wijeyewardene, who writes that Thaj Jaj "is a term usually applied to the people also known as 'Shan', and should probably include the Ahom and other Tai groups of Assam. The associated term is 'Tai Noi' (Lesser Tai) used to include, probably, all others in the southwestern branch [of the Tai speech groups]. These are 'Tai' terms and appear not to have superogatory or derogatory implications" (Wijeyewardene 1990: 48). The two terms seem to have been in use at least since the seventeenth century. Simon de La Loubère, a French diplomat who in 1687–88 visited Ayutthaya, then the capital of Thailand, reported that "In a word, the Siamese, of whom I treat, do call themselves *Tai Noe, little Siams.* There are others, as I was informed, altogether savage, which are called *Tai Yai, great Siams,* and which do live in the Northern Mountains. In several Relations of these Countries, I find a Kingdom of *Siammon,* or *Siami:* but all do not agree that the People thereof are savage" (La Loubère 1986: 7).

Although the Tai in Khun Yuam do not refer to themselves as "Thaj Jaj," or to the Thai as "Thai Nauj", many people, the elders in particular, are familiar with both terms. Some elderly town residents even recall the tales of both groups sharing a common origin, speaking similar languages and customs. The two groups were brothers: Thaj Jaj the elder, Thaj Nauj the younger. Several of them add that the difference between them was that the Thaj Jaj culture was close to the Burmese, but the Thaj Nauj was not.

"We were brothers": Narratives, Borderlands, and the Nation

The court of Siam (Thailand's old name) has concerned itself with the country's northern and northwestern frontier[5] at least since Rama III. Freshly aware of the increasing power of the British in Burma, the king ordered the ruler of the province of Chiang Mai to survey its frontier and encouraged new settlements of the Tai Karen- and Red Karen-speaking groups in the area. The king then claimed the new settlers as his subjects, who had send tribute to the capital, and the region as his territory. More than half a century later, disputes over British Burma and Siam's territories forced both countries to demarcate their frontiers, creating the border. Rajah, following Buzan's ideas on the state, argues that a "strong" or "weak" state is defined by its power to control the border, or, to be more precise, that the strength of the modern nation-state depends on "internally contested *or* imprecise boundaries and their, equally, administratively vague frontier areas contiguous with the borders of other neighboring states" (Rajah 1990: 124; original emphasis). He then suggests that Thailand be considered a "strong" state, partly owing to its control over the border and partly, I would add, because Thailand has succeeded in creating an official historical memory that dominates other memories or narratives in the country. The success of the national remembrance in the northwestern frontier is owed in part to the oral traditions in currency among the Tai-speaking people—in this case, the Thaj Jaj and the Thaj Nauj—that foster belief in a common origin (and, of course, also to the influence of the national education that was introduced to the area in the first half of the twentieth century).

The connections between such oral traditions and the national history may better be understood in light of Smith's (1991) hypothesis on national identity. Smith claims that national identity is not purely invented or imagined, but is connected with the ethnic community (or *ethnie* in French). As one of several features that define national identity, he notes that the people who claim "common myths and historical memories" share the same national identity, which in this understanding is a link to the elements that identify the same ethnic community. That is, the people believe they have "a myth of common ancestry" and "shared historical memories" (Smith 1991: 14, 20–1). By claiming that the Thaj Jaj and the Thaj Nauj were in the past "brothers", the Tai of Khun Yuam submit themselves to Thailand's national identity, believing that they share with the majority Thai a common ancestry and some historical memories. The Tai memories now become a part of the country's national history.

The Setting

Forming the majority of Khun Yuam's residents are the Tai and the Kon Müang, with a small number of Central Thai or Thai speakers. Most Tai speakers in Khun Yuam are descended from migrants who left the Shan States of Burma and arrived in the territory of Mae Hong Son Province in the nineteenth century. Their language is similar to the one spoken in the southern Shan States. Some Tai residents, however, originally came from nearby Tai villages, and some from villages in the territory of Mae Hong Son's Müang district. They had married locals and decided to settle in the town. Most Tai are rice farmers, but they are also involved in trade, part-time and full-time.

The Kon Müang speak the Kam Müang (Kham Müang or Mu'ang) language, which includes various related dialects spoken in northern Thai-

land. The Kam Müang spoken in Khun Yuam is said to share many simi-
larities with the Chiang Mai dialect. The written language, called Lanna,
Tua Müang, or Tua Tham, "is still in some use and is being locally revived"
(Diller 1994: 11–12). Davis (1984: 23) translates the term "Kon Müang" as
"the people of the principalities," noting that they do not "like being called
Lao." The Tai of Khun Yuam refer to the Kon Müang as *Joon* (in Central
Thai—*Juan* or *Yuan*), a term considered offensive by the latter. Numbering
among most Kon Müang town residents are the descendants of migrants
from Mae Chaem[6] as well as recent arrivals from this neighboring district.
According to many informants, the Kon Müang left Mae Chaem owing to
famine and drought in that area. In the past one or two decades many Kon
Müang from the provinces of Phayao, Chiang Rai, Lumpang, Nan, Phrae,
and other districts of Chiang Mai have migrated to Khun Yuam as well.
Some of them later married locals. Like the Tai, the Kon Müang make their
living in rice cultivation and trade.

The Birth of the Settlement: Whose Version?

There are several versions of Khun Yuam's establishment but no conclusions whether Khun Yuam was primarily settled because of its important
location for regional trading, logging, defense purposes, or political reasons. In the first half of the nineteenth century Tai speakers migrated from
the Shan States to settle in the Khun Yuam area in the first half of the nineteenth century. Other groups, such as the Karen, Lua and Kayah, also
occupied the area. The Thai historians Srisakr and Suchitt (1991) believe
that Khun Yuam and Mae Hong Son were established by Tai traders who
arrived with their caravans. The two settlements were therefore closely
related historically, economically, and politically. In the past the Tai of
Burma's Shan States had always traversed back and forth the Thai-
Burmese border, and most of the males were recognized by the locals as
doughty warriors, as well as long-distance traders and travelers. Their
homeland was in the valleys along the branches of the Salween River
(Srisakr and Suchitt 1991: 94–95). Because they had long been in contact
with the Burmese, many aspects of Tai everyday life, such as language,
architecture, music, and so forth, were influenced by Burmese culture.
Ratanaporn Sethakul (1989: 65–66), an expert on northern Thai history,
also notes that Tai traders in the nineteenth century traveled between the
Shan States and northern Thailand, usually "to Chiang Mai via Muang
Fang [north of Chiang Mai] or Mae Hong Son and a number of Shan settlements were established in those areas, particularly the latter which
came to be a predominately Shan place." It is not unlikely that these
traders probably stopped over in Khun Yuam to trade with the locals.

There is also a possibility that some of the early settlers in Khun Yuam
were war immigrants. According to elderly residents of a village some

twelve kilometers to the south of the town, the village of Müang Paun was established in the nineteenth century by Tai speakers, many of whom were escaping the fighting and bandits in the Shan States. During the first several years of the settlement of Müang Paun, life was hard but safer than in their homeland. Other immigrants then followed their predecessors, and the village of Müang Paun grew. Some of these newcomers moved to neighboring villages to find a new home, and some even went as far as Khun Yuam. Today, many Khun Yuam residents recall that their kin relationships with the locals of Müang Paun can be traced back several decades.

The oral history of the war migrants resettling in the area probably has some basis in fact. Ronald Renard confirms that the founding of Mae Hong Son occurred in the context of the political relations between the rulers of Chiang Mai and the Red Karens—or Kayah, as they call themselves. Renard writes: "As Chiang Mai's population grew and Red Karen strength mounted, Chang Phu'ak's successor, Putthawong, wished to survey conditions in the upper Salween. His *hona* [literally, the Front Palace, or the crown prince], Chao Mahot, sent Chao Kaeo Mu'angma to investigate the Red Karen boundary area in 1831." In establishing Mae Hong Son, the ruler of Chiang Mai hoped that it "would limit Red Karen influence more effectively than the treaties he felt the Red Karens were violating." The Red Karen kept migrating to and settling in the area and at the same time "also extended their influence over small Shan states on the Salween, successfully intimidating all the states except Mawkmai" (Renard 1980b: 129–30). The rulers of Mae Hong Son and Khun Yuam could not escape the intimidation of the Kayah's invasion and were forced to give tribute to the latter in exchange for their safety (Renard 1980b: 152).

One Thai author claims that the growth of Mae Hong Son and Paang Muu[7] was also related to logging activities in the area. In his account, the leaders of Mae Hong Son and Paang Muu, seeing that the British Bombay-Burma Trading Company had been logging in the forests on the territory of the Shan States, realized that teak was plentiful in the Mae Hong Son area and could be logged. They thus requested logging permission from the ruler of Chiang Mai and proposed that in return, the ruler would be given "khaa taumaj" (literally, the stump's price)[8] from every tree that was felled. The permission was soon granted and trees were felled and floated down the Pai River to the saw-mills in Burma. Eventually, new settlers arrived at Mae Hong Son and Paang Muu to take up a logging job. Both communities grew rapidly (Bunchuai 1961: 672).

In contrast, the official version of the history of Mae Hong Son and Khun Yuam given by Thai authorities emphasizes another issue. It states that in B.E. 2374 (A.D. 1831), Caw Kaew Müang Maa was ordered to survey the Burma frontier and to capture wild elephants for royal use. When he and his followers arrived at Paang Muu, he appointed a local Tai named Phakaamaung to be the village headman. There were already some Tai speakers dwelling in this area, but the former ordered the latter to assemble all these local Tai to found a new village. Another settlement, Mae Hong Son town, was also established, and the son of Phakaamaung, Saenkoom, was appointed headman (Mae Hong Son Provincial Office 1992: 1; Maitri 1980: 96–97; Athivaro Bhikkhu 1992: 31–32). The population of Paang Muu grew, so Shaankalee,[9] a son-in-law of Phakaamaung, later migrated together with a number of Tai people to the south, which was at the time mainly occupied by the Lua.[10] The Tai newcomers then established their own hamlet and called the place "Kun Jom"—"the hills of jom."[11] Shaankalee was later appointed by the ruler of Chiang Mai as *khun*, the chief, of the new settlement and was titled Phraya Sihanat (Khun Yuam District Office 1992: 2; Saadronnawid 1981: 5–10).

Trading Town

Located on a trade route between the Shan States and northern Thailand, Khun Yuam was economically active from the nineteenth century to the beginning of World War II. It became active again during Thailand's economic boom in the 1990s. Local and outside traders of Tai- Kon Müang- and Pa-O-speaking groups traveled via the town to buy and sell their goods. Local traders, mainly Tai, usually transported local products to the markets of Mae Hong Son, Mae Sariang, Mae Rim, Chiang Mai, and occasionally to the Shan States. On the return trip, local traders brought various kinds of commodities to sell in Khun Yuam. Outside traders from other northern provincial towns and Shan States' markets also came to trade. Arriving with these traders was news of the outside world. Kam Müang and Tai were spoken in the town; the latter was used more widely by speakers of other languages, especially among traders, as most of those who came from the Shan States did not speak Kam Müang. Culturally, Khun Yuam was close to the Shan States as well. Local people often crossed the mountains to the Shan States to hire Tai craftsmen and carpenters to build temples, stupas, Buddha images, or other religious works in Khun Yuam. Even learned monks would be brought from the Shan States for religious purposes, particularly when the town had no able monks to perform rituals. Occasionally local men went to find a wife, to visit relatives or friends, to get special kinds of food or cooking ingredients, to hire Tai musicians for entertainment. In the old days, the Shan States were always the place to go looking for Tai culture.

There were two groups of traders: full-time and part-time. All traders traveled on foot. Part-time traders, having no animals, normally carried the goods themselves, but full-time traders used oxen as pack animals and were therefore known as *phaukhaa wuataang* or "oxen caravan traders."[12] They were better off than part-time traders, who normally traded in the dry season after the harvest. Oxen caravan traders traveled in groups for safety reasons, for example, protection from wild animals, thieves, and bandits and for companionship. Traders thus often hired local men who were not traders to guard the trading caravans.

Many traders were said to be skillful in Tai martial arts—known as *laaj*-and had some knowledge of supernatural powers. Local oxen caravan traders owned many oxen—as many as thirty heads or more—as an indication of wealth.[13] Some even possessed horses. They preferred to have large houses, with particularly large living rooms at the front, to provide a living space for friends or fellow traders who came from other towns or villages. In the compounds, colossal rice house were built to keep enough grain on hand for their own consumption and for guests throughout the year. The hospitality that local traders offered to their trading counterparts from outside the town was reciprocated when they traveled to other towns to trade. Most caravan traders also owned rice-cultivated land, which in some cases was rented out to others to farm. Still other traders hired the locals to work on their land. Rent and wages were often paid in the form of rice, but cash was occasionally used as well. Wealthy traders also hired local women to work as servants or shopkeepers.

The Troubled Frontier

Life in the earlier days was difficult. There were wars between the Tai and the Kayah; both sides vied constantly to occupy the land, to assemble people for labor, to control the trade routes, and so forth. The rulers of Chiang Mai also tried to share control of the area. The fighting and conflicts in the area were serious enough to force the Thai government in Bangkok to reform its administration by the turn of the century. Despite the reforms, disputes continued, particularly between the British and the Thai. The latter decided to make more changes, in both the administrative and judicial systems. The following three or four decades also saw the administration trying to solve its disputes with the Tai who were British subjects. Taxes were reduced and individual land ownership was granted to the locals. For political reasons, more new settlers were persuaded to move into the area. New small settlements cropped up and Khun Yuam district slowly grew.

The fighting along the border in the territory of Mae Hong Son and Khun Yuam had continued even after the establishment of the two communities, forcing many residents of Mae Hong Son to seek refuge elsewhere. The town became almost deserted. The population of Khun Yuam, on the contrary, was slowly growing. In 1869–70[14] the ruler of Chiang Mai ordered his officials to inspect the territory around Khun Yuam again. Later Cakamöngsan, a local Tai, was appointed Phraya Sihanat; his wife, Nang Mia was put in charge of Khun Yuam administration. But in 1873–74 (?), "Nang Mia took her group to Mae Hong Son, where they cleared the land, prepared the soil for crops, and turned the place into a large town.... When Nang Mia took charge of Mae Hong Son and it grew, Müang Mai [the northern subordinate town of Mae Hong Son at that time, but now in Burmese territory] was placed under the jurisdiction of Mae Hong Son. Two towns were then under the jurisdiction of Mae Hong Son: Müang Mai and Müang Khunyuam" (Wilson 1985: 36). Khun Yuam was under the authority of Mae Hong Son rulers until 1884–85 (?) when the governor of Chiang Mai granted Khun Yuam its own administration (Wilson 1985: 36) and its own town ruler. As far as the Thai government was concerned, Khun Yuam was essential because of its militarily strategic location at the frontier between Thailand and Burma, which was occupied by the British. The Thai ruler in Bangkok was worried by the Burmese subjects of the British who traveled into the territory of Thailand to trade and seemed always to cause trouble to the local administration. The ruler of Khun Yuam, therefore, had to be a reliable and prudent person whom the Thai administration in Bangkok could trust (NA, R.5 RL-PS vol. 28).

After Phraya Sihanat died in 1884 (or in 1881–82, according to Wilson's manuscript), Nang Mia, who was also involved in teak logging, went to Chiang Mai for business purposes and was detained there for a while by Chiang Mai's ruler before returning to Mae Hong Son (NA, R.5 RL-PS vol. 28, p. 45). She was later appointed *caw müang,* the ruler of Mae Hong Son, while a local Tai man became the *khun* of Khun Yuam (Saadronnawid 1981: 10). She divided the local population into two groups, civilian and military, and ordered the groups' leaders to discuss and come up with solutions among themselves, and "do not follow the law practiced by Chiang Mai" (Wilson 1985: 36). Gradually, the rulers of Mae Hong Son and Khun Yuam became more independent from the caw (the ruler) of Chiang Mai.

In *rau sau* 119 (A.D. 1900), the "Regulations on the Administration of the Northwestern Monthon" were promulgated by the Thai court in Bangkok, integrating "Chiang Mai, Lampang, Lamphun, Phrae, and Nan into Thailand as one of eighteen *monthon* within the *thesaphiban* or centralized system of provincial administration" (Ratanaporn 1989: 255). Khun Yuam, Mae Hong Son, Mae Sariang, and Pai were also included in the Northwestern Monthon. These *müang* were all under the administration of the "*kha luang thesaphiban* [High Commissioner], a resident of Chiang Mai] whose deputies were in charge of different departments, including justice, revenue, treasury, public works, and forestry. The *monthon* was the highest level of government in the North, being directly responsible to Bangkok and all the officials of which were Bangkok appointees" (Ratanaporn 1989: 255). The titles of other officials were also changed by adopting some local terms (Phornphun 1974: 160–61). In the same year the Thai government also reorganized the administration of Khun Yuam. The rice paddy tax and the cattle slaughter tax, as well as the passport fee, were reimposed. The two roads in Khun Yuam town were widened by the communal cooperation of the locals so that one of them could be used as the market-place (in the past, selling and buying goods in Khun Yuam had usually been done on both road-sides in the center of the town) (NA, R.5 M. 58/175).

Ten years later, the local administration was reorganized. In 1910, Mae Hong Son was granted the status of a province of the northern region with Khun Yuam as one of its five *amphoe* (districts). Since then, a *phu-uwaaraatchakaan changwat*, or provincial governor, has been periodically appointed by the Ministry of Interior Affairs as the head of the provincial administration of Mae Hong Son, and a *naaj amphoe* heads up the district office in Khun Yuam (Raadchasenaa 1981: 16, fn. 2; Saadronnawid 1981: 12). New conflicts, however, emerged in the 1920s. Disputes among the locals, or between the locals and the authorities, over taxes and land or land ownership became too severe to be ignored. The Thai administration began to intervene and eventually made some progress.

After Khun Yuam was established, Phraya Sihanat, the first Tai *caw müang* of Mae Hong Son, ordered that the land surrounding Khun Yuam and Mae Hong Son, most of which was mountainous and covered with trees, be cleared for paddy fields. To encourage the settlers, all comers were allowed to clear as much new land as they wanted. The ruler supplied new settlers with some provisions, such as food and necessary equipment to clear the land (NA, MT.5.16/1). One of the first Tai settlers, Chaangnu, who migrated with his parents from the Shan States when he was thirteen years old, told Thai authorities that when the town of Mae Hong Son was founded there were only five hundred residents living in several *tambon* of Paang Muu, Mae Sauj, and Thung Mamuang. Many Tai people also already resided in Khun Yuam. At the time, land was not for sale. Anyone who wanted a piece of land just had to clear it and begin to cultivate it. If one stopped utilizing the land, it would be given to others who wanted it by the *caw müang*, who was in charge of ensuring that the cleared land was cultivated and the land tax collected (NA, MT.5.16/1). In other words, one could cultivate any land as long as one kept working on it and kept paying the tax. However, a peasant had neither title to nor owned the land. Anyone who cultivated the land had to pay *khaa nam* (the water tax) for the irrigation water that was used in the paddy fields as well (NA, MT.5.16/1).

Therefore, disputes between Thai authorities and the land users over land tax naturally occurred at times. In *rau sau* 131 (A.D. 1912), for example, four Tai landholders, who lived in Baan Paang Muu and were also British subjects, neglected their paddy fields. Their rights to land use therefore ceased. The four men appealed to the British Consul, accusing Thai authorities of prejudice against them. The British demanded that these four cases be reexamined. At the end of September in the same year, the Thai administration ordained that all cleared land to be registered by the *monthon's* authority, and a lease contract signed by both the land user and the authority. If the user stopped either cultivating the land or paying the rent, the lease would be terminated and the land would no longer be available to the lessee (NA, MT.5.16/1). Despite the above, disputes over land rights still occurred occasionally. Twenty-six years later, in 1938, Thai authorities decided to investigate the issue and discovered that the total area of the paddy fields in the territory of Mae Hong Son and Khun Yuam was approximately 735 *rai*, leased to 128 persons of several ethnic groups. But it was almost impossible to locate an individual land user's territory exactly. Also, the total "land-lease"[15] collected by the Mae Hong Son authorities at the time was only 60 baht annually. Most importantly, the Thai government was rather concerned that if the residents, many of whom were British subjects, were confronted with hardship, they might move to other places (and thus cause the Thai administration more troubles with the British). To forestall this, the Thai government, through the Ministry of Interior Affairs, finally decided to grant the residents of Mae Hong Son, Khun Yuam, and other districts along the border the right to own their land. This meant that any peasant who had leased the land from the authorities was now its owner (NA, MT.5.16/1). Since then, land ownership has been transferable from one individual to another.

Taxes and land ownership however were not the only causes of disputes between the locals and the authorities. Two serious insults were inflicted during this period. One was a prohibition imposed by the Thai administration on males wearing their hair long. The other was a case of sexual assault. Both sparked outrage among the locals, especially the Tai; some elders still recall these incidents bitterly. Like their fellows in the Shan States, the Tai in Khun Yuam, males and females, all had long hair.[16] Unfortunately, this custom was bound for extinction. Several elderly local Tai residents recall the prohibition of the Tai topknot hairstyle in Khun Yuam, apparently before the end of the nineteenth century: Tai males were no longer allowed to display their long hair. This prohibition, enforced by Thai authorities, was a great blow to the Tai men's morale because long hair was not only for the sake of beauty: the head and hair, as well as the combings, were considered *suung* (high) and sacred.[17] Thus, it would not be too surprising to find that many of these men fled across the border into the Shan States to avoid this new, heartbreaking regulation.

This new restriction applied to all Tai people, including those who lived in Khun Yuam, Mae Hong Son and along the Thai-Burmese border. In 1884 (or *cau sau* 1246, as recorded in the manuscript), the British Consul in Bangkok sent a letter to the Thai court protesting that the regulation was oppressive and could possibly result in many Tai from the Shan States, who were British subjects and often traveled across the border into the territory of Thailand, mistakenly being forced to have their hair cut. The Thai court replied that this regulation was intended to distinguish the Siamese Tai from the Burmese Tai, many of whom fled to Thailand when the fighting and the banditry along the Thai-Burmese border became intolerable. The court argued that having short hair had been traditional since ancient days. The men of Chiang Mai and other Thai towns in the northern region all had their hair cut. This regulation also served to prevent innocent Tai immigrants from the Shan States who had fled to Thailand from being mistakenly arrested, or even hurt, by Thai authorities. In the Thai court's view, if the Tai people wanted to be Thai subjects, they had to wear short hair like the Thai. If not, they would be regarded as Burmese. This was certainly not an oppression, but a matter of identity. Also, it was a means to learn who the allies and enemies of the country were (NA, R.5 RL-PS vol. 28, pp. 48–50).

The regulation was introduced because the Tai who were British subjects had become one of the Thai government's main concerns, often causing disputes between the Thai ruler and the British-Burmese administration. At the end of *rau sau* 112 (A.D.1893), for instance, the British Consul claimed that many of the Tai speakers who had fled conflicts in Mawkmai in the Shan States and taken refuge in Baan Mae La Luang (south of Khun Yuam) for the past seven years, wanted to return to their hometown of Mawkmai because the fighting had ceased, but were prevented from doing so by Thai officials at Müang Yuam (the former name of Mae Sariang town) and Mae Hong Son. The Thai government in Bangkok sent a letter to the British advising them that since these Tai residents had lived rather comfortably in Thai territory for many years, the Thai government was concerned that they might face hardship on return to their hometown. Several months later, however, after being detained by Thai officials, these Tai families were finally allowed to return to Mawkmai (NA, R.5 M.58/190). It is unclear why the Thai government did not want these Tai people to return to their hometown in the Shan States. Perhaps, however, it is related to the fact that at that time the border between Thailand and Burma was not yet settled. The Thai government was therefore trying to establish as many settlements as possible in the area it claimed was its territory, in order to provide evidence if a dispute concerning the territory should arise with the British-Burmese administration. In addition, it could also possibly be because the Thai government may have hoped that the settlers who were loyal to Thailand would defend the Thai frontier.[18]

The most grievous incident affecting relations between the rulers of Chiang Mai and of Khun Yuam, which proved a bitter experience for the locals of the latter, occured at the end of 1888. Nai Banchaphumasathan, who had recently visited Khun Yuam, told the story he had heard that "Cao Ratchaphakhinai of Chiang Mai had come to live as an official in Müang Khunyuam. He had abducted the daughters of the local people and the fathers and relatives of the women were angry. They joined together to attack Cao Ratchaphakhinai, and when he died, they fled, leaving Müang Khunyuam for the west bank of the Salween" (Wilson 1985: 33). One source found in Khun Yuam, however, gives some different details about the incident; namely, that Caw Raad (as he is called in the manuscript) was attracted to the daughter of Laeng, a very close friend of the ruler of Khun Yuam, but she did not have a crush on him. One day, Caw Raad visited the girl at home while her father was absent. Aflame with passion, he lost control of himself and raped her. Upon returning home, the girl's father saw Caw Raad leaving his daughter's room. Guessing what had happened, he was outraged and killed Caw Raad with his sword. The ruler of Khun Yuam reported the incident to Chiang Mai, which immediately demanded a full investigation. Caw Raad was found guilty of sexually assaulting the girl, so Laeng was not punished and continued to live in Khun Yuam. The body of Caw Raad was buried on a hilltop, east of the town,[19] which came to be called *Kung Caw Raad* (Saadronnawid 1981: 10–1).

Some locals say that Caw Raad hid behind the trees next to a pool and waited for some girls to come down to fetch water; then he came out and assaulted them. In this version, therefore, the incident takes place near the pool, not in the house. In another version of the same story told by a few elderly Tai informants, Caw Raad is not an official from Chiang Mai but the leader of a gang of bandits who robbed the locals of Khun Yuam and often abducted the women. He was finally arrested and taken to the top of a hill, where he was executed. Today, the story of Caw Raad seems to be forgotten; only some elderly town residents, as far as I know, recall the incident.

Lauj Krathong: A History Transformed

Throughout the northern region—in fact, in many places in both Thailand and the Shan States—the legendary tales of Phra Ubpakhud are handed down in various versions, so in the record the spelling of his name differs slightly from one version to another.[20] Almost all of these versions, however, relate Phra Ubpakhud to rainmaking or protecting a festival against disaster. In Khun Yuam, until recently Phra Ubpakhud was also associated with the *Lauj Krathong* festival, and with traders and being wealthy.[21] In this section I shall focus on the tales of Phra Ubpakhud and *Lauj Krathong*, which have been gradually replaced by the official narrative of Naang Nobphamaad's *Lauj Krathong*, a story of a woman who promoted a festival that linked celebrants with the Thai history several hundred years back of the Sukhothai period.

According to Przyluski (1967: 4), Phra Ubpakhud is said to have "a merchant origin."[22] His father was a perfume merchant in Mathurā, in the north of India, and Upagupta himself helped in his father's trade for some time before he was ordained as a Buddhist monk. His story is well-known for his adventures with King Aśoka and his victory over "Māra, the chief god of the realm of desire [kāmadhātu] who plays a somewhat satanic role as a tempter in Buddhism" (Strong 1983: 16). Phra Ubpakhud is also called a "Buddha without the marks" or "Alaksanaka Buddha". Strong explains that "[t]he implication is that he is like the Buddha in that he is enlightened and preaches sermons, but unlike him in that he does not possess the thirty-two major and eighty minor bodily marks of the Great Man [Mahāpurusa] (1983: 81, fn 27).

Phra Ubpakhud is a rather ambiguous and complex figure. Tambiah notes that at least three versions of the story of Phra Ubpakhud are told in the northeastern region. The first version is that Phra Ubpakhud "was a novice who lived in the water of the swamp (in a subterranean town). He was the son of Buddha and his mother was a mermaid. It is said that once the Buddha forced his semen … into the water and a mermaid swallowed it, became pregnant and gave birth to Uppakrut." The second version describes Phra Ubpakhud as "a *Naga* or serpent spirit," who "lives in the water. … He is invited to guard the proceedings; if he is not, then murder, storm and lightning will occur through the acts of Mara." The third version recounts the story of Phra Ubpakhud, who as a monk practicing "water meditating,"[23] was invited to preside over "a meeting of 1,000 monks in order to eliminate doctrinal differences. It was the third meeting of this sort since Lord Buddha's death" (Tambiah 1970: 169–70). Wells (1975) documents a story similar to Tambiah's second version in which "King Asoka once decided to build 84,000 *cetiyas* but Māra threatened to destroy them. The king appealed to the Lord of the Nāgas, Phra Upagota, to help him by capturing Māra. This the Nāga Lord did" (Wells 1975: 114). Sathiankoosed (Phya Anuman Rajadhon), a distinguished Thai scholar, states that some tellings say that Phra Ubpakhud lives at the "bottom of the sea." He also suggests that such versions of the story seem to confuse Phra Ubpakhud with the Lord of the Nagas, who also lives in the water (Sathiankoosed 1965: 194). A Burmese version, on the other hand, informs us that Phra Ubpakhud—or Shin Upago—as he is called by the Burmese, resides "down at the bottom of the river." This is because "[I]n a former existence he carried off the clothes of a bather, and for this mischievous pleasantry is condemned to remain in his present quarters till Arimadeya, the next Buddha, shall come. Then he will be set free, and entering the thenga will become a yahanda, and attain Ne'ban [Nirvana]" (Shway Yoe 1989: 228–9).

All the versions of the stories of Phra Ubpakhud appearing in the Kon Müang mythological tradition are similar to those mentioned above. According to Richard Davis, these versions can be recategorized into two main types: the literary and the oral. In both, "Upagutta is connected with the aquatic world" (Rhum 1987: 187; see also Davis 1984: 223–25). Rhum comments that "[I]t is surprising that Davis does not note that in the oral tradition [which of course is the one that concerns most villagers] Upagutta is considered to be a Buddhist novice… He is not fully a monk, but he is an ordained person. He is pre-eminently concerned with the control of water and is thought to live in rivers" (1987: 187). He continues to point out that both Davis (1984) and Tambiah (1970) agree that Phra Ubpakhud is said to dwell in the swamps (Rhum 1987: 187, fn. 24).

Because Phra Ubpakhud is best known for his triumph over Māra when the latter was trying to interfere with the former's preaching in Mathurā[24] (see details in Strong 1983: 77–78, 107–8, 185–96), he is usually worshipped as a protector, particularly of Buddhist festivals. Rhum (1987: 185) notes that from the Kon Müang's point of view, Phra Ubpakhud's job "is to protect the festival against the depredations of Māra and his hosts, who seek to disrupt these festivals. Their primary weapons are rain and fights amongst the festival-goers, which occur mainly between young men from different villages. Upagutta stops the rain and maintains social harmony... These festivals are major merit-making ceremonies whose theme is donation (*dāna*) by the laity to the temples. It should be noted that these festivals are not regular calendrical rites." It is rather clear, therefore, that Phra Ubpakhud lives in the water, either in the river or the swamp, and is so powerful that he is always invited to protect Buddhist festivals from disasters caused by both humans and nature.

Phra Ubpakhud is also associated with the rites of rain. Davis (1984: 228) provides an excellent summary: "Upagrutta's rites are performed in order to produce rain as well as to prevent it. His association with rain-making has been noted by a number of authorities. Phya Anuman thinks Upagrutta may be related to Phra Bua Khem, a type of Siamese Buddha image used in rain-making rites...Tambiah has interpreted the 'floating lights' festival [*Lauj Krathong*] as an offering of thanks to Upagrutta for the rain he has produced during the preceding *vassa*, and as a means of returning him to his watery abode once the rains are over.... Porée-Maspero has similarly deduced that Upagrutta is a rain deity, and that the floating of lighted vessels serves to return the forces of humidity to their ultimate source."

A rather different version of Phra Ubpakhud is told by an elderly, learned local Tai named Bunsii:

"Once, there was a fishing village. One day, several fishermen caught a big fish, about seven meters long. But when the head of the fish was cut off, it was still alive and its stomach was still moving. The fishermen thus decided to cut open the fish's body and they found a bag in its stomach. Inside the bag, there was a baby girl. They did not know what to do with the baby, so they thought they had better bring the baby to the king, who appeared to have no children. The king received the baby with joy and rewarded all the fishermen. Then, the baby was named Naang Misa.

The baby grew up to be a beautiful girl, but there was one problem; she had a terribly unpleasant body odor. The king tried by all means to have her cured, but no doctor could do anything. Time passed and the smell of her body became worse. The king's ministers and the nobles began to complain about her. They threatened to leave the country if the king did not do anything. Finally, the king had to order that the girl be put away on a raft in the river. She wept all the time until the raft came to the place where a *rishi* lived. The *rishi* heard her crying, so he rescued her and let her stay. He not only built a small hut for her (he himself lived in a cave), but also tried to help her to get rid of her unpleasant body odor by using the herbs he found in the forest until she was cured. As the days went by, she felt more and more grateful for his kindness until, though they had never had a sexual relationship, she became pregnant. The woman gave birth to a baby boy and she brought him up with great care and love.

One day, the *rishi* asked the woman whether or not she and her son wanted to return to her country. The woman said yes, so he accompanied them to her country. The king was very happy to see his daughter and grandson. He accepted them into his palace with a warm welcome. The boy grew to his teens in the palace. The king wanted his grandson to be his heir and become a king when he passed away, but his daughter wanted him to be ordained as a monk. Their argument went on for some time and upset the boy so much that one day he could no longer bear it. He jumped up into the air and began to fly to the heavens. Up there, he was ordained by *Phra In*[25] and was named Phra Ubpakhud. After the ordination, while he was flying down to the earth, he could see nothing but water. In the ocean, there was only one palace, made of gold, he thus had to land on that palace. Since then, Phra Ubpakhud has lived in the golden palace in the ocean."

Unlike the stories reported by Tambiah and Davis, this version depicts Phra Ubpakhud not as the son of Buddha and a mermaid, but of a *rishi* and a woman who is found in the stomach of a fish. Yet there are some similarities, such as that he is a Buddhist novice and resides in the water. Bunsii also reveals that according to Tai belief, offerings for Phra Ubpakhud are to be made twice a year, once on the full-moon day of the fourth lunar month and then again on the full-moon day of the twelfth lunar month. In the old days, Tai people would offer alms to the monks at the monasteries and listen to their sermons on the morning of the full-moon day of the fourth month. After nightfall, a gathering of mainly the elders of both sexes would assemble at the house of an elder to listen to a *caree* reading the Buddhist *jataka* tales (in Tai—*thaum lik*).[26] In Khun Yuam, however, observance of this tradition is in decline, and today only a small group of the elderly Tai still listen to the reading of the book.

A bigger, more important ceremony, was held on the night of the full-moon day of the twelfth month. On this night certain items, including a piece of *saang kaan* (the outer yellow robe of the monk),[27] fruit, sweets, betel, flowers, joss-sticks, and candles, were offered to Phra Ubpakhud. Because Phra Ubpakhud lives in the water, all of these offerings had to be put on a *phae* (raft) built from bamboo almost six meters long. Several householders would join together and combined their contribution atop a single *phae* to ensure that it would hold more than enough provisions. After dark, locals of all ages and sexes gathered at the monastery to listen to the monks preaching. At about midnight, the *phae*, accompanied by four Tai Buddhist monks, was carried to the riverbank. The candles were lit while the four monks preached to invite Phra Ubpakhud to come and take the offerings. When the monks finished their sermon, the *phae* was floated on the river. In the past, especially when the harvest or trade was good, there were more offerings, and a few *phae* would be built to float on the river. Again, fewer people, mainly the elderly Tai, continue to participate in the Phra Ubpakhud ceremony today. Since each year only a few households contribute offerings, the size of the *phae* is gradually decreasing.

In recent years in Khun Yuam, this "raft-floating" ceremony seems to have been replaced by the *Lauj Krathong* festival. Rhum (1987) describes Lauj Krathong, which is a term borrowed from the Thai language, as "to float banana-leaf cups [krathong]…containing offerings and a little candle, as an offering to Ganga and Upagutta." He reports that these *krathong* are floated in the river on the night of the full-moon day of the second lunar month according to the Kon Müang lunar calendar (Rhum 1987: 189).[28] In Khun Yuam the *Lauj Krathong* festival is rather magnificent. Although the day is rather quiet, the celebration at night is spectacular. A procession of trucks decorated with flowers and colored paper parades throughout the town. There is then a beauty contest, followed by a huge fireworks display. Finally, hundreds of *krathong*, big and small, are lit and floated in the town's reservoir. There are morning and nighttime sermons at the monasteries as well, and some elders, both males and females, spend the night there.[29]

However, many townspeople, the youngsters in particular, are inclined to believe that the *Lauj Krathong* festival is related to Naang Nobphamaad rather than Phra Ubpakhud. Naang Nobphamaad was the first-ranked concubine of Phra Ruang, the Great King of Sukhothai (Sathiankoosed 1965: 183–84, 1961: 5; Wells 1975: 114). Such a belief is probably due to the influence of the Thai educational system in which only the legend of Naang Nobphamaad is taught under the school curriculum. It is stated that King Chulalongkorn once wrote that

"the Loy Krathong had some connection with the floating lanterns as observed by Thai kings in the north when Sukhothaya was the Capital some six or seven hundred years ago. It was described ornately in a book written by Nang Nophamat, a beautiful and learned lady of the court of King Phra Ruang. The lady was the daughter of a Brahmin family priest attached to the Court. She said that in the twelfth month, November… the court was flooded. The King and his court went for a picnic on the river to witness the people enjoying themselves during the water festival at night. Nothing is said of the Loy Krathong of the people, but it can be taken as a fact that it took place. The *krathong* was most probably in the same shape as that which we see at the present day, for Lady Nophamat told in her book that she had introduced a new kind of *krathong* in the shape of a big lotus flower and many other styles for the king to float in the running stream, no doubt for his enjoyment. She further initiated certain recitations and songs to be sung for the King on the occasion" (Sathiankoosed 1961: 32–3).

The statement above is confirmed by a document issued by Thailand's Department of Fine Arts, which declares that "incidents [in Naang Nobphamaad's story] narrated by the author are in the Sukhothai period" and that "there are records of Brahmanic rituals containing more details than any other books. In comparison with those written in the Ayutthayan Palace Laws [*Kog Monthianlaan*], these rituals are older, probably dated to the Sukhothai period." It then concludes that Naang Nobphamaad "is a literature written in the Sukhothai period" (Department of Fine Arts 2002: 110).

Naang Nobphamaad, however, has recently become a topic of academic debate. Nidhi Aeosriwongse, a well-known Thai historian, has expressed some doubt about the date of this work. He argues that neither the subjects mentioned in Naang Nobphamaad's story nor its literary style is as old as it is claimed. Referring to the scholarship of Prince Damrong's writing, he notes that "in Naang Nobphamaad's text, there are statements in several places, for example, referring to the Americans, cannons, etc., demonstrating that it was not written in the Sukhothai period. In addition, its literary style was clearly of the Bangkok period. It is also believed that Rama III wrote as much as half of the work." He assumes that the story of Naang Nobphamaad was written in the early Bangkok period (Nidhi 2002: 114–5). As a matter of fact, Prince Damrong had written at least since 1914 that "considering its literary style, anyone who read Naang Nobphamaad carefully would see it clearly that the book was written between Rama II and Rama III of the early Bangkok period. Not before or after" (Damrong 2002: 5–6).

If both Nidhi and Prince Damrong are correct, then the literature of Naang Nobphamaad is nothing but another invention of the Thai state that has been reproduced by its own agents, that is, the Department of Fine Arts and the Ministry of Education, telling a memory of the nation's past that all different ethnic groups must believe they all share. And the tactic has succeeded: they now believe that it is a part of their ethnic memories.

Khun Yuam Today

There are few records on the region until the time of World War II. Between 1942 and 1945 Japanese troops stopped in the Khun Yuam-Mae Hong Son area before invading Burma. Unpaved roads were built, connecting this region with the Shan States. Airfields for military use were constructed in Mae Hong Son, Khun Yuam, and Mae Sariang. After the war, the Thai government decided to pay more attention to this northwestern frontier, partly owing to the communist movements that had become increasingly active. The old dirt tracks built by the Japanese were upgraded several times and have now become the main highways connecting Mae Hong Son and other towns with Chiang Mai Province. Airfields in Mae Hong Son and Mae Sariang have been upgraded for commercial plane landings, while the airstrip in Khun Yuam is reserved for military purposes. The region has become very important for the strategic defense of the country, so a Border Patrol Police unit is now located near the border. In the 1960s a highway was constructed, linking Mae Hong Son, Khun Yuam, and Mae Sariang with Chiang Mai. A bus service was soon operating, followed a decade later by tourism, another new development. Since then, travelers and tourists have become a common scene in the town.

Thailand's economic growth since the mid 1980s has drawn Khun Yuam closer to the capital. Almost all of the goods sold in Khun Yuam's shops today are imported. Oxen caravan traders have vanished, replaced by itinerant traders and Bangkok-based companies sales representatives, who transport much of the merchandise manufactured in the central region. Most sales representatives come once a month to check whether shop owners want more goods, to introduce new products, to hand in bills, to receive payments, and so on. These newcomers also come with a new language: almost all of them speak Central Thai and do not understand Tai and Kam Müang. In fact, the use of Central Thai has been gradually increasing. It is spoken far more often than in the past. Its written form is used in all business-related activities, such as banking transactions, purchase orders, bills and payment. Another group of outsiders are the independent itinerant traders, who occasionally visit the town in their utility trucks loaded with consumer products. Many traders are of Thai speakers and some are of Kon Müang.

Economic developments in the last few decades in Thailand have turned Khun Yuam, once a quiet backwater northwestern frontier, into an active market town. While the prosperity of the new economy has made local people aware that they are a part of a bigger economic system, the success of the creation of a national identity that relates to the local memories also generates among local people the sense of belonging to the nation among local people. The majority Thai have successfully persuaded the Tai that they all share a common ancestry, as well as historical memories, by mesmerizing them with oral traditions of Tai-Thai brotherhoods.

Notes

1. Rev. Cochrane, citing Hallett, notes that the Siamese, who were descendants of "the Lao branch of the Tai family," were driven south by the Burmese in the late thirteenth century. They later founded "Ayuthia" (Ayutthaya) in the Chao Phraya Delta in 1350 (Milne 1970: 24).
2. The term "Tai" contains at least two meanings: Tai as a language family and Tai as a self-reference of a specific group that speaks a Tai language. Keyes (1987: 213) states that the people who speak various languages of the Tai language family are "found throughout mainland Southeast Asia and southern China and include the Shan of Burma and southern China, the Tai Lue of northern Laos and southern China, the Lao of Laos, and various other Tai groups (such as the Tai Dam or Black Tai, Tho, Nung, and Chuang) of northern Vietnam, northern Laos, and southern China. The main Tai-speech groups found today in Thailand are the Siamese or Central Thai, the Lao or Isan (or Northeastern Thai), the Yuan or Kon Muang (or Northern Thai), and the Southern Thai." The word "Tai" as used in this essay, however, is a self-reference of an ethnic group living mainly in the Shan States and some parts of northern Thailand.
3. The transliteration of Thai and Tai languages in this essay follows the system in Haas (1956).
4. The Kon Müang also use the term "Ngiaw" when they refer to the Tai. However, this term is considered offensive by the Tai themselves.
5. The frontier here is defined as "an area on the peripheral regions of a state in which the political authority of the centre is diffused or thinly spread" (Giddens 1985: 50).
6. Mae Chaem is a district under Chiang Mai provincial administration and adjacent to Khun Yuam to the east. The locals of *amphoe* Mae Chaem are mainly Karen, Kon Müang, Lua and Hmong speakers (Chiang Mai Provincial Office 1986: 78–79). There are no Tai speakers living in Mae Chaem.
7. Paang Muu is a Tai village several kilometres north of Mae Hong Son town.
8. Phornphun (1974: 52–53) documents that the amount of the "khaa taumaj," varying from one to three rupees per tree, depended on the size of the trees that were cut. Later, the Thai administration in Bangkok ordered the rulers of Chiang Mai to add another two rupees for each tree. The additional money was to be sent to Bangkok.
9. He later had another wife named Nang Mia who was also a Tai. There is no record available about his first wife or why Shaankalee decided to take a new wife. In Wilson's paper, Shaankalee is referred to as Cakamöngsan (see below).
10. Today, none of the Lua people live in the Khun Yuam area. A large number of the Lua, however, reside in the territory of Mae La Noi, a neighboring district south of Khun Yuam.
11. Saadronnawid (1981: 6–7) states that "kun" literally means hills or mountains and "jom" is a kind of tree abundant in this area. The name of this place subsequently became "Khun Yuam."
12. This word is sometimes translated as "ox-train traders" or "bullock traders" see Bowie (1988), Chusit (1989), and Scott (1932). These oxen were used only for transporting goods and were looked after with great care.
13. Chusit (1982: 20; 1989: 5) documents that some oxen caravan traders might own up to one hundred heads of oxen.
14. Here and the next two places, I mark the dates with question marks because there is some doubt about the years in the document translated by Constance Wilson. According to a document in the National Achives (NA, R.5 RL-PS vol.

28) and in Saadronnawid (1981: 10), Phraya Sihanat, the husband of Nang Mia, died in 1884 (*cau sau* 1246 or B.E. 2427), but in Wilson's paper (1985: 36) it was in 1881–82, a few years earlier.

15. The manuscript cited here used the term *khaa chaw* or the rent.

16. Milne (1970: 114) reports that the Shans in Burma's Shan States in the nineteenth century were all seen to wear "long, straight black hair, which is washed, then oiled, once a week, sometimes twice, and even three or four times. Both men and women comb their hair carefully before twisting it into a coil or tight knot on the top of the head. As no hairpins are used, the twist often becomes loose, is taken down, then arranged and rearranged many times in a day."

17. Milne indicates that amongst the Shans, "To throw hair combings where they might be stepped upon would bring bad luck to the owner of the hair. Combings should be pushed into the thatch of the roof of the house, or hidden in a bush" (1970: 184). Hair was also considered an important part of the beginning of life. It is said that after a baby was born, his "first hair which is cut off is very carefully kept. It is put into a little bag and hung round his neck, a sure charm to prevent him crying in the night. If the child is ill, the bag, with the cut hair, is soaked in water, and the water is used to wash his little body, or he may have to drink it as a soothing draught" (1970: 37).

18. This issue perhaps becomes clearer if one considers the Karen people who dwelled along the Thai-Burmese border. Renard (1980a: 23–25) suggests that in the late nineteenth century, despite the fact that the Karen residents had paid less valuable *suai* (tribute) to the Thai authorities, they were considered satisfactory since they had played a significant role in negotiating and defending the frontier of Thailand. Thus, it would not be too far-fetched, learning from the Karen experience, for the Thai government to expect that settlements located along the border where the residents were Karen, Tai, and others would serve the Thai, in Renard's own words, "as border guards."

19. Its location is quite remarkable. To the south, at the foot of this hill, is a vast plain that is cultivated by the locals. Another hilltop to the west is the site of *Caung Khum*—one of the oldest Buddhist Tai temples in Khun Yuam. In the lowland between these two hills is a natural pool, where water is plentiful throughout the year and is used by the locals for drinking. It thus looks like a small valley with water running through the middle. To the north of the hill are residential areas, where most of the occupants are Tai speakers.

20. It is spelled "Upagrutta" (Davis 1984) or "Upagutta" (Rhum 1987) in the other provinces of the northern region, and "Phraa Uppakrut" (Tambiah 1970) in the northeastern region. He is sometimes referred to as "Phra Upagota" (Wells 1975: 114). Elsewhere, he is known as "Upagupta" (Przyluski 1967; Strong 1983). Rhum writes that in the Kam Müang language, his name is "usually spelled *Uppagrud*," but pronounced as Uppakhut. This indicates "a confusion with the word *garuda*" (Rhum 1987: 187, fn. 22).

21. The story of kind-hearted traders who offer alms to Phra Ubpakhud and later become rich is told in many places in the northern region. In Chiang Mai, for instance, the story of Luang Anusarn Sunthorn is probably the most well-known one. Wijeyewardene writes that Luang Anusarn Sunthorn was "a cultural and historical phenomenon in Chiangmai." A very wealthy entrepreneur and philanthropist, he "was largely responsible for the foundation of Wat Uppakut." Wijeyewardene (1992: 19) also notes that

"It is a belief Phra Uppakut walks the streets of Chiangmai on the full moon of the ninth month as a monk seeking alms. The first one to make an offering is blessed with good fortune. There is a story in Chiangmai that the future Luang Anusarn had walked overland to Chiangmai from China and was earning his living as a pedlar on the streets of Chiangmai. He had the good fortune to *tag bat uppakut* (place alms in Uppakut's bowl) which was the start of his successful trading career. The story goes on to say that the now jewel-encrusted pedlar's pole which he used is enshrined in the *uposata* of Wat Uppakut."

However, Wijeyewardene (1992: 19) comments further that "Unfortunately the truth is more prosaic, though not without its own excitement. Luang Anusarn's father was a successful businessman in neighbouring Lamphun who fell foul of the ruler, the *Caw Müang*, and fled with his young family to the protection of the Chiangmai Prince." The story of Phra Ubpakhud on laypeople conferring good fortune confirms that traders are the people most likely to be wealthy. Whatever the truth is or how a trader becomes rich is not important; the belief is that if one is a trader and earns merit regularly, one will have an opportunity to be successful and wealthy. Wealth comes after accumulating adequate merit.

22. Strong (1983: 76–77) comments that the life of Phra Ubpakhud is always "the subject of several legends.... In a previous life, on Mount Urumunda, Upagupta is said to have been the leader of a band of monkeys who converted five hundred Brahmanical ascetics by imitating in front of them the meditative postures of Buddhist monks." The legend continues describing how the here as subsequent life as a son of a perfume merchant was in fact foreseen and predicted by the Buddha himself one hundred years before Phra Ubpakhud was reborn (see details in Strong 1983: 174–76). None of my informants mentioned that the origin of Phra Ubpakhud was a merchant's son.

23. A similar version is told by Davis (1984). In this version Phra Ubpakhud "is a Buddhist ascetic whose solitary meditations at the bottom of the sea help him to achieve extraordinary psychic powers with which to vanquish violence, discord, and aggression" (1984: 228). Also note that the stories told of Ubpakhud's origin in all regions in Thailand, as far as I know, are quite different from the texts studied by Przyluski (1967) and Strong (1983).

24. Note that in Strong's version, Māra interrupts Phra Ubpakhud's own sermons in Mathurā, but in Davis's and Wells's versions, Phra Ubpakhud is invited by King Aśoka to prevent Māra from breaking up the cerebration of the "construction of 84,000 reliquaries built in honour of the Buddha" (Davis 1984: 223–24; see also Wells 1975: 114).

25. According to Tambiah (1970: 295), Phra In is God Indra.

26. The nighttime reading of the *jataka* was performed neither by Tai monks nor at the monasteries.

27. This item is most significant among the offerings. The outer yellow robe is needed because it is, in Tambiah's (1970: 302) words, a "conspicuous symbol of monkhood." In the *Bun Phraweet* festival held in some places in the northeastern region, there are even more offerings for Phra Ubpakhud: an almsbowl, an umbrella, a chamber pot, a kettle (Pricha 1991: 69), or even a triangle-shaped cushion and a water-basin (Kasem 1973: 32). Unlike the ceremony in Khun Yuam, moreover, these offerings are put on a small bamboo stool that stands about eyelevel.

28. The Tai lunar calendar differs from that of the Kon Müang. The first lunar month in the Kon Müang tradition begins after *auk phansaa,* or the End of

Buddhist Lent, which is approximately the eleventh lunar month in the Tai tradition. Therefore, the Tai twelfth lunar month is close to the Kon Müang second lunar month, and the Tai fourth lunar month is the Kon Müang sixth lunar month.

29. In the Kon Müang village where Rhum conducted his research, the celebration of *Lauj Krathong* is not less significant. There is one sermon in the morning and another at night at the village's monastery, and alms are given to the monks. Paper hot-air balloons are made and floated into the air. Small rockets and firecrackers are fired throughout the day. At night, a lot of *krathong* are floated in the nearby river (Rhum 1987: 189, fn. 26).

References

Athivaro Bhikkhu. B.E. 2535 (1992). *Wat kam kau changwat maehongson.* Mae Hong Son: Wat Kam Kau.

Bhabha, Homi K., ed. 1990. *Nation and Narration.* London and New York: Routledge.

Bowie, Katherine Ann. 1988. *Peasant Perspectives on the Political Economy of the Northern Thai Kingdom of Chiang Mai in the Nineteenth Century: Implications for the Understanding of Peasant Political Expression.* Ph.D. dissertation, University of Chicago.

Bunchuai Sisawat. B.E. 2504 (1961). *Chiangmai lae phaagnya* (Chiang Mai and the Northern Region). Bangkok: Khlang Witthaya.

Chiang Mai Provincial Office. B.E. 2529 (1986). *Prawad mahaadthaj suanphuumiphaag changwat chiangmai* (Ministry of Interior Affairs' Regional History of Chiang Mai Province). Chiang Mai: Chiang Mai Provincial Office.

Chusit Chuchart. B.E. 2525 (1982). *Phaukhaa wuathang phuubugboeg kaankhaakhaj naj muubaan phaagnya khaung phratheedthaj (phau sau 2398–2503)* (Phaukhaa wauthang: The Trading Pioneers in the Villages of Northern Thailand, 1855–1960). Chiang Mai: Chiang Mai Teachers College.

——. 1989. "From Peasant to Rural Trader: The Ox-Train Traders of Northern Thailand, 1855–1955." *Australian National University Thai-Yunnan Project Newsletter* 7, 2–8.

Damrong Rachanuphap, Prince. B.E. 2545 (2002). *"Ryang naang nobphamaad ryy tamrub thawsrichulaalag"* (The Text of Naang Nobphamaad or Thaw Srichulaalag). Suchitt Wongthes, 3rd ed., *Maj mii naang nobphamaad, maj mii lauj krathong, samaj sukhoothaj* (There are neither Naang Nobphamaad nor Lauj Krathong in the Sukhothai period), Bangkok: Matichon Publisher.

Davis, Richard. 1984. *Muang Metaphysics: A Study of Northern Thai Myth and Ritual.* Bangkok: Pandora.

Department of Fine Arts. B.E. 2545 (2002). *"Kam-athibaaj ryang Naang Nobphamaad"* (Explanation of Naang Nobphamaad's Story). In Suchitt Wongthes, 3rd ed., *Maj mii naang nobphamaad, maj mii lauj krathong, samaj sukhoothaj* (There are neither Naang Nobphamaad nor Lauj Krathong in the Sukhothai period),. Bangkok: Matichon Publisher.

Diller, Anthony. 1994. "Tai Languages: Varieties and Subgroup Terms." *Australian National University Thai-Yunnan Project Newsletter* 25, 8–17.

Giddens, Anthony. 1985. *The Nation-State and Violence.* Cambridge: Polity Press.

Haas, Mary R. 1956. *The Thai System of Writing.* Washington, D.C.: American Council of Learned Societies.

Keyes, Charles F. 1987. *Thailand: Buddhist Kingdom as Modern Nation-State.* Boulder and London: Westview Press.

Khun Yuam District Office. B.E. 2535 (1992). *Eegkasaanprakaub kaanbanjaasarub amphoe khunyuam* (Summary Report of Khun Yuam District). Khun Yuam: Khun Yuam District Office.

La Loubère, Simon de. 1986. *The Kingdom of Siam.* Singapore: Singapore University Press.

Mae Hong Son Provincial Office. B.E. 2535 (1992). *Eegkasaanbanjaasarub changwat maehongson* (Summary Report of Mae Hong Son Province). Mae Hong Son: Mae Hong Son Provincial Office.

Maitri Limpichat. B.E. 2523 (1980). *Khon naj phaalyang* (Man in a Yellow Robe). Samut Prakan: Naun.

Milne, Leslie. 1970 [1910]. *Shans at Home.* New York: Paragon Book Reprint Corp.

NA [The National Achives, Bangkok], MT.5.16/1. *Eegkasaan krasuangmahaadthaj ryang khamraungkhaung naj bunsiri theephaakham "naamyang" changwat maehongson, phau sau 2462–2481* (Documents of the Ministry of Interior Affairs, Naj Bunsiri Theephaakham's appeal regarding the agricultural land in Mae Hong Son Province, A.D. 1919–1938).

NA, R.5 M.58/175. *Eegkasaan kromraadchalekhaa radchakaanthiihaa krasuangmahaadthaj ryang cadraadchakaan myangkhunyuam 20 mithunaajon rau sau 119–16 kumphaaphan rau sau 119* (Documents of the Royal Secretary of the Fifth Reign, Ministry of Interior Affairs, Organizing the administration of Müang Khun Yuam. 20 June 1900–16 February 1901).

NA, R.5 M.58/190. *Eegkasaan kromraadchalekhaa radchakaanthiihaa krasuangmahaadthaj ryang angkryydtauwaa ryang ngiawcaklabpaj myangmaugmaj cawnaathiimajhajpaj 31 October rau sau 112–16 January rau sau 112* (Documents of the Royal Secretary of the Fifth Reign, Ministry of Interior Affairs, British's complaint about the Thai authority prohibited the Tai of Müang Mauk Mai from returning home. 31 October 1893–16 January 1894).

NA, R.5 RL-PS vol. 28. *Eegkasaanjeblem kromraadchalekhaa radchakaanthiihaa chudsamudphiseed (cau sau 1246)* (Documents of the Royal Secretary of the Fifth Reign, Special Volume, A.D. 1884).

Nidhi Aeosriwongse. B.E. 2545 (2002). *"Loog khaung naang nobphamaad"* (The World of Naang Nobphamaad). In *Maj mii naang nobphamaad, maj mii lauj krathong, samaj sukhoothaj* (There are neither Naang Nobphamaad nor Lauj Krathong in the Sukhothai Period), ed. Suchitt Wongthes. Bangkok: Matichon Publisher (3rd edition).

Phornphun Chongvatana. B.E. 2517 (1974). *Kauraniiphiphaad rawaang cawnakhaunchiangmai kab khonnajbangkhab-angkryd anpenhethaj radthabaansajaam cadkaanpogkraung monthonphaajab (phau sau 2401–2445)* (Disputes of British Subjects against the Ruler of Chiang

Mai resulting in the Siamese Government taking over the Administration of Northwest Siam [Payap Circle] [A.D. 1858–1902]), M.A. thesis, Chulalongkorn University.

Przyluski, J. 1967. *The Legend of Emperor Asoka in Indian and Chinese Texts.* trans. Dilip Kumar Biswas. Calcutta: Firma K. L. Mukhopadhyay.

Raadchasenaa, Phrajaa (Siri Thebhadsadin Na Ajudthajaa). B.E. 2524 (1981). *"Khanpogkraung rabaubtheesaaphibaan"* (Provincial Administration). In eds. Wutthichai Munlasilp and Somchote Ongsakun eds. *Monthontheesaaphibaan: Wikhraupriabthiab* (Comparative Study of Provincial Units), Bangkok: Siam Society.

Rajah, Ananda. 1990. "Ethnicity, Nationalism, and the Nation-State: The Karen in Burma and Thailand." In *Ethnic Groups across National Boundaries in Mainland Southeast Asia,* ed. Gehan Wijeyewardene. Singapore: Institute of Southeast Asian Studies.

Ratanaporn Sethakul. 1989. *Political, Social, and Economic Changes in the Northern States of Thailand Resulting from the Chiang Mai Treaties of 1874 and 1883.* Ph.D. dissertation, Northern Illinois University.

Renard, Ronald. 1980a. "The Role of the Karens in Thai Society during the Early Bangkok Period, 1782–1873." In Constance M. Wilson, Chrystal Stillings Smith, and George Vinal Smith eds. *Royalty and Commoners: Essays in Thai Administrative, Economic, and Social History,* Leiden: E. J. Brill.

———. 1980b. *Kariang: History of Karen-Tai Relations from the Beginnings to 1923,* Ph.D. dissertation, University of Hawaii.

Rhum, Michael. 1987. *Tutelary Spirits of a Northern Thai Village.* Ph.D. dissertation, Harvard University.

Saadronnawid. B.E. 2524 (1981). *Thiiralyg naj ngaanchalaung sanjaabadphadjodchanphised phrakhruu anusausaadsanakaan cawkhana amphoe khunyuam* (In Memory of the Celebration for Phrakhruu Anusaunsaadsanakaan, the District Ecclesiastical Head of Khun Yuam, who was awarded the Fan of the Special Ecclesiastical Rank). Chiang Mai: Thibphajaned Kaanphim.

Sathiankoosed (Phya Anuman Rajadhon). B.E. 2504 (1961). *Theedsakaan loj krathong. Anusaun naj ngaanphraraadchathaanpleongsob naawaaaakaadeeg wichian wiboonmongkon. Wat Makudkasadkridjaaraam* (Lauj Krathong Festival. Eulogy of the Royal Cremation of Air Force Captain Wichian Wiboonmongkon at Wat Makudkasadkridjaaraam, 22 November). Bangkok: Roongphim Rungryangthaam.

———. B.E. 2508 (1965). *Prapheeniithaj kiawkab theedsakaan trud-saad* (The Thai Custom of *Trud-saad* Festivals). Bangkok: Mongkhon Kanphim.

Scott, J. George. 1932. *Burma and Beyond.* London: Grayson and Grayson.

Shway Yoe (Sir James George Scott) 1989 [1910]. *The Burman: His Life and Notions.* Arran, Scotland: Kiscadale Publications.

Smith, Anthony D. 1991. *National Identity.* Reno: University of Nevada Press.

Srisakr Vallibhotama and Suchitt Wongthes. B.E. 2534 (1991). *Thajnauj thajjaj thajsajaam sinlapawadthanatham chababphiseed* (Lesser Tai, Greater Tai, Siamese Tai Arts and Culture, Special Issue). Bangkok: Samnakphim Mathichon.

Strong, John S. 1983. *The Legend of King Asoka: A Study and Translation of the Asokavadana.* Princeton: Princeton University Press.

Tambiah, S. J. 1970. *Buddhism and the Spirit Cults in North-East Thailand.* Cambridge: Cambridge University Press.

Wells, Kenneth E. 1975. *Thai Buddhism: Its Rites and Activities.* Bangkok: Suriyabun Publishers.

Wijeyewardene, Gehan. 1990. "Thailand and the Tai: Versions of Ethnic Identity." In Gehan Wijeyewardene, ed. *Ethnic Groups across National Boundaries in Mainland Southeast Asia.* Singapore: Institute of Southeast Asian Studies.

———. 1992. "Obituary: Kraisri Nimmanahaeminda, 1912–1992." *Australian National University Thai-Yunnan Project Newsletter* 17: 19–20.

Wilson, Constance M. 1985. "Thai-Shan Diplomacy in the 1840s and a Thai Government Survey of the Middle Salween, 1890." In Constance M. Wilson and Lucien M. Hanks, eds. *The Burma-Thailand Frontier over Sixteen Decades: Three Descriptive Documents.* Athens, Ohio: Ohio University.

2

WOULD-BE CENTERS: THE TEXTURE OF HISTORICAL DISCOURSE IN MAKASSAR

William Cummings

THIS CHAPTER EXPLORES THE MULTIPLE ways in which marginality is both created and challenged through the medium of historical discourse in Makassar, South Sulawesi. In Makassar, as in much of Southeast Asia, claims of status and identity are predicated on claims about heritage from the past. Would-be centers use a variety of subaltern strategies—most notably imitation—in order to press their claims for relevance and assert that their voice too is worthy of being heard.

The challenges to marginality that emerge from Makassar encourage us to recognize that border regions may be found throughout the geographical space of the nation. As scholars today increasingly recognize that borders can most productively be viewed as dynamic social spaces in which dominant and marginal peoples negotiate their relationships—rather than as simple geographical areas—we can better appreciate that borders and margins are not found only at the geographic frontiers where nations meet. Borders and margins mediating social relations permeate nation-states, particularly ethnically diverse nations such as Indonesia. Managing such internal border zones is as essential to the center's effort to maintain its social and political dominance through practices of exclusion and incorporation as managing its geographic frontiers. Populations in these internal borderlands face the same issues of resistance and accommodation, power and identity, as do those peoples who negotiate with the center from the position of geographic frontiers.

Makassar and the island of Sulawesi in general have long been part of the conceptual hinterland of the Indonesian state. Bound by neither history nor ethnicity to either Java or the Malay World, Makassar has been consigned to "eastern Indonesia," a convenient label that connoted backwardness in both the colonial and postcolonial Indonesian states. To the

Endnotes for this chapter begin on page 66.

Makassarese, of course, Makassar and Sulawesi have always been at the center of their social world. "Makassar" refers simultaneously to a language, those who speak it, and the region where they live. In contemporary terms, Makassar is a regional language, with approximately 1.5 million speakers, in the southern and western portions of Indonesia's South Sulawesi province. The Makassarese boast a rich history that stresses their fierce resistance to Dutch colonial rule, their Islamic piety, and their stubborn resistance to unjust domination by outsiders. Since their golden age in the seventeenth century, Makassar's fortunes have slid precipitously, and today it finds itself trying to reconcile its proud heritage with its comparative lack of influence within the Indonesian nation.

Makassar is itself a margin within the modern Indonesian nation state, but at a local level this marginal region possesses its own dynamics of status and peripheral areas. Against a backdrop of dominant notions about heritage and *sejarah*, this chapter narrates three attempts by local actors to move into the limelight. First, I look at how local agents conducting government-sponsored projects to collect and publish oral histories have placed Makassarese history within the framework of the dominant narrative of the Indonesian nation-state. Second, I examine a case in which a Makassarese from an area peripheral to Gowa—the dominant historical polity in Makassar—has constructed a history in hopes of being published and recognized as having a suitably important past. Third, I describe a historical recreation that takes place annually at the former royal palace of the kingdom of Gowa and explain how remnants of the royal family and provincial officials collaborate in this staged ritual to assert that Makassar is the equal of other major Indonesian kingdoms on Java and Sumatra.

Sejarah and Its Critics

The role of *serajah*—nationalist, state-sponsored history in modern Indonesia, especially under Suharto's New Order regime—has long been recognized by scholars. With what to outsiders has seemed ham-handed and blatant revisionism, an astonishing diversity of peoples, places, and histories has been cast into a single and simplistic mold. National unity was presumed to require a unity and unanimity of histories. The main lineaments of *sejarah* advanced the primary goal of legitimizing the existence of the unified Indonesian nation-state by promoting the concept of a unified national identity, declaring the anticolonial struggle the dominant historical experience of the nation, and glorifying precolonial kingdoms in the Archipelago as direct ancestors of modern Indonesia. The chief historical narrative that was applied across the new nation irregardless of local sensibilities and historical experiences was a linear tale of ancient kingdoms flourishing, a period of darkness under 350 years of colonial oppression, and then a heroic anticolonial struggle setting the stage for independent Indonesia to fulfill the promise inherent in the traditions of its ancient forebear. But upon closer inspection the inadequacy of the simple truisms became glaringly apparent. As Anthony Reid put it, the resulting nationalist history possessed "a somewhat brittle quality which did not invite too rich an elaboration" (1979: 298).

Indeed, there has long been argument among Indonesian historians about the role politics should or should not play in the production of histories. This simmering debate has oft encourage loyalty to the nation-state and acceptance of the New Order's authority (e.g., Pemberton 1994). Of course the overtly political and transparent goals of Indonesian nationalist historical discourse meant that it never required much sophistication or perception to see that promoting *sejarah* was a means to power in Indonesia. Yet even once this is recognized, when seen close up a much more ambivalent picture emerges.

In the case of eastern Indonesia, local groups (among the most marginal in the Indonesian nation) have engaged the promulgation of *sejarah* by Jakarta in complicated ways. Janet Hoskins (1993) describes how locals on the island of Sumba have looked to their past for figures that can fit into national notions of *sejarah,* particularly the new category of *pahlawan* or national hero. The headhunter Wona Kaka has been ideologically transformed from a raider whose actions derived from local feuds and motives into an anticolonial hero resisting Dutch oppression. As Hoskins colorfully puts it, "the people of Sumba have raided their own past, creating a new form of 'local history' that fits a mold cast in the steaming caldron of the struggle for national independence" (1993: 311–12). Many of Wona Kaka's descendants, however, have been reluctant to accept this transformation because the form and substance of *sejarah* is in fact ill suited to Sumba's past.

On the island of Sulawesi, too, the Pitu Ulunna Salu people of the hinterlands of the island's southwest coast have sought to make their past relevant to the present (George 1991). However, they have not been as successful in reshaping their traditions, which has left them frustrated at their apparent invisibility to outsiders. This is poignantly expressed in an annual headhunting expedition in which a surrogate coconut takes the place of a human head. For the Pitu Ulunna Salu, this perpetuation of an ancient custom is a means of keeping their past and identity alive. No one else, however, seems to notice that the rite is even taking place. Unlike Sumbanese reinterpretations and debates over Wona Kaka, here people have not reframed their past in ways acceptable (or even recognizable) to the center. Nor is it an issue of how a dominant historical discourse emanating from Jakarta has reworked or appropriated local historical traditions, beliefs, and practices. This marginal group has simply been left to labor in historiographical silence, removed from the historical concerns and narratives of *sejarah*.

The failure to fit into the mold cast by the discourse of *sejarah* results in marginality. Those without a recognized *pahlawan*, for example, have had no place in the nationalist history of anticolonial struggle so essential to the heritage of the nation-state. The case of the Pitu Ulunna Salu is even more dire, as their experience seems to lie beyond *sejarah's* ambit. It would be easy to conclude that the center presided over a massive campaign of disenfranchisement that deprived people across the Archipelago of their own historical narratives and foisted upon them misleading narrative forms that fail to reflect local experiences, memories, and traditions. In this view, center-periphery dynamics have been determined by the center alone, leaving regional societies in the position of trying to respond in a situation where they had little control over how the game was played. But those outside the center of authority were not simply downtrodden peoples trying in vain to voice local histories.

In fact, however blatant the political interestedness of *sejarah*, it was never a rigid, static discourse of the empowered and powerless, the dominant and the oppressed. *Sejarah* under the New Order created an arena full of lively contestation, albeit within the boundaries it had erected. Marginality, in other words, was certainly not a permanent condition faced by those outside Java. Further, marginality was not simply in the eye of the beholder, but subject to ongoing negotiation. In a variety of situations, historical discourse was manipulated in efforts to redefine where the border between center and periphery lay. This contestation is even evident in the flood of government publications about local history and culture across Indonesia's provinces, which we turn to now.

Collecting the Past

The effort to document satisfactorily the past of the nation has been an ongoing characteristic of Indonesian governments since independence. In the last several decades in particular, numerous Indonesian government projects have collected and published oral traditions about the origins and history of local communities in South Sulawesi. Such collecting in fact began with Dutch missionaries and colonial officials in the nineteenth century, who commissioned, requested, or by example inspired their Makassarese informants and assistants to write accounts of local folklore and traditions (e.g., Friedericy 1929; Matthes 1943). Building on these existing collections, Indonesian local history projects in each of the nation's provinces have produced hundreds of volumes containing these oral histories. Collected, edited, and set to paper, they are several steps removed from the world in which they were spoken. Instead of propagating their respective cultures, they are part of Indonesian nationalist historiography. Consider the oral histories from South Sulawesi published in one such book.

Ceritera Rakyat Daerah Sulawesi Selatan is one volume in a larger project devoted to "carrying out the excavation, investigation and recording of cultural inheritance for the creation, development, and endurance of national culture" (Suwondo 1977: n.p). Known as the Project for Investigating and Recording Regional Culture (*Proyek Penelitian dan Pencatatan Kebudayaan Daerah*), and carried out in 1976 and 1977, this nationwide initiative was coordinated by the Indonesian national Department of Education and Culture (*Departemen Pendidikan dan Kebudayaan*). It yielded fifty books from ten Indonesian provinces. Many of the volumes found their way onto shelves in Indonesian libraries, and many others sit decaying in boxes in government offices. It was in such an office, in fact, that I collected many of the books that provided material for my research. Indonesians themselves seem to pay these books little heed, and the fifty published from this project are only a small fraction of those that have been and continue to be harvested across the Archipelago.

In each of Indonesia's provinces, local cultural expressions—myths, dances, art, architecture, and popular stories—have been positioned as facets of a larger entity (Indonesian National Culture) manufactured at the behest of the New Order and its successor. Refracted through this lens, "popular stories" (*ceritera rakyat*) from South Sulawesi take their place literally and symbolically alongside volumes of popular stories from other regions in the national library system. That no one ever reads these books is beside the point. In a campaign to create an agreed-upon, unifying national culture in which all Indonesian citizens share, they are tangible proofs of the national motto "Unity in Diversity." Moreover, the equalizing and unifying function of these projects at the national level is reproduced at the local level. Within the pages of every volume coexist the stories and thus the cultures of all major ethnic groups from each province. All are made to share in the creation of a national culture.

These books-that-are-not-read are fascinating instances of the dedication with which the Indonesian government has woven together politics, education, and culture. While this discourse has helped set the terms within which political life is conducted in Indonesia, the books produced at its behest are far removed from Indonesians' everyday social life. It seems to be the assurance that comes from the ability to point at these collected works in libraries and government offices that is paramount; the form rather than the contents carries significance. In short, having been created is more crucial than being read.

If the product signifies only a generalized heritage, the process by which these volumes come to be is fertile terrain for defining and crossing margins. *Ceritera Rakyat Daerah Sulawesi Selatan* contains twenty oral traditions from South Sulawesi. A team of four investigators traveled through the province in pursuit of knowledgeable and willing informants able to narrate such stories. In the Introduction the team spells out four specific goals of their work:

1. To record, collect, order, and preserve examples of popular stories from the region of South Sulawesi in order to enrich national culture.

2. To document examples of popular stories from the region of South Sulawesi so they will not vanish swallowed up by time.

3. To create and develop examples of popular stories from the region of South Sulawesi so they can also be enjoyed by the people of Indonesia in general and South Sulawesi in particular.

4. To understand the function of popular stories from the region of South Sulawesi as instruments in the cultural development of that region.

The team followed a standard procedure. To avoid duplication they first pored over the stories that had already been published in newspapers, magazines, and books. Then they made inquiries about well-known local oral traditions, found people able to narrate the stories, and collected basic biographical information about the informants. The narration was tape recorded, transcribed, and translated into Indonesian. Then a summary of each oral tradition was made and the summaries compared to decide which stories best displayed "the distinctive features of the region and contained the cultural values that clearly reflect the thought-world of the storyteller's society." A number of questions were then asked of the chosen oral traditions and their narrators: At whom was this story aimed, by whom was it told, at what occasion and for what purpose was it recited? From whom had the informant heard the story—from their grandparents, mother, father, a storyteller? Had any other investigator elicited this story? Finally, the transcripts were edited for publication by systematically ensuring they had a similar style and voice.

The result is a volume of stories that are, for lack of a better term, *disembodied*. Gone are the emotions, surrounding geographical reference points, and social context of their telling. But so too do these stories poorly resemble contemporary Indonesian written literature, in large measure because they belong to the public as a shared cultural inheritance and are edited to avoid the distinctive styles and creative devices of individual authors.

The techniques used to produce this collection raise several issues. While the name, age, education, address, and language of the informant is appended to the end of each story, as are the name of the team member who translated the story and on which date it was taped, readers are not provided any information about the social context in which these "well-known" stories were narrated. That is, any information that team members gathered from informants on the history of the oral tradition and their understanding of its place in society is elided. Nor can we know what kind of prompting or editing took place during the process of recording it. Certainly the context of the investigation was a peculiar one.

It was a transaction between local informants, deputized representatives of the Indonesian national government, and the government itself, in which each gained something of value.

For local informants, there were several advantages to participating. Most obviously, they were in all likelihood paid for their time and expertise, but there were intangible benefits as well. In the eyes of their fellow community members, they gained status and prestige for having been recognized as experts by outsiders. This legitimation also extended to their community, for by contributing their stories local informants were able to bring recognition to their corner of Indonesia. As for the editors and researchers involved in the *cerita rakyat* projects, they too were paid for their efforts, but again far more was at stake. They too gained status and prestige for participating and being associated with a national project, affirmation of the historical importance of their province, and personal acknowledgment of their expertise. But being positioned one step up on the project's ladder also identified them as scholars capable of refining the gross work of informants and of judiciously determining what was an important contribution to national history. The key difference between these participants, and what creates the main boundary between them, is publication. For the Indonesian government, above all else through such projects it gains "buy-in" from provinces who become shareholders in a common endeavor. At this level the project acts as a province-by-province endorsement of the goals and nature of *sejarah*. The complexity of this transaction, and the multiple levels from which agents view the project and its outcomes, is a superb example of the kind of trading in cultural capital from which relative marginality or centrality is purchased or constructed. A very different dynamic applies to the efforts of a single individual to gain this capital and contest marginality, as described in the next section.

Asserting the Past

In describing the importance of recognition by the central government to Indonesians outside Jakarta, especially on outer islands like Sulawesi, James Siegel describes the sense of deep satisfaction this acknowledgment brings. "The nation seems to have found one; with that, one belongs to Indonesia in a profound sense. One supposes oneself truly at home; more so than in one's house of origin." In a poignant example, he cites observations by the late Japanese historian Tsuchiya Kenji that some men and women have been known to weep when they receive their civil service identification numbers (Siegel 1997: 7). For many Indonesians, this intense longing for recognition certainly extends into the realm of history, characterized by the hope that they may both take part in its construction and be officially acknowledged for their contributions.

A text that came into my possession in 1997 aptly represents the striving by some Makassarese to participate in and be validated by the discourse of *sejarah*. The text is a manuscript handwritten on about sixty empty pages of a dayplanner. The author, whose name I know only from the title page, is M. Taliu B., and in the manner of the Indonesian government productions discussed above, his work is titled *Kerajaan Siam (Siang)*. He passed the text to my Makassarese tutor at the time, Johan Salengke, so that I could know from him the history of Siang and include it in my writings. Since it was composed in Indonesian rather than Makassarese, we spent little time on it, and it has since languished at the bottom of a pile of miscellaneous material on a shelf in my office. Taliu was not the only acquaintance that had presented Johan with such material in the hope that I, an American historian with presumably (alas) great prestige and influence, could incorporate it into my work and thereby document their seminal contribution to Indonesian history.

Siang itself makes but a brief appearance in histories of South Sulawesi. Located north of the city of Makassar, it was a coastal community that until the middle of the sixteenth century attracted maritime traders to the region. Portuguese visitors commented on its importance as a commercial center on the west coast of South Sulawesi, and archaeological evidence supports the contention that Siang may have been a trade entrepot for centuries. It may also have been a political center of great importance, but we do not have local historical sources to evaluate how large an area it dominated. By the end of the sixteenth century Siang had become an insignificant backwater, commercially eclipsed and politically dominated by the kingdom of Gowa. We know little else about Siang, except that it never regained a position of significance within the histories told about South Sulawesi. With no chronicles and only a few Portuguese accounts of Siang in its decline, it remains a mystery teetering on the brink of historiographical oblivion. Taliu's hope was to regain for Siang a central place in history.

There are two impulses at work in Taliu's text: his desire to establish Siang's significance within the history of South Sulawesi and the Indonesian nation, and his desire to be recognized as an authority equal to the investigators deputized by the state to produce *Ceritera Rakyat Daerah Sulawesi Selatan*. Yet certain things have to be known about Siang to legitimate it as part of this discourse, and in fact they have to be known in a way that obeys particular dictates or forms. This is evident from the very beginning of the text, where Taliu's introduction reads much like one from any government publication.

Government publications like the *cerita rakyat* volumes have a formulaic, obligatory introduction that Taliu mimics perfectly.[1] His ambitions are appropriately modest: "May this book simply become a basic record that can be developed objectively" (*Sehingga buku ini hany a merupakan catatan dasar untuk bisa dikembangkan secara ilmiah*). At the same time he hints that this contribution gives only a glimpse into Siang's important history, stating that it "represents a small portion of the totality of the kingdom of Siang's era of greatness, which is still mostly veiled and in need of attention from cultural observers of South Sulawesi" (*merupakan sebahagian kecil dari kebesaran masa kejayaan kerajaan Siam (Siang) yang masih banyak terselubung dan perlu menjadi perhatian bagi tokoh-tokoh budayawan Sulawesi Selatan*). To ensure that the importance of this work, and of Siang's history itself, is recognized, Taliu concludes by affirming their contribution to the furthering of the values necessary in the modern Indonesian state: "For the kingdom of Siang since ancient times has been the site of ethical values both for governments as well as society" (*Karena kejaraan Siam (Siang) sejak dahulu kala sudah meletakkan nilai-nilai etis baik di bidang pemerintahan maupun pada masyarakatnya*). Alone missing in his mimicry of government publications are the obligatory forwards by government officials praising the work. With this exception, *Kerajaan Siam (Siang)* sets the same standard as that by which official histories are judged.

The effort to make his work equal to published histories obliged Taliu to observe the requirements of those histories. One element of this is format. *Kerajaan Siam (Siang)* follows the format common to the sort of local histories published as part of government projects. It begins, for example, with a section on geography that lists all the present-day communities located in the Siang area. It then discusses the origins of the kingdom, taking particular care both to push them as far back in time as possible and to connect these origins to other major kingdoms. In the case of Siang, its origins are tied to a legendary being (*tumanurung*) who descended from the mythical Upper World and married a local noble to establish the ruling line. Such a narrative is common throughout South Sulawesi and is intended to differentiate the kingdom in question from other communities by trumpeting its sacred and prestigious origins (Cummings 2002).

After relating this founding moment, the historical narrative moves on to catalog Siang's connections with the major historical kingdoms of the province, especially Bone and Gowa, but also noting similarities to powerful kingdoms beyond Sulawesi, such as Johor and Melaka. Taliu makes particular use of accounts by the Portuguese travelers who visited Siang as part of his fairly long and rather meandering history. These details bolster his claim that Siang had "an era of greatness" (*masa kejayaan*). Convincing the reader that this age existed, and that it was truly great, is Taliu's main rhetorical goal. The latter part of the book discusses an idealized form of government based on a division of the kingdom into four sections (known as the *Tokdo Appaka ri Siang*). The approximately sixty-page book ends with a special section on the connections between Siang and Melaka.

From this synopsis we can assess what, in Taliu's mind, a history of Siang needed to contain in order to be a fitting addition to the pantheon of successes that constitutes Indonesia's nationalist history. Put another way, we can determine the textual requirements that such a history must meet to be part of the discourse of *sejarah*. Minimally, the history of Siang must be told in such a way that obeys all the forms of objective history, and Taliu does an excellent job of modeling his hand-written work after published Indonesian histories. Beyond this there are three main requirements. First, the place in question must have known and suitably impressive origins. Second, it must have a past golden age. Third, it must have values that contribute to the nation today. Imitating published government histories, the author tries to establish Siang as a vetted contribution to historical discourse by meeting each of these standards. *Kerajaan Siam (Siang)* in effect creates Siang as a discursive object that can then be compared (favorably) to other discursive objects such as "Gowa" and "Melaka."

There is a desperate quality to this effort, as Taliu musters any and all evidence to convince the reader that Siang merits inclusion in the discourse of *sejarah*. Would that Siang too, he seems to be saying, could be a center of history, of authority, of status. Ultimately, nothing has come of his manuscript and his effort to take Siang from the margins to the center of Indonesian history. Nevertheless, we should recognize his efforts at least for their significance in illustrating how history mediates power and authority in Indonesia. The paucity of resources available to Taliu, and his ultimate failure to publish his manuscript, stand in stark contrast to another effort to harness the past in an annual celebration at Gowa's royal palace.

Staging the Past

In April 1997 I was urged by my Makassarese tutor Johan to attend a ceremony in which the royal regalia (*kalompoang*) were brought out and ritually cleansed at the royal palace (Ballaq Lompoa, or "Great House"). The annual event is held on the day before and the day of Idul Adha, the Islamic feast of sacrifice commemorating Ibrahim's sacrifice of Ismail. The culmination of massive effort and expense, it serves as the most important occasion for remnants of Gowa's royalty to display their heritage to honored guests and, via television, a nationwide audience.[2]

The first day consisted of preparations in three stages: collecting the sacred water that would be used to clean the *kalompoang*, the sacrifice of a water buffalo, and an evening feast and gathering that was part ceremony and part rehearsal dinner. That morning about forty costumed Makassarese set out from the Ballaq Lompoa in a solemn procession to the nearby sacred well. At the center of the march were four young children carried in a palanquin along with the empty water container. Musicians played as they walked, and once they reached the well (disturbing the bathing and washing of local residents), candles were lit, and popped rice and offerings in woven leaves dropped into the water to summon (I was told) the spirit of the well. The container was lowered on a rope and water from the well drawn back up. Some members of the procession anointed or washed themselves, or even drank some of this now holy water. With little discussion and without ritual speech of any kind, the procession traced its steps back toward the Ballaq Lompoa. After a brief stop to light candles and thrice circumambulate the ancient stone where rulers of Gowa were formally installed three times, the procession arrived back where they had begun. Not long afterward, a water buffalo was sacrificed after a short prayer and a plate of its blood gathered for use the next day. This took place behind the Ballaq Lompoa, and was witnessed a smaller audience of maybe twenty people. Then people disbanded during the heat of the day, but they would gather again that evening.

This first morning's activity was a kind of theater, but one whose participants were also its audience. The Makassarese involved were not making theater for outsiders, not troubling to make their actions convienent to watch or offering explanations and commentary on their activities. It was instead a private theater, in which Makassarese connected to the social network around the Ballaq Lompoa paid obeisance to their ancestors and their heritage. This preliminary phase gave way to a more organized, planned event that evening.

That evening, roughly double the number of participants in the earlier procession came together again for what amounted to a rehearsal dinner. In a back chamber where the royal regalia were kept, an elderly woman presided over the requisite rituals honoring their spirits. Sitting by the sacrificed water buffalo's head, she passed a pot of incense around the room three times counter-clockwise, then three times counterclockwise. Celebrants ate from great heaping plates of foods, particularly plates of yellow oiled rice in which fried chicken was buried (*kaqdoq minyak*) and also cooked meat from the slaughtered water buffalo. After this a rehearsal procession took place, and then the majority of the attendants departed.

The following day, after the Friday noon prayer, some two hundred people wearing traditional costume (mine rented for the occasion) came to the Ballaq Lompa. Again the old woman presided over an offering, invoking the spirits of the locked-up regalia in the inner back room, but the central activity of the day was a procession in which the regalia were brought out and ritually washed as people ate a large meal. A man read a short text about the kingdom of Gowa, its acceptance of Islam, and the beginning of annual regalia-washing ceremonies during Sultan Alauddin's reign in the seventeenth century. Bearers from the royal family carried major pieces of regalia from the small inner room out into the main room, preceded by ten teenage girls and six young boys holding aloft a rectangular piece of cloth under which all the regalia passed. The main pieces included the crown, four naga arm bracelets, a number of chains, cymbals, and medallions, and seven kris and swords. The regalia were placed on a stage in the main room around the member of the royal family chosen to do the washing this year. Incense was waved over each piece before it was washed with water taken from the well the previous morning. For the seven swords the process was more involved. Over each of the swords, a brief prayer was also spoken silently, incense waved, and popped rice thrown before the sword was handed to one of several men flanking the washer. These assistants each cleaned one of the blades by running lime slices over the edges, then rubbing them with bamboo shavings. Oil was rubbed onto the blades with pieces of cotton swabbing, and finally, the washer dabbed blood from the plate of sacrificed buffalo blood on to each item before they all were taken in a reverse procession back to the inner sanctum, not to be seen until the next year.

Fig. 2.1. Staging the past at Ballaq Lompoa (photo W. Cummings).

Yet for observers, the most striking thing about the ritual and meal was the presence of a cameraman from the television network RCTI (Rajawali Citra Televisi Indonesia) wearing jeans and a casual shirt in the midst of two hundred people dressed in traditional costume (Figure 1). Organizers had invited the network to televise the event in its entirety with the hope that it would be broadcast nationwide. Such a display would, they stated proudly, ensure that other Indonesians recognized the historical significance of Makassar in general and Gowa in particular. By this means the social network around the former court could gain a measure of the prestige and recognition accorded the other historically important kingdoms in the Archipelago, especially those on Java, and above all others the *kraton* of Yogyakarta. In other words, the cleansing ceremony at the Ballaq Lompoa embodied the same type of status-rivalry and concern with relative social position as Taliu demonstrated in submitting his history of

Siang. Like Taliu, who hoped some of Siang's newly acknowledged glory would accrue to him, participants at the Ballaq Lompoa ceremonies hoped some of the national recognition of Makassarese history would bolster their status by confirming their noteworthy identity.

Staging the past in hopes that their theater would be properly received and interpreted was the most ambitious of the Makassarese projects discussed here. In an effort to gain entrance to the most esteemed inner circle of Indonesian national culture, and recognition as one of the crown jewels of Indonesia's impressive cultural heritage, organizers and participants eagerly embraced the nationalist discourse of *sejarah*. By annually reenacting this event, they set out to make the deeds and legacy of the Gowa court a living history that cannot be forgotten, a heritage with which all Indonesians must reckon that will, at least in this respect, transport them from the margins of the nation toward its center.

Conclusion

A government-sponsored project, an individual toiling on his own, an annual historical reenactment at a former royal palace—these three projects represent efforts to negotiate the center-periphery dynamic characteristic of *serajah* in modern Indonesia. This dynamic was never fixed, and rather than being omnipotent, the center needed the participation and acceptance of marginal regions, groups, and even individuals across the Archipelago in order to function and gain legitimacy. Far from being only and always a disagreeable imposition by Jakarta, the discourse surrounding *sejarah* brought opportunities as well as strict requirements. Those marginal actors who were able to participate in government-sponsored initiatives had the best chance to parlay that opportunity into status and recognition, in effect gaining a seat at the table set by Jakarta. Similarly, those who were able to accurately divine the nature of *sejarah* and present their past within this framework had a chance to unmarginalize themselves. Mimicry alone, however, proved insufficient to this end, as Taliu's bold but unsuccessful undertaking suggests. Engaging the past in the present requires resources of the sort the sponsors and organizers of the Ballaq Lompoa historical re-creation were able to muster, though even their ultimate success is uncertain, given the level of their ambitions. Yet taken together, these three cases provide an important glimpse into the ways in which the past is used to construct centrality and marginality in modern Southeast Asia. These constructions by would-be centers are always improvised and unfinished, but what this indicates is not the futility of contesting the center, but the mercurial nature of marginality itself.

Notes

1. A reading of historical texts written by Raja Horo and given to Janet Hoskins during her research on Kodi might suggest similarities in how Indonesians— even those in authority—mimic government publications to assert a presence in the sphere of history; see Hoskins (1998: 84–91).
2. A similar filmed event in Makassar is discussed in Rössler (2000: 177–81).

References

Cummings, William. 2002. *Making Blood White: Historical Transformations in Early Modern Makassar.* Honolulu: University of Hawaii Press.

Curaming, Rommel. 2003 "Towards Reinventing Indonesian Nationalist Historiography." *Kyoto Review of Southeast Asia* 3 (March).

Friedericy, M. J. 1929. "De Gowa-Federatie (1926)." *Adatrechtbundels: Selebes.* Vol. 31. 364–427.

George, Kenneth M. 1991. "Headhunting, History, and Exchange in Upland Sulawesi." *Journal of Asian Studies* 50, no. 3: 536–64.

Hoskins, Janet. 1993. *The Play of Time: Kodi Perspectives on Calendars, History, and Exchange.* Berkeley: University of California Press.

———. 1998. *Biographical Objects: How Things Tell the Stories of People's Lives.* New York: Routledge.

Matthes, B. F. 1943. "Boegineesche en Makassaarsche Legenden." In *Dr. Benjamin Frederick Matthes: Zijn Leven en Arbeid in Dienst van het Nederlandsch Bijbelgenootschap,* ed. H. van den Brink. Amsterdam: Nederlandsch Bijbelgenootschap.

Pemberton, John. 1994. *On the Subject of "Java."* Ithaca: Cornell University Press.

Reid, Anthony. 1979. "The Nationalist Quest for an Indonesian Past." In Anthony Reid and David Marr, eds., *Perceptions of the Past in Southeast Asia,* eds. Singapore: Asian Studies Association of Australia.

Rössler, Martin. 2000. "From Divine Descent to Administration: Sacred Heirlooms and Political Change in Highland Gowa." In Roger Tol, Kees van Dijk, and Greg Acciaioli, eds., *Authority and Enterprise among the Peoples of South Sulawesi,* ed. Leiden: KITLV.

Siegel, James T. 1997. *Fetish, Recognition, Revolution.* Princeton: Princeton University Press.

Suwondo, Bambang, ed. 1980/81. *Cerita Rakyat (Mite dan Legenda) Daerah Sulawesi Selatan.* Jakarta: Departemen Pendidikan dan Kebudayaan.

Tsing, Anna. 1993. *In the Realm of the Diamond Queen: Marginality in an Out-of-the-Way Place.* Princeton: Princeton University Press.

van Klinken, Gerry. 2001. "The Battle for History After Suharto: Beyond Sacred Dates, Great Men, and Legal Milestones." *Critical Asian Studies* 33, No. 3: 323–50.

3

POLITICAL PERIPHERY, COSMOLOGICAL CENTER: THE REPRODUCTION OF RMEET SOCIOCOSMIC ORDER AND THE LAOS-THAILAND BORDER

Guido Sprenger

CREATION MYTHS ARE NOT SOMETHING THAT immediately springs to mind when the topic of crossing borders between modern nation-states is broached. Yet, as a form of narrative, they mirror valorizations and perceptions of the relations particular societies maintain with forces outside their domain. Even though the following myth makes no mention of nation-states, it provides a focal text for the understanding of Rmeet conceptions of the Laos-Thailand border.

The Story of the All-Overgrowing Tree

Two orphan boys catch a *jalook* bird in a trap. They take it home and keep it, but their father's sister (*al*) tricks them: They walk to the well together, but half way, the father's sister turns back, steals the bird, and kills it. The two boys find out only when the bird is already eaten. They manage to get its skull into their possession, and the younger brother puts it under his pillow. That following night, his parents appear in a dream and tell him to plant the skull in a termite mound. Next morning, he tells his dream to his brother, who does not believe him. So the next night, the older brother sleeps with the bird skull under his pillow and has the same dream. This time, they plant the skull as told, and soon a tree grows from the termite hill—its leaves being clothing; its fruit, gongs and money.

The other villagers want to participate in this wealth, so every house goes to perform a ritual blessing on the orphans, smearing their shins with chicken blood. This ritual obliges the orphans to make a counter gift of clothing and money. Only their father's sister refuses to perform it. Soon a thick layer of blood covers the shins of the two brothers, maggots grow in

---

it, and the orphans die. Father's sister and her husband, outraged, try to cut down the tree, but the husband's axe slips, and he hurts his leg and dies. The same happens to his wife.

Meanwhile the tree keeps growing to cover the entire land. There is no room left to grow rice or build houses. Nobody manages to fell it. Then two young men appear, Waang and Bii, offering themselves for the job on only one condition: that the day the felling begins and the day the tree falls be observed as taboo days by all Rmeet. The two men then cut down the tree and are killed by the falling trunk. The treetop falls into Thailand—or the neighboring areas in general—and thus its wealth is lost to the Rmeet. Since then, the Rmeet observe two taboo days within their 60-day cycle and invoke Waang and Bii at the beginning of all ritual formulas. The trunk, it is said, has turned into mineral coal since then and is mined by the Thai.

This is, in numerous variations, the most popular myth among the Rmeet. Considered to be *pawatsat priim*, "old history,"and to represent true events, it is offered as an explanation for the two taboo days, as well as for the wealth of Thai or Lao lowlanders. Several informants recounted the story after having seen Thai-run coal mines in Bokeo Province. So what is obvious at first glance is the following: Though they are dependent on trade with lowlanders and the Thai at present, the Rmeet claim to be the origin of the lowlanders' wealth. This is not connected with any sense of being "ripped off" by outsiders: the felling of the tree is felt to have been a necessity. But this is just one aspect of the complex relation between inside and outside in Rmeet society.

The Rmeet in the Laotian Nation-State

The Rmeet (or Lamet, as spelled in earlier literature) of Northern Laos are a marginal people, both in the sense of not being represented in national politics and in the sense of living close to the border of the Laotian nation-state. A trip from Takheung,[1] the village of fieldwork, to the Laos–Thailand border takes about two days, as does the journey to reach the provincial capital of Luang Nam Tha.

According to official definitions, Laos contains forty-nine different ethnic groups, the most numerous being the Lao. This number is actually quite contested, and various other ways of counting have been proposed (Pholsena 2002: 186). Besides the differentiation into forty-nine groups, another classification in general use among Laotian citizens and officials groups all ethnic groups into three large categories. The communist government adopted this tripartition after the revolution of 1975 from officials of the Lao Kingdom and it is used in most foreign-language handbooks on the country (2002: 179–80). It has replaced an older categorization that separated the Lao from the mountain-dwelling Kha (meaning "serfs").

The new tripartition classifies all Laotian natives according to settlement pattern and language. The Lao Loum (lowland Lao), including the Lao majority, speak Tai-Kadai languages. They are typically conceived to be Theravada Buddhists practicing wet rice agriculture on the plains. The Lao Theung (Lao of the heights) speak Mon-Khmer languages and are thought to have preceded the Lao Loum as inhabitants of Laos. Called Kha by the lowlanders, they have a history of marginalization and oppression in relation to the lowland kingdom before the revolution. Typically conceived to be mountain-dwelling swidden cultivators who practice "animism" (an ill-chosen generic term for non-Buddhist cosmologies in Laos), they are perceived as backward by many lowlanders. Finally, the Lao Soung (Lao of the mountain tops) who started to immigrate only in the mid-nineteenth century speak Miao-Yao and Tibeto-Burman languages. As many researchers have pointed out, these generalizations do not hold very well in reality (e.g., Ovesen 1993). Still, the "Lao Theung" characteristics fit the Rmeet I studied. This group of Mon-Khmer speakers, numbering about 17,000 people, mostly lives in mountain villages in the three north-western provinces Bokeo, Luang Nam Tha, and Udomsai, where Laos shares borders with China, Burma, and Thailand.

The Rmeet focus their rituals on various types of spirits, most prominently ancestor spirits, spirits of the soil and the sky, the house spirit, and the village spirit. The relations with spirits are mostly managed through the observance of taboos, and the taboo system is regarded a major feature of Rmeet tradition (*chiid Rmeet*). Yet, many taboos and the rituals connected with them have been abolished, in particular in Takheung. Two reasons are brought forward for this, both referring to external influence: first, a growing number of trade and labor trips have brought about encounters and comparison with other societies with lesser taboos; secondly, the government has demanded that the Rmeet stop the alleged waste of animal life in sacrifices and turn to modern medicine for cures. In their outward image of their relation to the government, the Rmeet of Takheung stress balance: the government makes proposals, and the Rmeet decide freely upon what to keep and what not. This does not indicate a move towards a secularized worldview: the spirits are still there, but many Rmeet decide to take their chances with them. After all, spirit attacks may often be countered by medicine (for example, in case of snakebite) or by a combination of medicine and shamanic healing.

But from the perspective of the central government, the Rmeet still fulfill many criteria of "backwardness." In Takheung village, where I collected most of my data, all households practice swidden cultivation. This type of agriculture is opposed by the Laotian government (Freeman 2002: 145). Especially during the decade after the revolution of 1975, the government tried to wipe out "superstition," meaning many local rituals and taboos (see e.g., Evans 1998: 71). Thus, both their agriculture and their cosmology put the Rmeet outside the official ideal of the modern Laotian nation-state. This is manifested in a common type of self-depreciation: when asked about the specificity of their culture, many Rmeet first mention their lack of education and technological skills, compared to the lowlands. On the other hand, they fully recognize their status as Laotian citizens. Appreciating the change from being called Kha to now Lao Theung, one household head claimed: "They used to call us slaves, but now we are friends—we are all Lao." Although the description of the relation as one of friendship is strongly influenced by national discourse transmitted by radio and visiting officials, it is based on a particular Rmeet concept, *kho am po*. This notion, meaning "loving and caring together," usually applies to family members or other close associates. Thus, values derived from family relations are transferred to the national community.

Besides that, it is mostly as a source of wealth and commodities that the lowlands are important for village society, in particular money for bride price and ritual objects like bronze drums (see Izikowitz 1979: 101–2). These two uses of money represent the most important sociocosmic relationships structuring Rmeet society. Bride price creates asymmetric wife-giving/wife-taking relationships. This type of relationship is not only the precondition of physical reproduction, but also the ritual source of fertility for the fields and health for the person. Bronze drums and gongs for their part are used to call the ancestors during sacrificial feasts, thus creating stable relationships with the dead. While bronze drums have for most part been replaced by smaller gongs, part of their meaning in ancestor rituals has been transferred to French colonial silver coins (*piastres de commerce* in French, *gemuul man* in Rmeet), another medium of status originating from outside of Rmeet society. These coins can be bought at local markets. Therefore, it is not simply wealth of a purely economic, utilitarian kind that is pursued; the labor relationship is an important means to propel the cycles of exchange between affines and the rituals concerning the dead. One could argue that relations with statebuilding, money-producing groups like the Thai and the Lao are essential to the maintenance of the internal sociocosmic order, thereby subordinating the local system to the dominant groups. But by telling the story of the tree, the Rmeet add another dimension to it.

Trade and Labor

In the most common form of trade relations, Rmeet villagers react to information from lowland traders. These make it known to the village headman that they will buy a type of forest produce on a certain day on the banks of the Nam Tha River. The price per kilo or grain container is fixed in advance, and the village headman passes the message to the villagers. The collecting of the forest produce—plant fibers, fruit, and edible caterpillars—is organized on a household level. On the date named by the traders, those who have collected sufficient amounts haul it down to the riverbanks. Most of the produce sold this way is destined for processing in Thailand, and the Rmeet are aware of that.

In contrast, produce destined for local markets is sold on market days. There is a monthly market on the bank of the Nam Tha, a walk of about four hours from Takheung. Some villagers are known to travel one to two days to reach this market place. The traders assembling there are usually not Rmeet, and I am not aware of traders based in Rmeet villages. The goods the Rmeet sell there are more basic than those traded to the cross-border merchants: rice, basketry, some vegetables from gardens and fields. The Rmeet in my study area have no regular cash crops.[2] I am not aware of any long-term relations between particular traders and villagers; the relationship is based on the exchange of goods for money, but entering this relationship does not require participants to conceive of it in terms of family or friendship. Another way to gain money, chosen mainly by young men, is to actively engage in trade. This is mostly trade with live-stock, which occasionally crosses the border. Selling livestock (in particular buffaloes) to neighboring countries is illegal in Laos, due to the shortage of animals inside the country. But still it is pursued, as prices in Thailand are much higher (by 50 to 100 percent). The practice of smuggling has led to several arrests of cunning Rmeet men. But not all trade involving the border is prosecuted.

Another important way of acquiring money is labor for wages. As Laos is among the poorest countries of Southeast Asia, many young Rmeet men and some women go to Thailand for this reason, sometimes for a year or more, sometimes for decades, or to never return. This relation has had a long history:[3] At least since the 1930s, wage labor in Thailand is among the most common way to acquire money (Izikowitz 1979: 101–2). The money earned is an important source of wealth for village society. Many households in Takheung have relatives working across the border, who occasionally bring remittances to their families of origin. Wage labor is also an opportunity for young men to earn bride price, sometimes before, sometimes after their marriage (the bride price sometimes being paid in installments). In these cases, Rmeet become employees of small or medium-sized firms in Thailand. They work as drivers and street vendors, or perform menial tasks (frequently, in rice mills). During their stay there, they often enter a relation modeled upon the family with their employers. Most of these are Thai, but also some migrated Lao and at least one Rmeet, who is occasionally called "father." These employers often provide them with food, thus enhancing the image of a family community. They also protect their employees in relation to the Thai administration. Many laborers from Laos lack proper passports or residence permits and are therefore constantly fearful of arrest or deportation. This stresses the laborers' dependence on their employers, combining familiarity with an acute sense of subordination.

Another widespread type of wage labor does not cross the border: groups of Rmeet men work as house builders for lowlanders. It is often lowland acquaintances (or friends of friends) who call for the Rmeet to form work teams. These teams comprised of friends or relatives from one village, live close with their employers, sharing their houses and tables. In contrast to workers in Thailand, they are often paid as a group and in kind (for example, with buffaloes). My impression is that labor away from the village, but inside Laos, stresses ideas of community, family relationships, and friendship much more than work in Thailand. Therefore, this type of work shares more features with relations inside the village than work in Thailand does. A parallel distinction is also found in the conception of the difference between Laos and Thailand, as I will show in the final section.

These experiences with societies outside the villages have markedly influenced Rmeet traditions, at least from the Rmeet point of view. The changes regarding the taboo system have already been mentioned, and have similarly affected marriage rules. First, traveling Rmeet would recognize different rules among different peoples, and second, travels would sometimes lead to interethnic sexual relations. Most of the Rmeet married to Khmu women had met their future wives on labor trips. Therefore, the outside is conceived as an agent of the blurring of distinctions maintained by taboos and the marriage system. Adopting a radical view of the dissolution of rules, some elderly informants claimed: "Today, everybody just marries whom they want!" But as data on old and recent marriages show, rules are still observed to a large degree. In fact, the concepts behind the rules, manifest in the types of relationships these rules create, are crucial to the concept of Rmeet society itself. One major effect of marriage rules is to separate inside relations from outside ones.

Trade Goods and Kinship

The Rmeet kinship system is closely connected to their marriage rules, which prescribe marrying matrilateral cross-cousins (e.g., a man marries his mother's brother's daughter). Prescription has to be understood here in Needham's (1973) sense: Kinship terminology turns every spouse, even entirely unrelated ones, and their families of origin into representatives of the prescribed category. The Rmeet use the same term for mother's brother and wife's father; prospective spouses have the same designation as mother's brother's daughter or father's sister's son, according to the sex of the speaker. It is considered best if a man marries a woman from his mother's group of origin, but if he does not, his wife automatically turns into a "mother's brother's daughter" terminologically.

This type of marriage prescription creates a hierarchical difference between wife-givers (*taa*) and wife-takers (*pesao/bäi*), here with wife-givers in the superior position. While this superiority implies a relationship of economic or political power, it is first of all a value statement. The wife-givers provide a taker with not just a wife, but the whole of the social unit basic to Rmeet society, for only after being married and having a child may a man move out of his parent's home, make a house himself, and cultivate a rice field. Thus, people would not say, "X's wife comes from Y's house," but "X's house comes from Y's house." This same idea of wife-givers as givers of life, health, and fertility accords them important roles in many of their wife-takers' rituals, including the rites of healing, sowing and harvesting, birth, and death. This legitimizes their claim for the allegiance of wife-takers and also their demands for bride price, which wife-givers may make until the end of the marriage.

The second most important kin relationship in Rmeet society is that of brotherhood, called *yuu-ääk* (younger sibling-elder brother). As is often the case in kinship terminologies that reflect asymmetric marriage rules, the terms for parallel cousins[4] are the same as those for siblings. The Rmeet also treat parallel cousins as siblings with regard to marriage and ritual roles. The *yuu-ääk* relationship is based on unnamed patrilineages of two to three generations' depth. These lineages should rather be called "grave clusters," as the shared burial place is a clearer reference to the groups' unity than actual genealogy. But it is the recognition of a common house of origin and the sharing of the same ancestors (via the graveyard) that creates these groups' identity. The *yuu-ääk* relationships are characterized by values of sharing and mutual help. Unequal relations are seldom stressed in institutionalized or ritualized contexts, not even among siblings, even though the elder-younger distinction is terminologically marked. This rule of equality contrasts markedly with the hierarchy between superior wife-givers and inferior wife-takers.

Both types of relationships, wife-giver/wife-taker and brother, are maintained by rituals that demand the use of imported objects. The piasters mentioned above mark a cycle of ritual reproduction. They are used as a part of bride price, and they also appear in rituals fixing the *klpu*-soul of a person to his or her body. In these contexts they reproduce families and the health of individuals. But they also appear in mortuary rituals, when all the silver coins in the possession of a group of brothers are exposed on the dead person's body. Coins are thus involved in the reproduction of affinal (bride price) and ancestral (mortuary ritual) relations. Another kind of imported object featured in rituals has already been mentioned—bronze drums and gongs. The large kettle drums have mostly been sold by now, but smaller gongs and cymbals are still used. Their most prominent use also relates them to the dead. As Izikowitz reports for the 1930s, these instruments may only be beaten during annual rituals performed by wealthy men for their ancestors (Izikowitz 1979: 117, 243). In Takheung, the instruments are used only during funerals and on the occasion of the sacrifice of a buffalo to the house spirit. This spirit is an aspect of the ancestors: the unity of all lineal male ancestors of a house and their wives, situated in a particular part of the house and protecting or punishing its inhabitants. Thus, the gongs relate to a similar social group to that supplying the coins in the mortuary ritual. But the beating of the gongs has another meaning: only up on buffalo sacrifices are the ancestors called by name from the edge of the village. This invocation is done by a ritual, but also by the sound of the gongs.

Clothing is another common item in ritual exchanges, and because the Rmeet usually do not weave, it has to be imported as well. Clothing may be part of a bride price as well as dowry, but it is characteristically a gift of the wife-givers to the wife-takers in healing rituals for the wife-takers.

The relationships structuring Rmeet village society are ordered by rituals that require gifts and objects originating from the outside. In the past, border crossing was a conspicuous part of this process of integration. The gongs and bronze drums were available only in Thailand, and were acquired by the assets from wage labor (Izikowitz 1979: 330). Nowadays, the link is more indirect: while ritual objects like piasters can be bought within Laos, the money for doing so is often obtained by work abroad. This is particularly true for Takheung. In many respects, this village performs larger rituals than some of its neighbors, and it is wealthier. The wealth displayed both in everyday life and in rituals is the fruit of more intense contacts across the Thai border, compared to other villages. Thus, crossing the border remains a vital part of the local system of ritual and kinship.

Inside and Outside in the Myth of the Tree

All these relationships are interwoven in the myth of the tree. In the following, I present a retelling of the myth, pointing out the aspects of Rmeet knowledge to which the myth appeals. It is an attempt at translating the notions and relations referred to in the myth into analytical language, linked with ethnographic data. I seek to make two points. First, the story links the inside order of Rmeet society, structured by kinship relations, to the outside, the realm of trade and nation-states. These two realms are complementary, but must be kept separate. Second, the use of the myth and its variations shows it to be a flexible means to relate the Rmeet to the outside world.

The heroes are orphans; that is, their parents have already become ancestors. Orphans often figure in Rmeet myths. Having lost the most important social relation for children, they are poor and isolated from society. This shifts their allegiance from mankind to spirits and wild animals, who pity them and help them. The result is often an innovation or the orphans' accession to high status. The "culture heroes" of the Rmeet are mostly orphans.

The two orphans engage in trapping, a mode of production that direct-ly relates to the space outside the village, namely the forest—a space of spirits and wild animals. They successfully capture a *jalook* bird (a species of finch) in the wilderness, but refuse to kill it. Instead, they treat it like a pet, an animal belonging to their house, thereby denying the difference between inside and outside. The killing is done by the father's sister. A father's sister is the closest relative on a young person's wife-taking side. She originates from his house, but does not belong to it any longer, having become an integral part of her husband's house, to be buried in his grave-yard when she dies. On the other hand, she maintains links to her original house, putting her on the subordinate and the superior sides of the affinal distinction at the same time. When father's sisters figure in myth, they are either treacherous or stupid, and their actions often lead to self-destruc-tion. On the level of myth, the values the father's sister embodies are con-tradictory and annihilate each other.

In this story, the stealing and killing of the bird is a clear violation of the wife-giver/wife-taker hierarchy. All that is left to the boys is the bird's skull. But the skull becomes fertile: The bird is integrated into the house, and then buried almost like a dead person—an animal of the wilderness becoming part of human society. The act is mediated by the dead parents of the boys; in other words, the lineal relationship to the ancestors, not the affinal one, is activated in order to integrate outside and inside. The result of this series of blurrings and reversals is stupen-dous wealth. All the objects imported from abroad grow on the tree, including clothing, iron tools, and money. Other local elaborations of the myth claim that writing too originates from the tree, as do radios and other commodities. The separation of objects provided through trade and labor relations and objects created by kinship relations, as experi-enced in everyday life, becomes conflated in the myth. It is the relation to the dead ancestors that create outside objects inside society.

The way the other villagers participate in this wealth extends this idea to affinal relations. Smearing the blood of a sacrificial animal on a person's shin is a generic act of blessing—one that is characteristically performed by wife-takers for their wife-givers. Both healing and harvest rites on the wife-taker's field feature this ritual, which obliges the wife-givers to pro-vide the wife-takers with gifts that are also characteristic of this relation—money in the form of silver coins and clothing, the products of the mythical tree. When the villagers perform the smearing ritual on the orphans in order to receive part of their wealth, they become ritualized wife-takers, making the orphans everybody's wife-giver. Ironically, only the single real wife-taker abstains from the exchange. The treacherous father's sister's house does not receive anything, and this interruption of the kinship system leads to anger and self-destruction.

But these manipulations do not benefit the orphans either. Each wife-giving relationship must be part of a chain of asymmetric affinal relations. Objects received from wife-takers may be passed over to one's own wife-givers. The superiority of the wife-givers is always balanced by their subordinate relation to their own wife-givers. In this respect, the orphans are the final link in the exchange chain and consequently die by virtually rotting away while still being alive. The creation of life and the maintenance of a person's physical being is closely associated with the flow of gifts and powers between wife-givers and wife-takers. This process fails in regard to the orphans (or only the elder brother, in some versions): fulfilling the role of universal wife-givers while having no wife-givers for themselves destroys them.

All of society suffers from the conflation of inside and outside relations: the growing tree takes up all the space for villages and fields; local society is almost entirely replaced by outside objects of value. This represents a conflict between two types of status. In the kinship system, absolute status differences only exist between parents and children, while between brothers status differences are subdued. On the affinal side, the wife-giver's superiority is balanced by his subordination to his own wife-givers. These hierarchical relations do not form pyramids, but rather "open cycles." Of course, this type of system may be used to create real political and economic dominance, as Leach (1954) has demonstrated for the Kachin. But achieving such dominance through asymmetric alliance is dependent on several traits, among them the association of certain lineages with the general fertility of the community (which is not the case among the Rmeet) and wealth imported from the outside. Furthermore, power based on asymmetric alliance is inherently unstable, as Leach and also Lévi-Strauss (1949: 327) have pointed out.

A different type of status derives from external wealth acquired through labor and trade. In the past, the absolute difference between rich owners of gongs, money, and buffaloes and poorer members of the community was even more marked than today. In the 1930s, in the western part of the Rmeet settlement area, there existed a named class distinction, based entirely on personal wealth. The *lem*, as the elite were called, were admitted by a ritual to their status. The status was neither inherited nor reproduced by kinship (Izikowitz 1979: 116–17). The Rmeet of Takheung do not remember such a named class, but they experienced a similar distinction between rich houses and poor ones, which depended on the rich for loans. The wealth of the rich houses was earned entirely by providing labor for the French and the Americans, the polarizing forces from outside before the Socialist Revolution of 1975.

What the myth shows is the irreconcilability of two principles—relative status and the kinship system on one hand, absolute status based on external wealth on the other. The ending provides the proper distinction between these two types of exchange. A number of Rmeet bachelors arrive (two in some, four in other versions) to fell the tree. Being bachelors, they are not fully integrated in the kinship system, having neither immediate wife-givers nor descendants. When they die, they become ancestors for all of society, or rather extend the ancestral type of relationship to the entire society. They are connected to two taboo days within the 60-day cycle, called "big Waang" and "small Waang," thought to demarcate the period needed to cut down the tree. On these days, people are not supposed to work outside the village, go to the fields, perform sacrifices, or trade animals. Very similar taboos must be observed by household members with regard to the dead of their family. The return of the day of burial in the 60 day cycle demands these observations for those descendants of the dead person, who were living in his/her house when he/she died. A single person's relation with the actual dead in his family is homologous to the relation of all generations of Rmeet everywhere to the bachelors who felled the tree.

The myth provides the Rmeet with a means to define their position within the field of ethnic identities in Laos. Although the felling of the tree benefited the whole world, it is only the Rmeet (and the closely related Khmu) who have to observe the Waang-Bii taboos. Both the orphans and the bachelors were Rmeet, and they provide Rmeet society with a specific evaluation in respect to the cosmos and to outside societies. Every formula accompanying a ritual gift or blessing begins with the words *hee hoo*, allegedly the bachelors' names. Thus, every gift is valorized by a reference to those who separated this type of giving and receiving from trade and labor. Just as the ancestors define the unity of the *yuu-ääk* groups (grave clusters), their relation to the tree fellers defines the Rmeet as a society with particular kinship and ritualized relationships, embedded in an environment that is governed by a different type of transactions.

On the level of myth as well as in everyday practice, the two types of relationships—with lowlanders and Thai on the base of trade and labor, and with kin in ritual—are complementary to each other. Anthropologists have repeatedly suggested that the introduction of money and the intensification of trade and other national and transnational economic activity are detrimental to traditional exchange patterns (Akin and Robbins 1999). At least for the Rmeet, the contrast of modernity and tradition, change and stability inherent in this argument does not necessarily apply. The myth constructs a difference between relations within and outside of society, but does not order them progressively; the acquisition of wealth objects by trade and labor is a necessary part of the entire system. Even looking back to the 1930s, when the Rmeet were much more isolated, the integration of external objects and the crossing of ethnic and national boundaries to this end was a precondition for the performance of rituals and the contraction of marriages.

Variations on the Myth and the Actor's View

A myth has its times and its times of change, as many writers have noted (e.g., Lawrence 1964; Morgan 1983: 83–84). The Lévi-Straussian view of myths relegates them to encapsulating the cultural unconscious of the societies that produce and transmit them (Lévi-Strauss 1970, 1977). But the obvious changes made to myths, raise the question of the relationship between conscious and unconscious use of representations. Although the Rmeet storytellers did not explain the myth to me in the way I interpreted it above, they still had obvious reasons to tell it. The motives of wealth and kinship are active issues for many Rmeet, and it is not surprising that they would transmit and transform a story that concerns them in a complex way. In this section I am going to deal with the variations on the story and the way they relate to particular points of view.

The myth of the tree is the single most often-told story I encountered during fieldwork. As *pawatsat priim,* "old history," it can be regarded as a creation myth, but it is not the only one. Earlier literature on the Rmeet suggests a different tale as the most widespread creation myth: A brother-sister couple survives a great flood and gives birth to a big gourd. After the gourd is cut open, all the peoples of the world emerge from it (Izikowitz 1979: 22). This story is known in many different versions all over mainland Southeast Asia and Southwestern China, but at least in popularity it takes second place among the present-day Rmeet. If this observation actually mirrors a historic shift in preference for specific myths, and not only a predilection of Western scientists for a particular type of story, it demands explanation. While the flood story accounts for the diversity of ethnic groups, the tree story addresses a matter of greater importance in the present: differentiated sets of status types and reproductive relationships. Therefore, it is a more appropriate means to discuss and understand the specific inside/outside relationships of current society.

The story of a tree overgrowing the land and threatening society is found in a number of variants within Laos (Suksavang 1997: 3–6, fn. 28; Annales de Lan Xang 1956). But the growth of trade goods and valuable objects on it is, as far as I know, unique to the Rmeet versions. Whatever meaning the analysis of other peoples' versions may reveal about their relation to their cultural setting, the story is particularly apt to represent Rmeet perceptions about the complementarity of wealth-producing and life-reproducing relations. The expansion of market opportunities, the frequent travels to Thailand, and the perceived changes brought about by them are likely to have stimulated an urge to formulate the myth in regard to these phenomena. Storytellers may relate in several ways to the myth, addressing several layers of signification (see Molenaar 1987: 257) and stressing different categories.

It is in this context that the relationship of the Rmeet to the nation-state border can be determined. The myth is a part of shifting solidarities in regard to the lowland Lao and the Thai. When discussing their relationship to the outside, the line between "us" and "them" sometimes runs between the Rmeet and the lowland Lao, sometimes between Laotian citizens and the Thai. These shifts appear when differences in wealth and education are discussed for it is then that the distinctions between Laos and Thailand and between the Rmeet and the Lao are modeled upon the same set of terms. These two sets can be summarized as follows: "We are stupid, uneducated, poor—but loving and caring for each other; they are successful, educated, wealthy—but not caring for each other." Thus, in cases discussing Rmeet identity, the line is usually drawn between them and the lowland Lao. But when they speak of their experience as labor migrants in Thailand, the distinction shifts and the Rmeet see themselves as representatives of Laos. In these cases, they would stress the "loving and caring" (*kho am po*) of all members of the Laotian nation-state, understood to have the values of a family. One man returning from Thailand even described the difference between his relationship with Lao and with Thai officials in terms of the "loving and caring" relationship. It is along these lines that the myth of the tree is understood: in some versions, its top falls into the lowlands and causes the wealth of the Lao; in others, it is the Thai who benefit from the tree.

The conflation of Rmeet and Laotian in the latter case is illustrated in a version told by a 26-year old father who had often worked construction jobs for lowlanders, but never in Thailand. His story revolves entirely around the contrast between Laos and Thailand. The tree planters are not distinctively Rmeet, but people from Laos in general. The story basically explains the difference in wealth between the two countries. For this storyteller, the difference between inside and outside relationships of Rmeet society is muted in favor of the distinction of two national economies. As demonstrated in the section on trade and labor, a number of features are common to relations within villages: close bonds with the employer, in terms of shared space and commensurality; and work teams made up of friends and relatives. It is therefore not surprising that a man with much experience in this line of work would draw a more distinctive boundary between Laos and Thailand. But to what extent this version can be considered as more "nationalist" than others is hard to say. After all, the linking of Rmeet society to the Laotian nation-state is still accomplished by ideas of kinship; the specific features of "imagined communities," in Anderson's (1991) sense, that create supralocal national identities are not clearly operative.

This idea is extended onto a more global level in the rendition offered by an elderly storyteller. Now about 70, he participated in the Second Indochina War as a soldier of the Royal Laotian Army. Although he does not share the ideological background of this war party, he draws his identity very much from these events. He portrays himself as a knowledgeable man, based on his experience outside the Rmeet area and his involvement with foreigners. In general, knowledge of local traditions and local history is less valued by most Rmeet than knowledge derived from beyond. This storyteller liked to sprinkle his Rmeet with Lao words when talking to me and often pronounced his few words of French and English. His version of the tree story is the most "modern" one I heard: All types of technological objects, radios, and tape recorders grow from the tree. Furthermore, all writing, another sign of cultural sophistication, originates from it. When it falls, it falls into the rich countries, including Thailand, the U.S., and France. From the old man's perspective, the difference between rich and poor nation-states subordinates the one between the Rmeet and the Lao. His version was the most expansive and creative, the others were recounted by people who were much less eager to demonstrate their knowledge and cosmopolitanism.

In contrast, the myth as told by a young mother stresses the internal aspects of the story: She does not specify which rich and poor areas were created by the fall of the tree, either Rmeet and lowlanders or Laotians and Thai. But in her version, the interactions between Rmeet are more detailed. There is an additional part about beads made into necklaces involving a second father's sister, and the tree fellers give specific instructions about the taboo days: "Waang and Bii said these taboos shall be observed for every following generation (*juu*)." This phrase stresses the similarity to the taboos observed in regard to dead ancestors, as their duration is also measured in terms of *juu*. (Ancestor taboos have to be observed for one *juu*; that is, until the children of the dead have died themselves.) In her wording, the Waang-Bii taboos come across as an extension of domestic ancestor taboos, both in time and in terms of the social entity involved. Although this particular woman lived in Thailand as a girl, she speaks from a distinctively female point of view: most Rmeet women regard themselves as bound to the village and the domestic sphere, and rarely get involved in trade and migration.

As we can see, the myth provides individual storytellers with a wide range of possibilities to relate to it and adapt it according to their own position within society. This position, in the cases mentioned, always involves particular experiences with inside and outside relations. Telling the myth enables people to define their relationship to the nation-state, to the border to Thailand, to a market economy and to the kinship system.

Conclusion

Border crossings and the integration of valuable objects and money by trade or labor migration are not recent innovations to Rmeet society. Within living memory as well as on the horizon of earlier anthropological records, labor migration to Thailand has always fueled the contraction of marriages and the performance of rituals. Still, the Rmeet conceive their society as based on a distinction that poses inside and outside relationships as complementary to one another: the interplay of inside relations—those between the living and the dead as well as those between different types of kin—is a prerequisite to seeking wealth from the outside. On the other hand, relations with spirits and with affines can be maintained only by integrating this type of wealth.

The double periphery at which the Rmeet are situated is a major factor in this self-image. First, the Rmeet are marginalized in respect to the nation-state. Their rituals and their economy define them as "backward" from an official point of view, and the Rmeet have hardly been involved in any supravillage administration.[5] The marginalization fuels the easy separation of inside and outside that forms the base of the concept of sociality in this society. This is not to argue that marginalization promotes the maintenance of local identity, but rather to show that local representations of society and the political situation are linked and produce each other to some degree.

The second periphery is the geographical one—the closeness to the Thai border—which extends the inside/outside relations to another level. Because Thailand is a more potent source of wealth than the Lao-dominated lowlands, the distinction between inside and outside may also be understood to represent the divisions between nation-states. There is a tendency to understand the myth as a conflation of the Lao-Rmeet distinction in favor of a more general distinction between Laos and Thailand. In this respect, the same conceptual strategy of inside and outside may apply to the Laotian nation-state as a community. In the versions of the myth that contrast Laos with Thailand, the Laotian nation-state appears as an extension of Rmeet society, thereby muting their marginal position. This shifting in the geographical range of sociality leads to an interplay of notions of difference and similarity of Lao and Rmeet that I have explored elsewhere (Sprenger 2004). Among them is the idea that many of the hallmarks of lowland culture derive from the Rmeet, including its wealth, its kings, and even the entire people, all documented in mythical history. In this way, the Rmeet take their own present marginality into account even as they situate themselves at the center of cosmological production.

Notes

1. Fieldwork was conducted from 2000 to 2002, 14 months in all, and was supported by the German Research Council in the framework of the Research Group for Southeast Asia, University of Münster.
2. Some Rmeet villages produce opium, but not those I did research in, so I have no data on trade relations regarding this cash crop.
3. In the system of galactic polities (*muang*), which existed until late in the nineteenth century, there were no fixed territorial borders between political entities; sovereignty was understood less in territorial terms, than as control of manpower (Tambiah 1985). The French-Siamese crisis of 1893 first established the need to draw a line between Siam and Laos, which the Siamese had considered their region of influence until the French claimed the parts east of the Mekong (Stuart-Fox 1996: 22–23; Thongchai 1994: 141–44). Because the border between Laos and Siam in the northwest was the river Mekong, it was relatively easy to detect, yet it remains unclear when this border was administratively controlled.
4. Parallel cousins are the children of one's parents' same-sex siblings. The logic of this is the following: Children of brothers belong (in a patrilineal society) to the same exogamous group and therefore cannot marry; thus, they are designated with the same terms as siblings. If every man marries his mother's brother's daughter, as he should, then a pair of sisters would marry a pair of brothers or parallel cousins. Therefore, also children of sisters are designated as siblings. This homology of marriage rules and kin terms is what Needham (1973) calls prescription, a structural feature independent of the statistical occurrence of normative marriages.
5. There is at least one Rmeet in a high party position, but the Rmeet I have been talking to are not aware of him.

References

Akin, David, and Joel Robbins. 1999. "Introduction to Melanesian currencies." In D. Akin and J. Robbins, eds., *Money and Modernity: State and Local Currencies in Melanesia.* Pittsburgh: University of Pittsburgh Press.

Anderson, Benedict. 1991. *Imagined Communities: Reflections on the Origin and Spread of Nationalism.* Revised edition. London and New York: Verso.

Annales de Lan Xang. 1956. *Annales de Lan Xang: origines légendaires.* Trans. Louis Finot. *France-Asie* 12 (Présence du Royaume Lao): 1047–49.

Evans, Grant. 1998. *The Politics of Ritual and Remembrance: Laos since 1975.* Chiang Mai: Silkworm.

Freeman, Nick. 2002. "Laos: Sedately Seguing into the Twenty-first Century." *Southeast Asian Affairs:* 145–56.

Izikowitz, Karl Gustav. 1979. *Lamet: Hill Peasants in French Indochina.* 2nd edition. New York: AMS Press.

Leach, Edmund. 1964. *Political Systems of Highland Burma.* 2nd edition. London: Bell.

Lawrence, Peter. 1964. *Road Belong Cargo: A Study of the Cargo Movement in the Southern Madang District, New Guinea.* Manchester: Manchester University Press.

Lévi-Strauss, Claude. 1949. *Les Structures Élémentaires de la Parenté.* Paris: Presses Universitaires de France.

——. 1970. *The Raw and the Cooked: Introduction to a Science of Mythology 1.* London: Cape.

——. 1977. "The story of Asdiwal." In Claude Lévi-Strauss, ed., *Structural Anthropology II.* London: Lane.

Molenaar, Henk. 1987. "The Labyrinth of Time, Myth and the Individual: Considerations on the Rationality Debate as a Step towards a Historical Epistemology." In *The Leiden Tradition of Structural Anthropology,* eds. R. de Ridder and J.A.J. Kattemans. Leiden: Brill.

Morgan, Prys. 1983. "From a Death to a View: The Hunt for the Welsh Past in the Romantic Period." In *The Invention of Tradition,* eds. E. Hobsbawm and T. Ranger. Cambridge: Cambridge University Press.

Needham, Rodney. 1973. "Prescription." *Oceania* 43: 166–81.

Ovesen, Jan. 1993. *Anthropological Reconnaissance in Central Laos: A Survey of Local Communities in a Hydropower Project Area.* Uppsala: Department of Cultural Anthropology, Uppsala University.

Pholsena, Vatthana. 2002. "Nation/Representation: Ethnic Classification and Mapping Nationhood in Contemporary Laos." *Asian Ethnicity* 3, no. 2: 175–97.

Sprenger, Guido. 2004. "Encompassment and Its Discontents: Rmeet and Lowland Lao Relationships." In Gerd Baumann and André Gingrich, eds. *Grammars of Identity/Alterity: A Structural Approach*, London: Berghahn.

Stuart-Fox, Martin. 1996. *Buddhist Kingdom, Marxist State: The Making of Modern Laos.* Bangkok: White Lotus.

Suksavang Simana. 1997. *Kmhmu' Livelihood: Farming the Forest.* Trans. Elisabeth Preisig. Vientiane: Ministry of Information and Culture, Institute for Cultural Research.

Tambiah, Stanley J. 1985. "The Galactic Polity in Southeast Asia." In *Culture, Thought and Social Action.* Cambridge: Harvard University Press.

Thongchai Winichakul. 1994. *Siam Mapped: A History of the Geo-body of a Nation.* Chiang Mai: Silkworm.

CENTERING THE MARGIN II:
ETHNIC MINORITIES IN
SOUTHEAST ASIAN BORDERLANDS

4

Premodern Flows in Postmodern China: Globalization and the Sipsongpanna Tais

Sara Davis

AT THIS TIME, WORD ARRIVED that the Lord Buddha had descended from the heavens to live among people, and that he had brought with him good fortune, wisdom, and a written alphabet. Thereupon, everyone went to the Lord Buddha to request the written alphabet. The different ethnic groups each took their own tools for preserving the alphabet: Hans took paper, Tais took palm leaves, and Akhas took buffalo hides. They followed the same route, climbing mountains and fording rivers, traveling many months and years before they finally arrived at the sacred mountain where the Lord Buddha preached to the people. Together they kneeled before the Lord Buddha and requested the alphabet. The Lord Buddha wrote the same alphabet on the paper, palm leaves, and buffalo hides.

As the people returned, they swam across rivers. The currents were strong and rapid, the waves surged to and fro, the paper brought by the Hans was soaked through, and the letters on the paper changed to resemble bird scratches; [as for] the buffalo hides the Akha had brought, because they got hungry along the way, they [the Akha] roasted and ate the buffalo hides. Only the letters that were carved on the palm leaves, which were not affected when wet and could not be roasted and eaten, preserved the form of the alphabet given by the Lord Buddha for later times. This became the graceful, elegant Tai alphabet of today. (Chuba Meng [Khruba Muang] 1981: 31)

Introduction

The anecdote above is translated from a Chinese Tai minority Buddhist treatise that dates from the seventeenth century.[1, 2] Tai minority informants interviewed in China recently told the same tale. In the past, textual transmission, Buddhist sacrality, travel, and ethnic identity were closely inter-

---

Endnotes for this chapter begin on page 105.

woven for this Theravada Buddhist border people. Today, as China lowers the barriers on its southwestern borders and increasingly cooperates with neighboring countries on trade and development projects, Tai Buddhist monks once again move back and forth across the national borders of China, Thailand, Laos, and Burma[3] (the so-called Golden Triangle). These monks are bringing back to China a classical Tai alphabet that was banished in recent decades, though today they carry it not on palm leaves but on floppy disks, videos, and CDs. In many border regions of the world, new transnational ethnic discourses and technologies are emerging. Yet some of the ways in which they are transmitted look surprisingly ancient.

Much has changed in this region: hills have been leveled to make way for new roads, power lines have replaced the canopy of the rain forest, and new migrants from the coast are building cities in place of villages. Yet the persistence of these ethnic oral legends and practices of culture-bearing exemplifies some of the ways in which globalization happens along channels worn deep by history. One reason for the persistence of old exchange systems may lie in the nature of the march of globalization as it advances on new and more remote terrain. While trade and business dramatically reshape the Chinese coastal and urban areas on a regular basis, such inland ethnic villages, marginalized within the nation-state, are the last to benefit from China's rapid economic development and lack new communications systems that facilitate information flows. Thus premodern routes, such as the pan-Tai transborder Buddhist network, revive longstanding regional systems that carried information, technology, and culture back and forth between rural villages over difficult mountain terrain.

Discussions of globalization have tended to take a top-down view, emphasizing the role played by mass media and other supraterritorial flows in the emergence of new ethnic spheres (Appadurai 1996; Castles and Davidson 2000; Ong and Nonini 1997; Scholte 2000). This article draws on fieldwork research in minority languages in border villages, using the local as a tool with which to analyze the global. By examining this particular form of transnationalism in all its folkloric and sociolinguistic specificities, we may gain insights about global ethnic flows in general. Transnational ethnic communities, after all, are in many ways social movements, which are organized—as social movements always have been—by people. Like the palm leaf texts that preceded them, videos and floppy disks require someone to obtain them, carry them, and interpret them to the laity. This article aims to reveal a social system that transmits modernity across the borders.

As we will see, pan-Tai ethnicity in southwest China is created and sustained in large part through a network of minority temples, which function as schools, political centers operating below the radar, and inns for traveling monks. This horizontal temple network once spanned the many fiercely independent local Tai states. Here, I argue, the weak warp of a multicentered, consensus based political system was held together by a horizontal woof of mobile intellectuals.

In the twentieth century, national expansion into Tai regions led not to the incorporation of these independent minorities into larger nations, but rather to their marginalization. Efforts to secularize Tais, to make them into good communists or national citizens, in fact merely forced former Buddhist monks and local oral traditions underground, creating a radical sense of shared ethnic oppression around the borderlands. Today, these minority institutions are resurfacing in a new form, re-creating a historical geography and promoting new notions of ethnic identity.

The Sipsongpanna Tai Lüe constitute one small branch of a Tai-Kadai language family spreading across Vietnam, Burma, Thailand, Laos, and India. This vast and diverse language family incorporates the peoples of Thailand, with whom Tais feel a strong affinity. It also includes the Burmese Shan; "Shan" is an etic Burmese ethnonym that, like the Chinese *Daizu*, includes many Tai-speaking groups. While Thai and Tai Lüe are separate languages, northern Thais and Sipsongpanna Tai Lües can often communicate. Yet despite their many lexical similarities, the languages also display differences; Tai Lüe has its own unique grammatical, lexical, and tonal variations, as well as additional politeness registers that are usually expressed through pronoun selection. Thus, most central Thai speakers have difficulty understanding Tai Lüe. The Thai and Tai Lüe writing systems are also related, although again not mutually intelligible. The classical Sipsongpanna Tai Lüe alphabet has more than sixty letters, and more closely resembles the Lanna Thai alphabet (Lanna was a historical northern Thai kingdom) and the Tai Khün alphabet (the Khün are another Tai branch in Kengtung, Burma).

As is true of other ethnic minority regions of China, since the 1980s the Chinese government has officially promoted mass tourism to Sipsongpanna, aimed largely at Han Chinese tourists; but here wealthy Thais are also targeted (Davis 2001; Evans 2000; Hyde 2001). Such mass tourism booms attract urban visitors to exoticized dance revues, minority theme parks, and the like. This form of development has been part of a national policy aimed at incorporating troublesome border tribes into China, and the results have been mixed (Schein 2000; Swain 1995). It has brought an economic boom-and-bust cycle to Sipsongpanna, as well as a flood of Han Chinese migrants seeking economic opportunities. Parallel with the development of Yunnanese tourism has been the revival of Tai Buddhism, which has reemerged dramatically in Sipsongpanna since the 1980s.

The importance of Buddhist temples, both as centers of an emerging ethnic resistance and as the nexus of a transborder network, became clear during my field research in 1997–98. My research began in China's southwestern Yunnan province, where I wrote a dissertation (Davis 1999, 2005) on the political significance of reemerging Tai Buddhist oral traditions. In order to translate oral texts and interview performers, I studied the Tai spoken and written language in a Buddhist temple. Subsequent field trips in 1999 and 2001 expanded the research into Tai Buddhist temples in northeastern Burma and northern Thailand. My language teacher during my initial research in Sipsongpanna was a Chinese-speaking Tai monk at Wat Pajay (Chinese: *Zong Fosi*), the main Buddhist temple in Jinghong and the head temple of Sipsongpanna.[5]

The Tai temples are a unique institution within China, though they resemble similar institutions in Southeast Asia. Tai novices are initiated at the age of eight or nine in major village ceremonies, and the brightest novices can be invited to the main seminary, Wat Pajay. There they study the classical Tai alphabet, Buddhist sutras, and other Tai texts. This classical Tai alphabet differs from the "new" Tai alphabet (Chinese: *xin Dai wen*) taught in the Chinese schools, to which we will return. Most novices find temple life congenial, as there are few restrictions and many peers to play with. Those who have not left monastic life by their early twenties may be fully ordained, and can then be selected to study at the Nationalities Institute in Kunming, or at Buddhist seminaries in Thailand. As Mette Hansen (1999) observes, the temples' attempt to fill a deeply felt gap in rural education has at times brought the monks into conflict with the government. Given its connections with universities in other regions, Wat Pajay certainly offers many opportunities to impoverished rural families that they would not otherwise have.

One day after my language classes began, my teacher asked me to examine a faulty temple printer. In the midst of this rustic temple building, I found the monks maintained an air-conditioned, carpeted room with three new Macintosh computers, a scanner, and a laser printer, together with cheerful posters from Thailand; in a fusion of Tai and Chinese, they called it the *hong diannao* (computer room). Thereafter, I often stayed at the temple after classes to fix technical problems when I could, to coauthor a Tai-English primer, and to chat and observe. I attended and recorded Buddhist holiday celebrations, traveled with monks to their home villages and to village rituals, and was pressured into singing Tai songs at public festivals. Despite some initial hesitancy about the presence of a foreign woman, the monks quickly became supportive of my research into oral epics, which they saw as underscoring the importance of a kind of rich local culture that the government did not encourage or support.

In turn, I began to recognize the centrality of the Tai Buddhist temple not only to local religious life but also to political life. Village temples were often home to community meetings on problems of education, infrastructure, and taxation. Villages with particular needs used invitations for Buddhist holiday feasts as a way to get Jinghong Tai government officials onto their turf, as it were, then to overwhelm them with generosity and hospitality, and finally to politely but firmly instruct these officials on how to act for the village. Once or twice, Tai monks organized holiday processions through downtown Jinghong; these spontaneously turned into unplanned demonstrations of hundreds of Tai villagers, who emerged from their houses silently and marched behind the monks to the temple to make donations. Such public gatherings of hundreds, even thousands of Tais were common at the temples, and were an unmistakable public show of support, although they were never reported in the state-owned news media.

These local institutions also had a transnational reach into both Thailand and Burma, and monastic movements re-created a symbolic geography while bringing new fuel to local cultural traditions. Thai Buddhist supporters have given significant aid to Sipsongpanna temples. The large golden Buddha image in Wat Pajay was a gift from supporters in Thailand, and most Tai village temples had smaller Thai images in their main halls. Monks who traveled back and forth to study in Thailand often stopped over at temples in Burma. The most popular route from Jinghong ran southwest to Muang Long (Chinese *Da Menglong*) on the Chinese border with Burma, then southwest again to the Burmese Tai city of Kengtung, and due south from Kengtung into northern Thailand. In 1998, when six Muang Long monks were promoted to the status of Buddhist master (Tai, *khuba*),[6] the Burmese Tai "saint" Khruba Bunchum constructed a reliquary on the Burmese side of the border with Muang Long, and hundreds of Tai villagers walked across the border to pay homage.

This route has considerable local significance in Buddhist history. Jinghong, Kengtung, and Chiang Rai are important *muang*, capitals of former Tai kingdoms, which continue to act as market centers that serve outlying villages. Muang Long, while not a former capital, was a historical center of Buddhist activity. According to local legend, a reliquary there preserves a footprint left by the Buddha on his first visit to Sipsongpanna, when he traveled north from Kengtung to Muang Long and then Jinghong. Oral histories say that the first missionizing Buddhist monks to arrive in Sipsongpanna in the eighth century came from Kengtung to Muang Long.[7] In recent years, when Khruba Bunchum has visited Sipsongpanna, he has often entered Sipsongpanna along the same route. In 1998, Muang Long still had the most Buddhist masters of any town in Sipsongpanna. Traveling to and from Jinghong, Kengtung, and northern Thailand, young Chinese Tai monks and pilgrims move along a road with a centuries-old history of Buddhist transmission, re-creating a Tai religious and political geography. In the same way, Paul Cohen (2000) notes, Khruba Bunchum's extensive building projects of Buddhist reliquaries and temples across upland Southeast Asia re-creates a symbolic geography and places him in the traditions of Theravada Buddhist kingship.

As the towns they visit are former capitals, when Tai monks move about with new robes, candles, posters, scriptures, books, amulets, cassettes, and videos, these objects circulate quickly around villages. They are shared between friends and followers, copied and passed around further still, and are the focus of intense interest and discussion. Because Thai, Lao, Shan, and Tai Lüe are closely related languages, and perhaps because of a well-developed oral tradition that trains Tais to memorize lyrics, an intent listener or reader can rapidly absorb the contents of CDs, cassettes, and books. Song lyrics in particular are memorized, practiced, sung aloud with friends, and revised to adapt to local conditions. By singing political pop songs in Shan, studying the Thai text that accompanies sung lyrics on music videos, and memorizing Buddhist sutras, monks and friends in even remote villages in Yunnan are knit together with monks in Burma and Thailand. Its dual role in providing underground community centers and transborder hubs for monastic travel makes Sipsongpanna's revived Buddhist temple system a way to channel information and technology.

China, Thailand, and Burma may or may not intentionally tolerate this movement. (In 2001, Khruba Bunchum's annual visit to Sipsongpanna was delayed for some days because of government reluctance to allow him into China). Yet like the borders they cross, Buddhist monks can be difficult to manage. As many Theravada Buddhist monks are roughly in their late teens to early thirties, all shave their heads, and all wear orange robes, so it is easy for a traveling monk to blend in locally. That monks of all ages are widely respected also eases the way. While villagers must return home to their farms, monks live unstructured lives; any monk sitting in any temple can be said to be doing his job, no matter where he is. Monks travel cheaply, sleeping and eating at local temples; and as sacred personages and teachers, their words carry weight. In sum, they make ideal culture-bearers. It should not be surprising that monks transmitting ideas, texts, practices, rituals, and organizational models have a long history in many parts of Asia (Mair 1988).

Before the twentieth century, the Tai monastic network held together a group of independent small polities. Tai societies, I argue, were run by fluid, consensus-based systems connecting several small capitals. While they paid tribute to several empires, these small kingdoms were not actually incorporated into larger empires until the midtwentieth century. The monastic network helped these multiple centers exchange information, and thus helped hold them together, creating a multicentered region. Subsequent national domination of ethnic minorities, while temporarily forcing this Buddhist network underground, did not eradicate it but instead created fertile conditions for its revival as a conduit for pan-ethnic flows.

Premodern Flows

Although contemporary Chinese histories tend to stress that ethnic minority regions have always been "inseparable" parts of a geographic whole, Chinese dynastic histories indicate that some frontier tribes that ceded sovereignty in name maintained their independence in fact.[8]

Through a variety of strategies, Sipsongpanna appears to have ceded sovereignty in name only, while maintaining de facto political autonomy and close ties with nearby small states. The integrity of Sipsongpanna's own kingdom was itself often in flux, owing to the multicentered, village-based nature of its politics and the constant mobility of its people. The pan-regional alliance of monks, who were indigenous intellectuals, was one of several glues that held the disparate regions together. They and their broad-based educational system created a regional Buddhist culture and an alliance of former monks in the villages, which provided a horizontal form of stability. This region, as Andrew Walker observes, offers grounds for a powerful critique to traditional center-periphery political models (Walker 1999: 11).

Historical records as early as the Han dynasty report that the empire was aware of contemporary Jinghong. In Chinese annals such as the *Shi ji* (*Records of the Historian;* Sima 1997), *Ming shi* (*History of the Ming Dynasty;* Zhang 1997), and *Yuan shi* (*History of the Yuan Dynasty;* Song 1997), it was called *Cheli*—loosely, "wagon station" or even "truck stop"—in Chinese because of its key position on long-distance trade routes. Yet the first conquest of the region appears to have happened no earlier than the late thirteenth century, when a Mongol invasion caused mass migration of Tais to Burma and subsequently to contemporary Assam (Gogoi 1968).

This Mongol conquest was tenuous at first. Sometimes Cheli sent tribute to the Mongol emperor; more often Cheli troops mounted on elephants fought Mongol troops on horses. For instance, the *Yuan shi* (Song 1997) reports that Cheli made tributary gifts of domesticated elephants to the Mongol emperor (*Basic Annals* chap. 29), before a subsequent uprising lost the town again. Again, the *Ming shi* (Zhang 1997) reports that a pacification command was "established" at Cheli, fell, and was reestablished (*Records,* chap. 46, *Record 22, Geography 7,* Yunnan province, Cheli city).

Even at times of more stable colonization by Sinitic empires, Sipsongpanna appears to have maintained self-rule through a number of strategies, including the payment of multiple tribute, split rule, and the creation of "bogus notables." As Thongchai Winichakul (1994) notes, Sipsongpanna and other neighboring states ceded multiple sovereignty to several larger empires at various times, including Thailand and Burma. Indigenous scholars in Sipsongpanna also report that alliances with Burmese empires were made through royal marriages (*Xishuangbanna Daizu zizhizhou wenhua ju* 1993: 140). Thongchai writes, "unlike the modern concept of a sovereign state, a tributary's overt and formal submission did not prevent it from attempting to preserve its own autonomy or 'independence,' nor did the quest for autonomy prevent a state from submitting itself to more than one supreme power at the same time" (1994: 88). This strategy prevented more thorough forms of domination. As Shih-Chung

Hsieh pungently writes of Sipsongpanna, "The best strategy was to declare oneself a vassal, then do as one pleased" (1995: 309).

Another apparent strategy characteristic of Sipsongpanna appears to have been the creation of two centers in one capital: in the early twentieth century, two foreign visitors note that the quiet fort of the imperial pacification commissioner stood in contrast to the bustling palace of the Tai prince, where the real business of running the kingdom was done (Dodd 1996 [1923]: 184; Medford 1936: 200). C. Patterson Giersch (2001: 79) reports a geography that sounds quite similar in another Tai region of Yunnan.

That the officials listed as local rulers (Chinese: *tusi*) in much of the Yuan and Ming dynastic histories are surnamed Dao also raises questions. Under the *tusi* system, local rulers of Chinese border peoples were chosen as delegates of the Chinese empire. The Tai surname Dao is a title for members of the noble class, a rank of equals who were subordinate to the prince, surnamed Chao. It is possible that at certain stages in the history of colonization, the imperial official selected by Tais as the Chinese empire's representative was not the ruling prince, but someone of rank equal to or lower than that of the ruling prince.[9] Certainly, it is curious that a Tai-language collection of rulers' biographies takes little notice of the Chinese empire (Dao 1990). James Scott notes the creation of "bogus notables" in rural Laos, officials whose task it was to hold visiting French imperial officials at bay (Scott 1990: 132), and it could be that the promotion of Daos to the role of *tusi* had something to do with this. The position of ruling prince, or *Chao*, was apparently maintained throughout; the last heir to the title, Chao Cun Xin, later served as the first governor of the autonomous prefecture. Whoever the imperial official was in name, such strategies— multiple sovereignty, split rule, and bogus officials—would have made Chinese imperial conquest on the southwest border largely a matter of "public transcript" (Scott 1990), while local politics continued to be carried on in their own way (on this point, see also Hsieh 1995).

What was their own way? Retroactively analyzing the indigenous Tai political system poses challenges to contemporary scholars. We who live in a world organized around nations are trained to conceive of political sovereignty as singular, bounded, and hierarchical, and of ethnic minorities as contained or "possessed" by a nation (Handler 1988; Hsieh 1995). Thus, Chinese state-sanctioned histories today note the existence of a hereditary Tai class of princes and nobility, and mistakenly characterize Tais as "feudal" (Chinese: *fengjian zhidu*). Georges Condominas, noting their sometime conquests of lowland regions, describes them similarly as *emboîte* (boxed in) in a feudal system that they in turn imposed on others (Condominas 1990).

However, both such descriptions, in emphasizing the verticality of the Tai system, at once miss its horizontal, decentered, and fluid aspects and fail to account for the well-documented mobility of the "serfs." Villagers shifted about between villages and towns, federations of villages and states split and reformed, and the nobility were sometimes compelled to travel far and wide in order to hold a constituency together. Trade networks and circulating markets contributed to this mobility, adding to the cultural vitality of a multicentered region (Walker 1999). Such continual and steady movement and change make the region difficult to characterize, though we can note three constants: village affiliation, strong traditions of independence, and freedom of movement.

Because primary affiliations were to the village and township, these could form alliances, or split and re-ally in new federations, as situations dictated. Tais had strong affiliations with home villages (Tai: *ban*), each of which was in turn allied with a township (Tai: *muang*), where a regular market drew individuals from other villages. As one Tai informant observed, "[Chinese scholars] talk about the Water Dai (Chinese: *Shui Dai*), Han Dai, and Flower-waisted Dai (Chinese: *Huayao Dai*), but in fact we Tais have always organized ourselves according to places." Thus the "twelve townships" of Sipsong-panna were at various times in its history nine or fifteen townships, and at other times riven by intertownship warfare (Dodd 1996: 190).

The nobility who ruled the township shared equal rank, and were often required to answer to village constituents. Several Tai informants argued that in fact the so-called feudal society "had relatively democratic qualities." "If people did not like the prince, and if he was not following the people's will, then they made him retire, and replaced him with someone else from the family," recalled one elderly villager. A younger Tai man in the room commented quietly, "Some people might say we had more democracy then than we do now." Writing in *Cultural Survival*, the Burmese Shan author Sao Ying Sita concurs, emphasizing that "the consent of the ruled was essential" in Tai villages, and that a village chief "who frequently ignored the consensus of the villagers…would soon cease to have influence." She adds, "[T]he rulers made it a point to embark on frequent tours of even remote corners of their states in order to keep themselves informed of the opinions and prejudices of the villagers. In some of the older Shan principalities, any man could walk into the courtyard of the ruler's abode, strike the brass gong customarily kept there to summon the ruler, and air his grievance or lament" (Sao Ying Sita 1989: 10).

Indeed, constant travel appears to have been essential to this system. While villages are connected to their township by a road, the villages are also connected to each other. A web of paths traces much of Yunnan province, and dirt trails wind between rice fields, over hills, through forests, and across borders. To this day, these have never been completely mapped. Boundaries between townships "did not forbid people to trespass or to earn their living in the area[;]…the borders were 'golden, silver paths, free for traders'" (Thongchai 1994: 73). Political leaders, monks, laborers, market traders, and carts of villagers off to visit family for a festival (Tai: *boi*) moved constantly to and fro between one such hub and another, staying for a day or a year. Such routes provided for quick escape in times of turmoil, and local knowledge of forest paths made the region difficult for outsiders to conquer.[10]

Given such movement and independence along a widespread network, the stability and hierarchy of this lowland system of kingdoms may have been overstated in the past. Rather than envisioning a box, we might usefully imagine the capital of a federation as the center of a spiderweb of such silver trails, a hub on the network. The Buddhist thinker Sivaraksa Sulak (1990) suggests a social model, "Indra's Net," that could be used here to describe the Tai system. Indra's Net is "a spider's web in which at each node appears a mirror which reflects all the other mirrors and vice versa indefinitely. In this way, each infinitesimal part encodes the entire whole within it[,]…a form of political organisation that emphasises…[i]nter and independence in which power is not centralised but exists equally in every node….Relationship and connection between groups is thus vital" (Sulak 1990: 37).

In the Tai system, villages reflect the independence and interdependence that characterize both the alliance of townships and the diplomatic relationships between capitals. Breakaways and new alliances could happen freely without threatening the integrity of the whole. Combining elements of monarchy and anarchy with multivalent paths and connections, this system of rural groups was able to adapt quickly to constantly changing political and environmental conditions. In an era of upheaval and globalization, such mobile, networked small polities may begin to make new kinds of sense.

These independent groups were held together by a number of elements that permitted interdependence: trade, kinship networks, and a horizontal system of Buddhist temples that reinforced a shared culture. Monks moved to and fro between townships to study and convene. As culture-bearers between these centers, they made temples into forums for the arts and created a shared regional Buddhist tradition known as "Yuan Buddhism" (Cohen 2000). The temple-based school system also created an educated substratum of former monks across regional villages who acted as community leaders.

Thus there are a number of records of traveling monks in this region, some of whom covered great distances. These include records of visits from Sri Lanka to the Mon kingdom of Burma and the Thai kingdom of Sukhothai (Ling 1979: 18); visits by monks from Chiang Mai, Thailand, to the Burmese Pagan kingdom in the late fourteenth and early fifteenth centuries (Ling 1979: 14–5); travels by Han Chinese monks to Burma and India via the Burma road through Dali (Jia 1994); and contact between monks from Burma's Pagan kingdom and India (Gogoi 1968). Moreover, Wang Zhiyi reports Tai pilgrimages to India and Sri Lanka via Muang Long as early as 76 C.E, and again in 82 C.E. and 225 C.E., in order to obtain Buddha images and scriptures (Wang 1990: 411). In the early twentieth century, foreign missionaries stationed in Burma report monks still in motion: the medical missionary Gordon Seagrave reports treating "an opium-eating Buddhist priest come to us from way up in China, somewhere" (1930: 135).

The larger temples also served as centers for visual and literary arts, some of which emerged from transborder contact. Temple buildings were decorated with narrative murals depicting tales from the Buddhist scriptures, and from local legends. Li Weiqing reports that an artisan from Burma taught Sipsongpanna Tai monks the art of temple mural painting during the Ming dynasty (Li 1990: 460), and that travel by princes and former monks to and from Burma brought scriptures, musical instruments, and painters to Tai temples (1990: 459). Festivals on temple grounds brought together dancers, musicians, and oral poets.

Through the temple educational system, these texts and other arts spread throughout villages. Even today, some former monks (Tai: *khanan*) maintain private collections of hand-copied literature in their houses. Others drew on their familiarity with Buddhist literature to compose epic tales and became oral poets (Tai: *changkhap;* see Davis 1999). Though many monks leave temple life in order to start families in their twenties and thirties, after "coming out" (Tai: *auk ma*) these former monks are respected because of their education, and they continue to take a prominent role in community politics and in temple committees.

Thus, while the premodern Tai system was based on fluidity and decenteredness, it shared a horizontal, pan-regional association of Buddhist teachers and their students—an association of religious and secular intellectuals that could be mobilized for a variety of purposes. Such former monks managed to maintain an underground Buddhist culture during the period of systematic government oppression from the 1950 to the 1970s. It is this system that has been reemerging in the late twentieth and the early twenty-first century.

Modern (and Postmodern) China

The expansion of the contiguous nations into this transborder region during the first half of the twentieth century drove Tai Buddhist monks and former monks underground and over borders into Burma, Laos, and Thailand. At the same time, the massive instability created by attempts to "stabilize" national borders created a shared sense of oppression among related ethnic peoples, radicalizing many. In the 1980s and 1990s, with increased liberalization and the new permeability of national borders to trade, this underground movement resurfaced and quickly grew. A period of severe repression followed by a period of liberalization appears to be a potent combination for creating religious and ethnic revivals.

From the 1950s until the 1970s, Chinese government religious policy forced hundreds of Tai monks to unfrock. Centuries-old temples were systematically destroyed, sacred sites were desecrated, and Buddha images were publicly smashed and burned. As elsewhere in China, the few Buddhist temples left standing in the region were used to store farm machinery or animals. The elaborate Buddhist murals were scraped off temple walls and replaced with Maoist slogans. Old Tai texts were seized and taken away or destroyed, and Tai elites, first hailed as part of a new minority cadre, were then denounced and sent to labor camps. Still, as one informant put it, "We sang the old Buddhist songs in the villages, but we sang them in secret." An aura of fear persists around Buddhist practice today; some Tais are reluctant to discuss Buddhism with a foreigner, and others carefully close doors and windows in their homes before praying.

While government policy toward religion was uniformly harsh after 1953, minority language policy was conflicting and confusing. The product of an approach taken with many other minority languages, a "new Tai alphabet" was invented by Chinese and Tai scholars and officials in the 1950s and promoted as an improvement that would increase literacy rates—although in fact Tai literacy had always been high among the men permitted to study it. This new alphabet was taught in schools and used in official prefectural publications, and the old alphabet was banned. During the Cultural Revolution, minority language and alphabets were forbidden altogether as minorities were expected to assimilate to the Chinese nation completely. In the early 1990s, the government briefly caved in to popular pressure to bring back the old alphabet, and then reversed that policy for good. The new alphabet was once again mandated.

Despite decades of government policy promoting the new alphabet, it is still used only in official government documents. Many Tais are quietly resentful of it. They report that those who know it can use it for nothing except reading a relentlessly cheerful two-page, state-published newspaper. No Chinese–Tai dictionary using either the new alphabet or the old alphabet was published by the state for nearly fifty years. Those literate in the new script say they cannot read the old script, and complain that the new alphabet in effect cuts a generation of Tais off from their centuries of written traditions. The persistence of the government's relentless promotion of the new script strongly suggests a cynical motive behind the language policy: is the aim really to increase literacy in Tai, or to gradually eliminate it?[11]

National expansion caused similar kinds of ethnic upheaval on the borders of Burma, Thailand, and Laos, creating a growing sense of shared oppression. After a military coup in Burma, Tais in Kengtung became embroiled in a brutal war for the right to secession, and politically radicalized monks in Kengtung took on the task of preserving and promoting the Tai script, publishing Buddhist sutras and language primers, and organizing language classes (Chao Tzang 1987). In Thailand in 1976, a military massacre of student protestors drove left-wing students, academics, and monks together into the forests of northern Thailand, creating a loose network of left-wing temples. Thus Chinese Tais who fled to Burma or Thailand during the Chinese Cultural Revolution encountered other Tais with similar experiences, as well as a model of Buddhism that advocated active participation in community politics. Inevitably, this encounter radicalized some Tais from China.

In the 1980s, with the Chinese government loosening some restrictions on religion and a tourism boom bringing floods of Han Chinese migrants into the region, Chinese Tai villagers launched a dramatic movement to rebuild and revive the Buddhist temple. Kiyoshi Hasegawa reports that in the 1950s, there were 574 temples in Sipsongpanna and 6,449 monks and novices. In 1981, after the Cultural Revolution, this number had dropped to 145 temples and 655 novices—there were no longer any fully ordained monks in Sipsongpanna (Hasegawa 2000: 4–5). In 1998, Wat Pajay reported to me that there were 560 temples and about 7,500 monks and novices. In the early days of the revival, the cost of stupa and temple restoration was split among all households of each related village (Hasegawa 2000: 4). By 1997, villages raised the funds themselves, sometimes with donations from relatives overseas, but the temples were rebuilt under the guidance of monks trained in building and decorative techniques in northern Thailand. Many parents, especially those living in villages with little or poor schooling, have taken their children out of public schools to educate them in temples (Hansen 1999). The temples are cared for by former monks; for instance, in the town of Gasa (Tai: *Gatsai*), dozens of elder Tais gather in a designated temple one day a week to sweep up, repaint damaged images, and instruct young novices.

The resurfaced Buddhist temple and renewed ethnic pride brought back many former exiles who had fled over the borders. In 1990, Tai villagers joined with the prefectural government in rebuilding the former chief temple of the region, Wat Pajay, which had in the past stood behind the prince's palace in Jinghong. To lead the temple, they invited Dubi Long Zhaum,[12] a popular Tai monk and orator whose parents had fled with him over the border to Burma during the Cultural Revolution. As a novice and monk, Dubi Long Zhaum took his orders at a temple in Kengtung, the home of much of the Tai language teaching and publishing activity of the Shan States. The connection with temples in Kengtung remains a vibrant one, and Kengtung temple activities and publications provided a template for those later published in Jinghong.

Chinese government officials increasingly express worries about the connections between radicalized Tai monks in Burma, where ethnic temples have long stood at the forefront of the struggle for ethnic autonomy, and disaffected Tai monks in China. Yet the premodern monastic system survived because of the failure of projects of national integration, which largely continued previous center-periphery "civilizing projects" (Harrell 1995). Had the Chinese and Burmese governments not banned the Tai alphabet, systematically repressed local religion, neglected ethnic education, and driven many over the borders, the sympathy felt now between Chinese and Burmese minority monks would not be so great. The growth of pan-Tai sentiment owes as much to preceding—and continuing—experiences of hegemonic nationalism as to contemporary global transnational openings. As Tai villagers visiting Wat Pajay often say, "No one cares about our Tai culture; only our temple cares."

Popular Culture

The core of the transmissions between Burmese, Thai, and Chinese Tai monks is interwoven with language politics, oral traditions, and new music. Cassette tapes, music videos, and Macintosh software all carry Tai spoken dialects and Tai alphabets, materials not otherwise available in China, and they weave together an ethnic sphere out of modern media. Cassettes, videos, and software expand a sense of Tai subjectivity in China to include new visions of a transborder modernity. Monks share these objects among themselves.

Perhaps unsurprisingly, considering that monks are after all teenage boys and young men, rock music has played a catalytic role in this expanding sensibility. Chinese and American popular music, replete with urgent disco rhythms, blatant sex, and (in the Chinese case) patriotism, dominates music shops in Jinghong. Despite the state's opening of the borders to some kinds of economic trade, popular and traditional music from Southeast Asia are still unavailable. Some Tais wondered openly why it was easier in Jinghong to find a music cassette in English than a cassette from Thailand.

Monks who travel to study in Thailand hear, for the first time, songs whose lyrics they can understand the lyrics. Those who returned to Sipsongpanna with their tapes have helped create a growing market for Southeast Asian pop music in Sipsongpanna. Many who lived in Thailand became ardent fans of a kind of Thai political country music called *lukthoong*, which is sung in a northeastern Thai dialect close to Tai. The monks at Wat Pajay were especially fond of a *lukthoong* ballad about a Thai villager who is forced to sell the beloved water buffalo he has had since childhood in order to buy medicine for his sick mother. They played it over and over in the computer room and were sometimes visibly moved. One monk said, "We like this song, because this is what our lives are really like. You never hear a song like this in Chinese." One returned monk began to write song lyrics about social issues in Tai, and soon temple rock concerts and Tai-language pop cassettes spread across Sipsongpanna (Davis 2001). Bootlegged copies of Thai and Burmese pop songs with photocopied liner notes soon began to appear in village markets.

Tai monks who traveled in Thailand and Burma also brought back Thai and Burmese Shan music videos, mounting a sort of small-scale insurgency against Chinese karaoke. With the influx of Han Chinese tourists and migrants to Sipsongpanna have, inevitably, come karaoke bars. In these ubiquitous storefront lounges, tourists gather with groups of friends to sing along with Chinese-language lyrics displayed on TV screens. Tais have a long tradition of group antiphonal song, and many Tai village homes are replacing or supplementing these a cappella traditions with karaoke machines (VCDs, which are much like DVD machines with a microphone attachment). Some Tai activists expressed serious concern about the role played by karaoke in speeding up the pace of language loss and Hanification among youth. "We long for the day when you will see classical Tai script on the karaoke screen," said one concert organizer in 1998.[13]

One monk returned from a trip to Thailand with a *lukthoong* music video, made by the singer who sang about the buffalo, that was watched by every monk and novice in Wat Pajay. When we visited his home village, the monk from Wat Pajay brought along the tape to show to some teenage novices there, one of whom had recently had a motorcycle accident and was feeling depressed. The small cluster of monks sat riveted on the floor in front of the Thai music video, intently watching the entire tape three times in the course of an afternoon without moving.

The material was both alien and familiar; one monk murmured, "Thailand is more developed than we are," and the monk from Wat Pajay agreed with him. Here was someone they all recognized: a rural Thai farm boy wearing a jaunty baseball cap, singing in their dialect about love, heartbreak, and the harshness of farm life. Yet in contrast to visual representations of Tai minorities in Chinese mass media, nothing about this Thai singer said that he was primitive, backward, or exotic. On the contrary: he was "cool," modern, on the cutting edge of Thai youth culture. The afternoon had qualities of revelation about it, and at its end, the senior Wat Pajay monk was gravely thanked as he carefully rewound the video, put it back in his satchel, and took it with him.

The notion of *lukthoong* standing for modernity in Sipsongpanna carries certain peculiar ironies. *Lukthoong* is popular in Thailand because of a national nostalgia for the simpler rural life it depicts. Deborah Wong (1994) observes similar processes of ethnic nostalgia in Asian American karaoke videos, which create an "imagined community" of nostalgic Vietnamese immigrants who gather to sing along in the United States. Thais in Thailand have their own nostalgic visions of Sipsongpanna, which is depicted in Thai television documentaries as home to the kingdom's ancestors. Video appears to have a peculiar ability to provoke such multi-centered yearnings for other lives and places. Yet unlike the television documentaries in Thailand disseminated via the airwaves, the videos played in Sipsongpanna are circulating through face-to-face contact and exchange, even a kind of intentional transmission, by Buddhist monks.

Along these lines, and with an even more explicitly activist sensibility, the monks who return from Thailand and Burma have brought floppy disks carrying a classical Tai font that can be installed on any Macintosh with a Thai language platform. (While most of China uses Windows-based computers, Macintoshes are more popular in Thailand.) The font was created by Tai monks studying in Thailand, who took computer classes at a Chiang Mai seminary. The Mac font is viewed as one of the most significant benefits coming from Buddhist contact with Tais across the borders.

Thus in 1998, Wat Pajay, alone in southern Yunnan, ran a Tai-, Thai-, and Lao-language printing office in downtown Jinghong. This Tai "Kinko's" typeset Buddhist scriptures, language primers, AIDS education pamphlets, and posters. Unfortunately, its Thai benefactors had not arranged for training in the use and maintenance of the computers, and after a series of system crashes the shop closed. Nonetheless, the monks still have a functioning publishing center for themselves, and have successfully produced a multivolume edition of *Vesaenthala* (the Buddhist legend of Vessantara) and, with some triumph, a Chinese–Tai dictionary (*Xishuangbanna Daizu zizhizhou renmin zhengfu* 2002). The dictionary was compiled by monks and community activists in Jinghong, but credited to a prefectural government editorial collective and published by a Kunming-based publishing company. Such projects are part of larger temple efforts to encourage Tais to speak Tai and use the Tai classical alphabet, an effort that has been gaining support among many villagers and some elites, but one that needs to be negotiated carefully with the authorities.

This last venture, the dictionary, caused upset among high-ranking prefectural government officials, because the dictionary developed by the temple uses the classical Tai script taught in the temples, not the new script promoted by the government. Thus far, the Chinese government has been more tolerant of Tai Buddhist revivalism than it has of other ethnic movements in Tibet and Xinjiang—in part because of Yunnan's culture of relative tolerance, in part because of material interests that have kept the southwestern border open, and in part because the Tai Buddhist temple has carefully avoided direct challenges to the state. But as the movement continues to grow, Chinese policy will likely change as well. Recently, a senior minister of Sipsongpanna prefecture, speaking of the dictionary project, expressed grave concern that it was an example of a reviving "feudal culture" and voiced outrage about the transmission of the Tai alphabet from outside of China. He said, "If you want to use a real Tai script, then the new Tai script was created by people right here in Sipsongpanna," adding, somewhat ominously, "Strictly speaking, the Buddhist temple is not illegal, but one could say that they are illegal."

When told this, one of the activists involved in the dictionary project appeared unconcerned about the possible threat of a crackdown on Tai publishing projects. Tais in other regions of Yunnan are expressing excitement about learning to use the Tai font, he said, and the temples are spreading the software across Yunnan rapidly. There were even hopes among younger Tais that a unified script could be created for all Tais everywhere. "The classical Tai alphabet will be a popular folk move- ment," he said, "and eventually, the government will have to accept it." Like the alphabet developed by language committees in China's nation- building phase, this new Macintosh font does not conform to traditional usage, though with it at least younger Tais who live within Sipsongpanna will be able to read some of the old handwritten texts preserved in village stilt houses and temples. However, the key issue here appears to be, as ever, not print but politics.

As Benedict Anderson (1991) tells us, historical empires, and in their wake nations, have coalesced in varying ways around empires of print, texts that have created a shared identity. Chinese national identity includes the use of characters, and here a widely used minority written alphabet and spoken language is creating a resistant transnational ethnic group. Shared between a senior monk and a novice, these postmodern objects are luminous with a premodern text, a new "fetishisation of the commodi- ty"—one that takes us far, in fact, into the "misty realm of religion" where Marx hesitates to tread (Marx 1976: 165). What is fetishized and thus potent about these objects is their simultaneous familiarity and foreignness, the ways in which they are at once classical and modern. Like the *kula* objects that circulate between Melanesian islands, these Tai-language tapes and disks rarely stay in one pair of hands for long, and like *kula* exchanges these exchanges also create a fluid "network of relationships" that "forms one interwoven fabric" (Malinowski 1961 [1922]: 92). Here as well, "it is easy to see that in the long run, not only objects of material culture, but also customs, songs, art motives and general cultural influences [and, we might add, ethnic identity] travel along the Kula route."

Globalization Travels along Old Roads

To conclude, we can draw three larger points from the Tai case: about con- tinuity and rupture, about the local and the global, and about possibilities for comparison.

No one would dispute that globalization has brought us into a world that is radically unlike the one that preceded it—with more forms of supraterri- toriality; a higher velocity of flows along emerging systems of communica- tions, finance, and trade; and new notions of group identity that exceed the boundaries set by nations. Much about the emergence of pan-Tai ethnicity in the border areas of China and Southeast Asia does constitute a radical break with what came before, especially the kinds of technology used and the kinds of identity promoted. Cassette tapes, videos, and computers are radically different from the classical oral poetry and palm-leaf scriptures of earlier times. They contain different aesthetics, are avatars of new global businesses, and in many ways stand for the osmotic absorption of a grow-ing—some would say hegemonic—global culture. With their arrival, some elements of a past Tai oral tradition may be preserved, such as the language itself; and other elements may gradually vanish forever, such as the ability to compose oral poetry based on Buddhist literature.

Similarly, as Charles Keyes (1995) points out, the notion of a horizontal pan-Tai ethnicity, now potentially rallying around a single alphabet, is a new development explicitly responsive to the growth of nation-states. Jinghong, Kengtung, Chiang Rai, and Chiang Mai never had need of an aggressively promoted pan-Tai ethnicity before. Wherever they traveled, Tais—identified by village first and foremost—could communicate through an overlapping set of languages. The emergence of a pan-Tai community is in fact symptomatic of the significant break with that sys-tem caused by hegemonic nationalism in the twentieth century.

Yet even as the world Tais live in now often appears to be characterized by rupture, difference, chaos, and "a general break with all sorts of pasts" (Appadurai 1996: 3), a closer look at modernity's front lines has revealed a few continuous threads: institutions, routes, and folk practices that link localities. The emergence of a pan-Tai community relies in part on the historical insti-tution of a horizontal transregional temple. Intriguingly, while drawing some support from Thailand, this network has not made the apparently obvious connections with global Buddhist movements such as Soka Gakkai, but remains something akin to the same closed circuit it was in the past. It also remains as decentered as it was before: there is no one single "Tai homeland" for which all Tais yearn, but rather a system of equal hubs, towns in neigh-boring regions that each boast different strengths, with multivalent nostalgias from varying points. Moreover, despite the pan-Thai aspirations held by some leaders of post–World War II Thailand, this community is geographi-cally bounded to the borderlands of northern Thailand, northern Laos, north-eastern Burma, and Southwest China: the marginalized areas of four nations that share the same river delta and a long history of contact and exchange.

While the "Golden Triangle" is unique in many ways, looked at in this light possible comparisons come to mind—with Xinjiang and the states along the Silk Road, border regions of several nations in Central Asia and the Near East, and indigenous peoples in border areas of Mexico and Guatemala, among others. Many rural areas of the world have been man-aged by networks of multicentered ethnic tribes. Like Sipsongpanna, many of these small states had historically retained their independence from larger polities through face-giving diplomacy, yet found their net-works disrupted by the border drawing of nation-states. Today, many such marginalized groups are banding together across borders to form powerful ethnic and religious communities.

On a macro scale, the new phenomena of globalization—mass migration, global flows of finance and media, simultaneous and speeded-up processes of movement and contact—present a picture of bewildering chaos and confusion. Yet while we attend to the new content of videos, films, and other mass media that promote shared identities, in the villages where we can watch modernity in the process of conquering new terrain such objects are shared through the oldest form of communication in the world: something we might call folklore. The chief conduits here are indigenous systems of face-to-face contact, hand-to-hand exchange, systems of remembering and performing done in living rooms, on stilt-house porches, and in temple halls.

Thus we should attend not only to the video itself but to the person who carries the video, who puts it into the machine and presses "play," who explains the images that appear in terms a village teenager can understand. In the right hands, modernity is made to feel not foreign or alienating but as familiar, remembered, and natural as an old legend. It is a gift from teacher to student, from priest to congregant, that expands a personal sense of subjectivity to include new possibilities.

Notes

1. The Yale Council on East Asian Studies and the UCLA Center for Southeast Asian Studies each provided postdoctoral fellowships and other support while this essay was being written, and the UCLA Center for Chinese Studies provided a forum for an early draft. A Kao fellowship from the Yale Council on East Asian Studies supported field research in 2001. I am grateful to Kathryn Bernhardt, C. Patterson Giersch, and Stevan Harrell, who offered valuable comments and questions. Thanks also to Wendy Cadge, Valerie Hansen, Galen Joseph, Charles Keyes, and Katherine Rupp for reading early drafts; and to Tom Borchert, Gardner Bovingdon, Paul Cohen, Victor Mair, Margaret Mills, Joseph Roach, James Scott, Donald Swearer, and many in China and Burma who must be anonymous, for conversations and correspondence.

2. As the Tai Lüe original of this valuable text is not available, the passage is translated from a recently published Chinese translation, which often appears to favor contemporary terminology. The translator uses such official post–1949 terms as *minzu* (nationalities), *Hanzu* (Han nationality), *Daizu* (Dai nationality), and *Hanizu* (Hani nationality). The originals in Tai Lüe would probably have been *phasaa* (in Sipsongpanna Tai Lüe, meaning "race"; a homophone in central Thai means "language"), *Haw* (Han Chinese), *Tai*, and *Kaw* (inclusive of Akha, Aini, and Hani). Note also that the spelling "Tai" (not "Dai") is favored by most scholars outside of China to represent the aspirated initial consonant, and is used here.

3. The official name of Burma is now Myanmar. However, the name change was instituted after a military coup refused to cede power to the winners of a

democratic election in 1990, and many foreign scholars continue to call the country Burma.

4. No standard romanization system currently exists for Tai Lüe. For the most part this essay follows standard conventions used in romanization of Thai. The exception is "Wat Pajay," which is the spelling used by the temple. The name for the region, Sipsongpanna, has been erroneously translated by some scholars as "The ten thousand rice fields." This is a confusion of the Tai Lüe term *pan*, "village" or "township," with the Thai term *phan*, "ten thousand." *Sipsong*, everyone agrees, means "twelve," and *panna* means "township rice field"—a reference to the traditional organization of townships in the federation around their allied village rice fields.

5. My teacher left monastic life in 1999, and not long after I helped him to emigrate to the United States, where he still lives.

6. *Khuba* is the Tai Lüe pronunciation; the same term appears in Thai as *khruba*.

7. Chinese historians of the Tai vary in the date they set on Buddhist transmission to Sipsongpanna, which tends to range between the thirteenth and fifteenth centuries (Liu 1993; Wang and Chang 1990; Zheng 1993; Zhu 1993). Ai Feng (Yan Feng), who unlike many historians draws on Tai-language written histories in the original, puts the first transmission to Sipsongpanna in the sixth to eighth centuries (Yan, Wang, and Dao 1988). Oral traditions that I heard in Sipsongpanna supported these earlier dates. Regrettably, Tai-language texts are not archived anywhere and are in a state of chaos. Given the many political agendas behind early and late dates (which implicitly confer "civilizedness" on Sipsongpanna via the Buddhist tradition), the dating of Buddhist transmission to Sipsongpanna should be regarded as contested.

8. Rohan D'Souza (personal communication, 20 February 2001) rightly observes that many precapitalist empires "functioned through systems of alliances at their fringes and outposts," and that in this regard Tai self-rule would be typical of imperial border regions in a comparative context. However, in China as elsewhere, earlier self-rule tends not to be stressed in official histories, which legitimize contemporary national agendas by reading retroactively.

9. The Tai Lüe term *chao phaendin* literally translates as "prince of the earth." It parallels similar terminologies in other Tai-speaking regions of the Mekong valley, such as the term used among Shans and Thais, *chao fa*, literally "prince of the heavens" (in Burmanized form, the term often appears as *sawbwa*). One local Tai-language chronicle lists Daos as rulers at various stages of Tai history (Dao 1990). C. Patterson Giersch (personal communication, 25 June 2001) notes similar uses of the term *chao suen vi fa* in Kengtung chronicles that suggest an incorporation of the Chinese *xuanwei* with the Tai *chao fa*. My suggestion of the possible existence of "bogus notables" in Sipsongpanna must remain speculative until more local Tai-language annals become available.

10. Scott (1985, 1990) explores these and other forms of rural resistance to domination and conquest in more depth.

11. Stevan Harrell (personal communication, 8 August 2002) suggests that the motivation behind promoting the new script is its standardization, adding, "I know standardisation has been a big motive in the development of new Yi scripts; the old ones certainly had no standard." But this seems unlikely in the case of Tai Lüe; the policy has not aimed to produce a unified alphabet with other Tai peoples in China, such as those in Dehong, but has created separate new simplified scripts in each region. The lack of any Chinese–Tai dictionary

until the language policy had been in place for more than forty years also suggests that standardization was not the goal. In any event, with the exception of only a few letters, the old Tai Lüe alphabet and the alphabet used by Tai Khun neighbors in Kengtung, in the Shan States, of Burma, are virtually identical; if anything, this offers another state motivation to stick to the simplified script policy in the face of widespread grassroots resistance to it.

12. Sipsongpanna Tai Lüe do not have surnames, but they bear titles that indicate rank. On entering the temple, Tai novices keep their given names but exchange their male titles (*Aye*) for the title of novice (*Pha*, like the Thai *Phra*); thus a boy named Aye Tai would become Pha Tai as a novice. If Pha Tai ordains as a monk at the age of 18 or 19, he becomes Du Tai, and if he is promoted again in his twenties the title becomes *Dubi*. Dubi Long Zhaum is the abbot of Wat Pajay; thus his title is *Dubi Long* or "Great Dubi." Were he to leave monastic life after being ordained, he would become a *khanan* or former monk. Novices who leave before being ordained are not *khanan*.

13. In 2001, several Tai musicians, including a former monk turned singer, did succeed in recording two pop VCDs (music videos) with Tai classical script on them.

References

Anderson, Benedict R. 1991. *Imagined Communities: Reflections on the Origin and Spread of Nationalism.* Rev. ed. London: Verso.

Appadurai, Arjun. 1996. *Modernity at Large: Cultural Dimensions of Globalization.* Minneapolis: University of Minnesota Press.

Castles, Stephen, and Alastair Davidson. 2000. *Citizenship and Migration: Globalization and the Politics of Belonging.* London: Macmillan.

Chao Tzang, Yawnghwe. 1987. *The Shan of Burma: Memoirs of a Shan Exile.* Singapore: Institute of Southeast Asian Studies.

Chuba Meng [Khuba Muang], ed. 1981. *Lun Daizu shige* (A Discussion of Tai Poetry and Song) (Tai: *Wa du ma yaw gamkhap Tai*). Trans. Ai Wen Pian. Kunming: Zhongguo minjian wenxue chubanshe.

Cohen, Paul. 2000. "A Buddhist Kingdom in the Golden Triangle: Buddhist Revivalism and the Charismatic Monk Khruba Bunchum." *Australian Journal of Anthropology* 11, no. 2: 141–54.

Condominas, Georges. 1990. *From Lawa to Mon, from Saa' to Thai: Historical and Anthropological Aspects of Southeast Asian Social Spaces.* Trans. Stephanie Anderson, Maria Magannon, and Gehan Wijeyewardene. Ed. Gehan Wijeyewardene. Canberra: Department of Anthropology, Research School of Pacific Studies, Australian National University.

Dao Gaung Siang, ed. 1990. *Cheua kheua chao sianvi Sipsongpanna* (Chronology of the Princes of Sipsongpanna). Kunming: Yunnan minzu chubanshe.

Davis, Sara. 1999. "Singers of Sipsongpanna: Folklore and Authenticity in Contemporary China." Ph.D. dissertation, University of Pennsylvania.

———. 2001. "The Hawaiification of Xishuangbanna: Orality, Power, and Cultural Survival in Southwest China." *The Drama Review: TDR* 45, no. 4: 25–41.

Dodd, William Clifton. 1996 [1923]. *The Tai Race, Elder Brother of the Chinese: Results of Experience, Exploration, and Research of William Clifton Dodd, D.D., Thirty-three Years a Missionary to the Tai People of Siam, Burma, and China, Compiled and Edited by His Wife*. Bangkok: White Lotus Press.

Davis, Sara L.M. 2005. *Song and Silence: Ethnic Revival on China's Southwest Borders*. New York: Columbia University Press.

Evans, Grant. 2000. "The Transformation of Jinghong." In Grant Evans, Christopher Hutton, and Kuah Khun Eng, eds., *Where China Meets Southeast Asia: Social and Cultural Change in the Border Regions*. Singapore: Institute of Southeast Asian Studies.

Giersch, C. Patterson. 2001 "'A Motley Throng: Social Change on Southwest China's Early Modern Frontier, 1700–1880." *Journal of Asian Studies* 60, no. 1: 67–94.

Gogoi, Padmeswar. 1968. *The Tai and the Tai Kingdoms, with a Fuller Treatment of the Tai-Ahom Kingdom in the Brahmaputra Valley*. Gauhati, Assam: Gauhati University, Department of Publications.

Handler, Richard. 1988. *Nationalism and the Politics of Culture in Quebec*. Madison: University of Wisconsin Press.

Hansen, Mette Halskov. 1999. *Lessons in Being Chinese: Minority Education and Ethnic Identity in Southwest China*. Seattle: University of Washington Press.

Harrell, Stevan. 1995. "Civilizing Projects and the Reaction to Them." In Stevan Harrell, ed., *Cultural Encounters on China's Ethnic Frontiers*. Seattle: University of Washington Press.

Hasegawa, Kiyoshi. 2000. "Cultural Revival and Ethnicity: The Case of the Tai Lüe in the Sipsong Panna, Yunnan Province." In *Dynamics of Ethnic Cultures across National Boundaries in Southwestern China and Mainland Southeast Asia: Relations, Societies, and Languages*. Proceedings of "Making Regions: Proto-Areas, Transformation and New Formation in Asia and Africa," 16–17 October 1999, Kunming, China. Chiang Mai, Thailand: Ming Muang Printing House. Also posted March 2000 to http://coe.asafas.kyoto-u.ac.jp/research/sea/social/hayashi/Hayashi_Unnan_8Hasegawa.htm (24 January 2001).

Hsieh, Shih-Chung. 1995. "On the Dynamics of Tai/Dai-Lue Ethnicity: An Ethnohistorical Analysis." In Stevan Harrell, ed., *Cultural Encounters on China's Ethnic Frontiers*, Seattle: University of Washington Press.

Hyde, Sandra Teresa. 2001. "Sex Tourism Practices on the Periphery: Eroticizing Ethnicity and Pathologizing Sex on the Lancang." In Nancy N. Chen et al, eds., *China Urban: Ethnographies of Contemporary Culture*. Durham, N.C.: Duke University Press.

Jia Xu. 1994. *Zhongguo xinan dui wai guanxi shi yanjiu: yi xinan sizhoulü wei zhongxin* (Study of the History of Southwest Chinese Foreign Relations: Taking the Southwestern Silk Road as the Center). Kunming: Yunnan meishu chubanshe.

Keyes, Charles F. 1995. "Who are the Tai? Reflections on the Invention of Identities." In Lola Romanucci-Ross and George A. De Vos, eds., *Ethnic Identity: Creation, Conflict, and Accommodation*, 3rd ed. Walnut Creek, Calif.: AltaMira Press.

Li Weiqing. 1990. *"Daizu foside huihua yishu"* (The Art of Dai Nationality Temple Paintings). In *Beiye wenhua lun* (Discussion of Carved-Leaf Culture), eds. Wang Zhiyi and Yang Shiguang. Kunming: Yunnan renmin chubanshe.

Ling, Trevor. 1979. *Buddhism, Imperialism, and War: Burma and Thailand in Modern History.* London: George Allen & Unwin.

Liu Yan. 1993. *Nanchuan fojiao yu Daizu wenhua* (Southern-Transmitted Buddhism and Dai Nationality Culture). Kunming: Yunnan minzu chubanshe.

Mair, Victor H. 1988. *Painting and Performance: Chinese Picture Recitation and Its Indian Genesis.* Honolulu: University of Hawaii Press.

Malinowski, Bronislaw. 1961 [1922]. *Argonauts of the Western Pacific: An Account of Native Enterprise and Adventure in the Archipelagoes of Melanesian New Guinea.* New York: E. P. Dutton.

Marx, Karl. 1976. *Capital, Volume 1.* trans. Ben Fowkes. London: Penguin.

Medford, Beatrix. 1936. *Where China Meets Burma: Life and Travel in the Burma–China Borderlands.* London: Blackie & Son.

Ong, Aihwa, and Donald M. Nonini, eds. 1997. *Ungrounded Empires: The Cultural Politics of Modern Chinese Transnationalism.* New York: Routledge.

Sao Ying Sita. 1989. "The Tradition of Democracy in the Shan State." *Cultural Survival* 13, 4: 10–2.

Schein, Louisa. 2000. *Minority Rules: The Miao and the Feminine in China's Cultural Politics.* Durham, NC: Duke University Press.

Scholte, Jan Aart. 2000. *Globalization: A Critical Introduction.* New York: St. Martin's.

Scott, James C. 1985. *Weapons of the Weak: Everyday Forms of Peasant Resistance.* New Haven: Yale University Press.

———. 1990. *Domination and the Arts of Resistance: Hidden Transcripts.* New Haven: Yale University Press.

Seagrave, Gordon S. 1930. *Waste-Basket Surgery.* Philadelphia: Judson Press.

Sima Qian. 1997. *Shi ji* (Records of the Historian [ca. 145–ca. 86 B.C.E.]). Scripta Sinica (*Han ji dianzi wenxuan*), Academia Sinica Computing Centre, November www.sinica.edu/ftms-bin/ftmsw3 (29 January 2001).

Song Lian. 1997. *Yuan shi* (History of the Yuan dynasty [1310–1381]). Scripta Sinica (*Han ji dianzi wenxuan*), Academia Sinica Computing Centre, November www.sinica.edu/ftms-bin/ftmsw3 (29 January 2001).

Sulak, Sivaraksa. 1999. *Global Healing: Essays and Interviews on Structural Violence, Social Development, and Spiritual Transformation.* Bangkok: Thai Inter-Religious Commission for Development.

Swain, Margaret Byrne. 1995. "A Comparison of State and Private Artisan Production for Tourism in Yunnan." In Alan A. Lew and Lawrence Yu., eds., *Tourism in China: Geographic, Political, and Economic Perspectives*, Boulder, Colo.: Westview Press.

Thongchai Winichakul. 1994. *Siam Mapped: A History of the Geo-body of a Nation.* Bangkok: Silkworm Books.

Walker, Andrew. 1999. *The Legend of the Golden Boat: Regulation, Trade, and Traders in the Borderlands of Laos, Thailand, China, and Burma.* Surrey, UK: Curzon Press.

Wang Zhiyi. 1990 "*Xishuangbanna xiaocheng fojiao lishi kaocha*" (Survey of Xishuangbanna Hinayana Buddhist History). In Wang Zhiyi and Yang Shiguang, eds., *Beiye wenhua lun* (Discussion of Carved-Leaf Culture),. Kunming: Yunnan renmin chubanshe.

Wang Yizhi and Chang Shiguang, eds. 1990. *Beiye wenhua lun* (Discussion of Palm-Leaf Manuscripts). Kunming: Yunnan renmin chubanshe.

Wong, Deborah. 1994. "'I Want the Microphone': Mass Mediation and Agency in Asian-American Popular Music." *The Drama Review: TDR* 38, 3: 152–67.

Xishuangbanna Daizu zizhizhou renmin zhengfu (Xishuangbanna Dai Nationality Autonomous Prefecture People's Government), ed. 2002. *Dai Han cidian* (Dai-Chinese Dictionary). Kunming: Yunnan minzu chubanshe.

Xishuangbanna Daizu zizhizhou wenhua ju (Xishuangbanna Dai Autonomous Region Culture Bureau), ed. 1993. *Zanha ju zhi* (Record of Zhangkhap Opera). Kunming: Wenhua yishu chubanshe.

Yan Feng [Ai Feng], Wang Song, and Dao Bao En, eds. 1988. *Daizu wenxue shi* [History of Dai Nationality Literature]. Kunming: Yunnan minzu chubanshe.

Zhang Tingyu. 1997. *Ming shi* (History of the Ming Dynasty [1672–1755]). Scripta Sinica (*Han ji dianzi wenxuan*), Academia Sinica Computing Centre, November www.sinica.edu/ftms-bin/ftmsw3 (29 January 2001).

Zheng Peng. 1993. *Xishuangbanna gailan* (An Introduction to Xishuangbanna). Kunming: Yunnan minzu chubanshe.

Zhu Depu. 1993. *Leshi yanjiu* (An Examination of Lüe History). Kunming: Yunnan renmin chubanshe.

5

Borders and Multiple Realities: The Orang Suku Laut of Riau, Indonesia

Cynthia Chou

Introduction

IN THIS ERA OF REVOLUTIONARY changes, processes of globalization, internationalization, and supranationalization are seen as rearranging and restructuring spatial relations to form a borderless world or "space of flows" (Castells 1989, 1993, 1996). The prime purpose of this chapter is to argue that such processes may not necessarily lead to the advent of a system of "variegated citizenship" (Ong 1999: 215) in a more global world of "multinational" (1999: 221) and "graduated sovereignty" (1999: 215). Instead, state borders are, in fact, gaining in importance. Most importantly, this essay argues for the need to move to a comprehensive analysis of the paradoxical strengthening of state borders within these so called borderless worlds.

Today's borderless worlds do not come into being merely by allowing things to take their own course. They are, in fact, political choices made within a context of assessment and enforced by the states concerned (Bienefeld 1994). Thus, contrary to the prevailing view that nation-states are evolving towards larger and borderless worlds, it is in fact the case that the governments of the nation-states are by no means presiding over the demise of their own borders.

The study of borders—their significance and processes—remains crucial. Borders rarely match the simplicity of their representation on maps, but are themselves structures of policy making and tools of control and order (Baud and van Schendel 1997: 222). They delineate simultaneously zones of sociohistorical and cultural production, as well as spaces where processes of "meaning-making" and "meaning-breaking" happen (Donnan and Wilson 1999: 64).

Endnotes for this chapter begin on page 131.

This chapter focuses on the predicaments of the Orang Suku Laut ("tribe of sea people") of Riau, Indonesia. They are presently confronted with challenges imposed on their maritime world by the emergence of new borders resulting from the recently created Growth Triangle zone. For centuries, the Orang Suku Laut have regarded themselves as the indigenous people and owners of a vast maritime world known as the *Alam Melayu* (Malay World). As a people who practice a mobile lifestyle and economy, they have navigated the sea and coastal areas within this region as their life and living space for generations.

The *Alam Melayu* is currently divided among five nation-states—namely Indonesia, Singapore, Malaysia, Brunei, and Thailand. Since European colonizers arrived in the sixteenth century, this region has been subject to a succession of border changes that mapped it into different divisions of sovereignty, economies, knowledge, and social landscapes (Wee 1988; Wee and Chou 1997). The difference today lies in the extent of the changes in the region's inhabitants as well as on their habitat brought about by current border manipulations.

State borders, themselves molded by human agencies and the physical environment, in turn shape the human landscape around them (Donnan and Wilson 1999: 47). This chapter is thus distinguished by four main research themes. The first of these sees the border as a product of the sociopolitical landscape and elucidates the form and practices of state political systems and other institutional structures embodied in the border. The second examines how the border affects the cultural, economic, and demographic landscape that stretches away from the border on either side. The third examines the effect of the border on national policies and the attitudes of, and to, the border inhabitants. The fourth departs from the traditional view of borders as seen from the center, but follows what Baud and van Schendel (1997: 212) have proposed: a new view of borders from the perspective of a state's periphery, i.e., from the borders themselves.[1]

One of the greatest impacts contemporary border constructions have on a region is the convergence of intense and conflicting demands on resources. These demands are further exacerbated as each of the resultant spatial realities strives toward higher economic growth in response to the forces of globalization. In this context, the new borders have forced the Orang Suku Laut into new forms of territorial tenure, which have shifted them out of their traditional life and living spaces. Thus, the Orang Suku Laut provides a case study of the tensions that have arisen as a consequence of the increasingly complicated relation between global forces, state powers, and local identities.

Three main arenas of contestations and conflicts are examined here. The first concerns the impact on the Orang Suku Laut's tenure of territory. The second depicts how the making of borders has led to the gendering of spaces. The third involves the reclassification of what have served as life and livelihood resources for the Orang Suku Laut by way of a redefinition of what constitutes resources by the new sovereign powers. In these three areas of discussion, the gendering of the border is highlighted to show how Orang Suku Laut women are doubly affected by differential values that can exist on either side of the border.

The Setting

The Orang Suku Laut are found scattered throughout the Riau–Lingga Archipelago of Indonesia and the southern coasts of the Malay Peninsula (Johor), the east coast of Sumatra, and the larger islands of Bangka and Belitung (Sandbukt 1982: 17). Until recently, they were also found along the north coast of Singapore (Mariam 2002).

The Orang Suku Laut are divided into various *suku* (tribes), such as that of *Suku* Tambus, *Suku* Galang, *Suku* Mantang, and *Suku* Barok (Sopher 1977; Sandbukt 1982). Further subdivisions occur within these *suku* along the lines of kinship and territorial occupation. The most senior male member is usually made the *kepala* (head) of the community—a position often appointed by the Indonesian authorities. Although a *kepala* wields more power, he is not recognized by his *suku* members as possessing absolute authority over the community. The head of a *suku* is often verbally acknowledged and officially recognized to be a man, yet it is not uncommon that the actual power to make and carry out decisions, on a daily basis as well as on crucial matters, lies with a woman. No rights to ownership and division of labor among the Orang Suku Laut are clearly defined by sex. For example, during fishing expeditions, men often spear for fish while women row the boats, tasks that are deemed complimentary, but men often praise the women for being skillful spearers too. Both men and women possess the potential to become *dukun* (practioners of indigenous medicine)—a position held in great esteem in Orang Suku Laut communities. There is no distinct division in the type of *ilmu* (knowledge or magic) practiced by either men or women.

The Orang Suku Laut are a fishing people, and the sea and coastal areas constitute their life and living spaces. As they live a maritime way of life from birth, they possess an outstanding knowledge of the winds, currents, and tides that govern the sea; of rich fishing grounds and mangrove swamps; and of the position of the sun, moon, and stars whereby they navigate their way through their maritime world. They depend predominantly on the sea for their food, and what surplus maritime products they may have are sold to the Chinese *thau-ke* (bosses) for extra income.

Historically, the Orang Suku Laut played an important role in support of the Sultan's position during the period of the Malacca-Johor-Riau Sultanate. As vessels, they roamed the peripheries of the Sultanate extending its influence and, because of this, they gained in political importance.

However, their influence began to wane when the Dutch arrived on the scene in the eighteenth century. There are now 3,609 Orang Suku Laut (roughly half men and half women)[2]—a figure that amounts to approximately 6 percent of the total 50,000-strong population of the Riau Archipelago consisting of Malays, Javanese, Bawanese, Minangakabau, Buton, Orang Dalam, and Chinese (Kepulauan Riau Dalam Angka 1987: 32). From the perspective of government officials and other local Indonesians, the Orang Suku Laut are "smelly people who never bathe," "people who do not wear clothes," "people who do not have bathrooms," and "people who live and do everything in their boats." Furthermore, they are said to have no religion and not to pray at all.[3] The majority Malays, with the support of the Indonesian authorities, have been exerting pressure on the Orang Suku Laut to convert to the Muslim faith. Some have converted, but most continue to abide by their own religion of worshiping sea and land spirits. Whatever is said of them, the Orang Suku Laut identify themselves as the *orang asli* (indigenous people) and *asli Melayu* (indigenous Malays) of the *Alam Melayu*—a point that even the Muslim Malays and the other non-Malay local inhabitants of Riau freely acknowledge.

For centuries the maritime waters of what now encompasses the five nation states of Indonesia, Singapore, Malaysia, Brunei, and Thailand have constituted the life and living spaces of the Orang Suku Laut. The mobile lifestyle of the Orang Suku Laut and their houseboats forms a basic but crucial premise for the Orang Suku Laut's perception of space and formulation of communities. Their mobility enables them to conceive of communities that need not be bound to immediate and specific localities; indeed, it enables them to construct their communities in networks covering large expanses of space with no definable borders (see Chou 2000).

Riau is one of Indonesia's twenty-seven provinces and comprises Riau mainland on the central part of eastern Sumatra and the Riau Archipelago which stretches from the Straits of Malacca in the west to the South China Sea in the east. Riau of Indonesia today coincides approximately to the former indigenous kingdom of the Riau-Lingga Sultanate, which had a history of over 400 years and was one of the last areas to be subsumed under direct Dutch administration (Figure 1).

Although Riau is now a province of Indonesia, both the Orang Suku Laut and the Muslim Malays continue to consider it a part of a wider Malay world that transgresses all modern day-borders to encompass parts or entireties of what we know today as Riau in Indonesia, Singapore, Malaysia, Brunei, and southern Thailand. This vast spatial expanse that the Orang Suku Laut regard as theirs is currently facing the imposition of external agendas once again. Presently, Riau is increasingly perceived by the Indonesian, Singaporean, and Malaysian governments to fall onto a collective agenda known as the Growth Triangle.

Fig. 5.1. Riau and the Growth Triangle.

In late 1989, Mr. Goh Chok Tong, then Deputy Prime Minister of Singapore, coined the term "Growth Triangle" to promote the establishment of a trilateral economic development program among Riau in Indonesia, Singapore, and Johor in Malaysia. The program was to interweave the comparative advantages of these three nation-states in order to form synergies that would increase the overall well-being of the industrial countries and the collective (Kumar and Lee 1991; Lee 1997) by creating a spatial configuration that would collapse national borders to service a "spaceless" (Macleod and McGee 1996: 425) and "borderless" economy (Chen and Kwan 1997).

As a result, the past few years have seen a startling increase in the flow of goods, capital, information, and people between Singapore and Johor, and between Singapore and Riau. Figures provided by Macleod and McGee (1996: 425) show that population movements across the causeway between Singapore and Johor escalated at about 17 percent per annum. Approximately 25,000 Johoreans cross into Singapore to work each day, and about 12.2 million people from Singapore cross over to Johor each year. With regard to border crossings between Batam and Singapore, the 69,000 tourists who entered Batam (mostly from Singapore) in 1980 had swelled by 1985 to over 500,000 (Batam Industrial Development Authority 1991).

Other cross-border initiatives between Riau and Singapore have included (Macleod and McGee 1996: 425): (1) an increase in speedboat shuttle service to Riau from Singapore to intervals of only thirty minutes; (2) the development of Batam Island's international telephone system, which is routed through Singapore and not Jakarta (a first); (3) a joint Singaporean and Indonesian governmental agreement to issue "smart cards" in place of passports to allow Singaporean managers quicker cross-border transit time through customs in Batam; and (4) a new Singapore consulate in Riau to boost economic links (Straits Times 15 February 2001: A1). Cross-border schemes for the future between Johor and Singapore have included (Macleod and McGee 1996: 425): (1) the installation of a second causeway linking Johor and Singapore at a cost of S$1 billion; (2) a possible extension of the Singapore subway or Mass Rapid Transport into Johor Bahru; and (3) a proposal to form a joint Malaysian and Singaporean governmental agreement to issue "smart cards" in place of passports to allow selected Malaysians and Singaporeans quicker cross-border transit time through customs at the Malaysian and Singaporean immigration checkpoints.

Also critical within the scope of the Growth Triangle, are the intergovernment and private business propositions are focused on establishing marine complexes housing oil terminals and chemical supply bases, an agro-processing center, residential developments, marine tourism, and light industries. The province of Riau is seen as boasting "an Archipelago of virgin islands" (Soh and Chuang 1990: 34). Golf courses have also been part of the scheme to turn Riau into an ideal tourist belt. In the perspectives and plans of the governments and private business investors, the ambition is to transform the island chain into the "Caribbean of the East" (1990: 34): a place that is all things to all people.

Theoretical Considerations

Ong (1999) has maintained that in borderless zones such as the Growth Triangle, localized political and social organizations, while not having come to an end, are becoming more flexible in their management of border sovereignty. This flexibility is the result of the links that localized political organizations are forming with multi- and transnational institutions to promote the flows of global capital. Ong (1999: 215) views this flexibility of sovereignty as a strategy adopted by localized political organizations to accommodate transnational foreign corporate institutions, which possess a "mix of legal protections, controls and disciplinary regimes." Furthermore, "globalization has induced a situation of graduated sovereignty, whereby even as the state maintains control over its territory, it is also willing in some cases to let corporate entities set the terms for constituting and regulating some domains. Sometimes, weaker and less-desirable groups are given over to the regulation of supranational entities. What results is a system of variegated citizenship in which population subjected to different regimes of value enjoy different kinds of rights, discipline, caring and security" (1999: 215).

Ong (1999: 221) sees the Growth Triangle as moving toward forming "multinational zones of sovereignty." The challenge that she (1999: 222) proposes for the study of the construction of borderless zones is to discover the kinds of "conducive regulatory environment" that prevail under supranational management while more multinational networks of partnerships are being set up within and between national borders.

Noting Ong's highly convincing arguments and other more adamant assertions on the demise of the state and borders (e.g., Sassen 1995: xiv)[4] in the current era of globalization, I shall nevertheless suggest that the state remains to be a key institution in structuring spatial realities via border constructions. In spite of the creation of global or borderless zones such as the Growth Triangle, I believe that it is the state that continues to hold the monopoly on defining the borders of such spaces and on determining who will be allowed to participate in such zones. In other words, would-be participants must first affiliate themselves to a specific state-defined spatial order, and then be accorded a legitimate citizenship, before they can participate with any legitimate right in such spaces or exercise flexibility in their movements within such spaces.

At this point, it is important to keep in mind that zones such as the Growth Triangle are created under certain circumstances. First, several individual states must believe that, although they lie in close geographical proximity to one another, they are in different stages of development; and second, each state must consider itself to possess what it deems as a different sort of comparative advantage—be it in human, capital, or material resources—over its neighbor states. Thus, the creation of the Growth Triangle and other such zones are necessarily premised upon divisions and differences that are marked by state borders. Indeed, it is only when the individual states clearly see such divisions and differences that they are willing to form multilateral relationships and zones such as the Growth Triangle. A network of interdependency between these states is then established to interweave their comparative advantages and so increase the overall well-being of both the individual states and the collective zone. In other words, a zone such as the Growth Triangle exists by virtue of two conditions: first, its own opposition to other communities or zones, and second, the oppositions among the communities that form the zone itself.

The sovereignty of the state in defining borders—even in these so-called borderless Growth Triangle zones—can be seen in the proceedings of the recent meeting of the foreign ministers of the Association of Southeast Asian Nations (ASEAN), where the ASEAN Troika was established. It was agreed that the resolution of any sort of problem must be premised on all participants knowing "precisely" what each member state's "respective position" is. This assumes that transnational problems can be solved "without compromising ASEAN's cardinal principle of non-intervention" in "domestic" issues (Jakarta Post 2000).

The notion of zones such as the Growth Triangle is thus relational, implying both difference and similarity. I believe that the Growth Triangle is one of the best places to examine the relational nature of borders and everyday practices of exclusion and inclusion, and will show that spaces such as the Growth Triangle are not "graduated zones of sovereignty," but actually spaces marked by borders reflecting overlapping multiple realities.

Borders are "simultaneously structures and processes, things and relationships, histories and events" (Donnan and Wilson 1999: 62; see also Anderson 1996: 1). In these overlapping positions the role of the border is that of "a marker and agent of tradition and change" (Donnan and Wilson 1999: 62). Borders inscribe the edge of a social system (Wallman 1978: 205), and are, at the same time, the interface and identity lines between inside and outside, and between "us" and "them" (see Ross 1975). This important role of the border in the selectivity and reclassification of peoples, interest groups, territories, and resources underscores the reason why borders have also become a term of discourse in narratives of multiple repertoires of identities and realities.

Borders as representing "the edge of a social system" (Wallman 1978: 206) and the interface between two systems of activity, organization, and meaning are, following Douglas (1966), also predisposed to be characterized by ambiguity and danger. By this, I mean that members of respective systems regard the border as a screening mechanism to mark off members from nonmembers, and acceptable from non-acceptable participants of the two systems. One of the significant byproducts of this function within the Growth Triangle has been that of the gendering of the borders.

Diverging from Ong's theory (1999: 215) that the Growth Triangle has become a multinational zone of greater flexible sovereignty where even "sometimes, weaker and less-desirable groups are given over to the regulation of supranational entities," I argue to the contrary by presenting the case example of the Orang Suku Laut women in Riau.

The Orang Suku Laut, and in particular Orang Suku Laut women, are seen by both the Indonesian state and the other neighboring states as anomalous citizens inclined toward subversion of state order and policies. In an apparent attempt to control these women, the governments and their agents have turned to borders as a tool to forbid them to enter this supposedly global zone or move from one system to another. This gendered construction of the state, in addition to selecting and rejecting acceptable participants for the global sphere, is also the gendering of the border. The gendering of the border has thus acted both as an impediment to and a stimulus for new definitions in the tenure of territory, modification of resources, and gender relations, especially at the level of the individual and local communities who need most to participate in the Growth Triangle.

Multiple Realities: Redefining the Tenure of Territory

The Orang Suku Laut do not regard the inception of the Growth Triangle and its resultant new order of sovereignty and spatial ownership as a new phenomenon. They are fully aware that various border constructions symbolizing and signifying different eras of political domination in Riau have been superimposed on their maritime world. These changes are clearly remembered by many Orang Suku Laut in various ways. In a conversation I had with Buntot, an Orang Suku Laut woman from Teluk Nipah Island, she explained that she had seen many borders in her lifetime. These borders signified the domination of the area by the Malay sultans, Japanese, Portuguese, Dutch, and the Republic of Indonesia. Buntot was able to recount experiences of hardship during food shortages and the torture of women during the Japanese Occupation. These hardships compared unfavorably to the relative comfort of being left alone by the Dutch colonizers.

In another conversation I had with three Orang Suku Laut women, Imah, Suri, and Yang from the neighboring island Pulau Nanga, they spoke of changing impositions of borders that signaled various changing realities and everyday practices in Riau. For these three women, the changes were perceived in terms of the different currencies that had been used in Riau. For example, they recollected that initially they "did not use any money" but "just *tukar barang* (bartered goods)" before they proceeded to use "*uang dollar* (dollar money)," and then money with the "*cap burung* (bird seal),…*pakai layah* ([currency] with [the seal of a] sail),…and now it is the bird."[5]

The Orang Suku Laut see borders as byproducts of particular historical circumstances. While politicians and geographers wrangle with the definitions of the spatial dimension of borders and their roles in nation and state relations, the Orang Suku Laut perceive them in temporal and gendered terms.

The Orang Suku Laut understand that the changing border constructions by external entities on their maritime world connote different eras of political domination and thus different political realities. Yet these realities are not viewed as superseding their perspective of what constitutes their maritime world. First, the definition of their world is not constrained by borders. The Orang Suku Laut's maritime world is as wide as their mobility will allow them to cover. Second, Riau is a part of a wider Malay world that overrides all other temporary and temporal borders. Third, they are the custodians of this Malay maritime world. Such claims by the Orang Suku Laut are known to the other local inhabitants of Riau.

One of the most important aspects of the Orang Suku Laut' perception of borders is the fact that they acknowledge borders only in a temporal sense; that is, borders are temporary markers that inevitably will change someday. They believe that they possess an unbroken historical tradition that overrides all temporal borders, and that the ultimate sovereignty lies with the *Raja Laut* (Ruler of the Sea) in their borderless world. They deem their sovereign the ruler of the maritime world, even though there may be, within this expanse of space, borders conventional to the passing eras of different political dominations.

The Orang Suku Laut believe that the *Raja Laut* is more *"khuat"* (powerful) than all other Rajas. They claim that "even the Raja in [the current state of] Malaysia" and "the Raja of Galang [in Indonesia]" are descendants of the *Raja Laut*. Below are excerpts from a conversation that I had with the Orang Suku Laut from Dapur Enam. In these excerpts, they explain the sovereignty of the *Raja Laut*.

> Cynthia: Who is *Raja Laut?*
>
> Sman: The *Raja Laut* is *orang kami* (one of us).
>
> Bego: The *Raja Laut* is *Orang Daik* (person from Daik).
>
> Cynthia: You mean to say that the *Raja Laut* is Raja to all the different groups of Orang Suku Laut?
>
> Sman: Yes. The *Raja Laut* is Raja of all the islands. In Malaysia, they also have a *Raja Laut*. However, their *keturunan* (descent) and our descent are from Daik.
>
> Bego: [The present *Raja Laut*] is *Orang Tua* (senior person) Bosor...[who] lives in *bagain* (province) Daik in Pulau Buloh Konkee. *Dia* (He/She) possesses incredible strength. *Dia* is able to uproot a coconut tree...and throw it into the sea. *Dia* is also able to overturn ships.
>
> Sman: When a *Raja Melayu* (Malay Raja) meets a *Raja Laut* (Raja of the Sea), [the former] is unable to lift his hands and legs against the latter.

In the event of the death of a *Raja Laut*, a child of the *Raja Laut* will become the next *Raja Laut*. According to Sman, the news of such a succession will be made known to them in the following way.

> Sman: Our people will come and tell us about it. We are [also] the *orang asli* of Singapore, Malaysia and here [Riau, Indonesia].

Although the Orang Suku Laut from Dapur Enam speak of being descendants of Daik and having a *Raja Laut* who is an Orang Daik, there were other tribes of Orang Suku Laut who did not perceive their origins as stemming from Daik. Nor did they agree that the *Raja Laut* is an Orang Daik. In spite of variations in details, a few key points in all the conversations that I had with the Orang Suku Laut can be noted. First, they all stressed that they and the non-Orang Suku Laut Malays or Muslim Malays share a common origin, descent, and habitat. Therefore, in spite of existing borders that divide the region into various nation states, the Orang Suku Laut see these borders as but recently constructed phenomena that do not change the basic fact that this entire space was discovered by them. Second, the Orang Suku Laut maintain that it was by their very mobility that the region was discovered, formed, and expanded. Third, the Orang Suku Laut see that the cohesion of the entire region has long been based on their network of genealogical and kinship ties, which continue to prevail in spite of the interference of modern-day political borders. Based upon these premises, the Orang Suku Laut claim ownership of and sovereignty over this entire space.

For the Orang Suku Laut, all space is equally accessible to men and women. Both men and women possess equal claims to the tenure of territory, and women are just as able to be the *Raja Laut* of the maritime world. This is reflected in Bego's and Sman's answers to my query below.

Cynthia: Can a woman be a *Raja Laut?*

Bego: Yes. The *Raja Laut* can either be a man or a woman.

Sman: The *Raja Hutan* (Raja of the Forest) can also be a woman.

It is just as interesting to note that, according to various written historical sources (the *Tuflat;* Matheson 1989) and the oral histories of my non-Orang Suku Laut Malay informants, a woman named Raja Hamidah, also known as Engku Puteri (Raja Ali Haji 1982: 32), became the wife of Sultan Mahmud in 1804. The island of Penyengat in Riau was her *mas kawin* (dowry). The Sultan gave instructions for "the island to be cleared, and a royal residence with fortifications, a mosque, and audience hall be constructed" (Matheson 1989: 159). My Malay informants maintain that it was thus Raja Hamidah who opened up the rest of Riau from Penyengat Island. Hence, the Malays deem it necessary for everyone to pay homage to Raja Hamidah's grave in order to win her permission to journey through the Archipelago. Although the Orang Suku Laut acknowledge the existence of Raja Hamidah, they maintain that even she would be subject to the sovereignty of their *Raja Laut.* The Orang Suku Laut explain why this is so in the conversation below.

Cynthia: You mean the Raja for the Orang Suku Laut is not from Penyenget?

Bego: Penyenget is *orang baru* (newcomers).

Cynthia: I ask this because I was told [by the Muslim-Malay Raja] that before I go anywhere in Riau, I should obtain the permission of Raja Hamidah who opened up Riau.

Sman: Raja Hamidah was a woman. Yes, you may have had to obtain permission from her. However, her *keturunan* (descent) is also *orang kami* (from our people). All *Rajas*…are descendants from us. Formerly, we all lived in the boat in the sea. We had no houses. If it had not been for us, the *orang asli,* how could there be islands etc. now? Now we say that we own all the islands. In our history, the *Raja Laut* had fifteen children and gave each of them rings and islands. That is how the islands came into being … People will say that the *kota besar* (capital city) is Jakarta—and the *Sultan besar* (big Sultan) is from the big city. However, for us, the *Raja Laut* and *Raja Hutan* are number one.

The issue of contention here for the Orang Suku Laut over the legitimacy of Raja Hamidah's claim of sovereignty over Riau is not her gender, but the fact that they consider her a descendant of the Orang Suku Laut.

The superimposition of borders on the Orang Suku Laut's tenure of territory happened many a time before. What is different today is the extent of changes—in particular on the lives of the Orang Suku Laut women—brought about by these new borders. The borders of the Growth Triangle, which function as instruments of the three respective states' policies to attract multinational investments into the region, have radically redefined the tenure of territory in Riau. Unlike the borders imposed previously, the Growth Triangle borders have led to the dismantling of entire communities and the wiping out of landscapes that once formed bases of livelihoods for the Orang Suku Laut and other local communities. Although resettlement and compensation fees have in some cases been paid to those who have been affected, these payments have been made only to men. This assumes that men are the heads of households and sole title-holders of the tenure of territory. No such recognition is awarded to women. Looking to the future, in cases where programs for the retraining of skills are offered, women are once again not included in the scheme of things.

Thus, from the perspective of the Orang Suku Laut, the Growth Triangle borders have functioned as a structure and symbol of differential in gender and status. In other words, these borders have become places of specific gender relations. This stands in stark contrast to the way in which the Orang Suku Laut have mapped out their maritime world. In the everyday lives and practices of the Orang Suku Laut, their maritime world comprises a complex network of collective and interrelated tenures of territories (Chou 1997) where men and women share equal rights and privileges.

The tenure of territory pivots on the stories that Orang Suku Laut men and women possess exclusively (Chou 1997). The inhabitants of Riau recognize these stories as the Orang Suku Laut's indigenous collective title deed, an oral tradition that reflects and confirms which Orang Suku Laut tribe was the first to discover the potential of an area or areas as moorage and settlement zones. These title deeds modify and organize the sea and coastal spaces into areas of custodianship for the Orang Suku Laut. Although they are thus recognized as the owners and custodians of these territories, everyone else continues to enjoy free access to sea and land space. Any outsider who wishes to enter such territories must first seek the permission of the head (*kepala*) of the Orang Suku Laut tribe that owns the area. As custodians of sea and coastal spaces, the Orang Suku Laut shoulder the responsibility of *jaga* (protecting and looking after), maintaining (*piara*), and reproducing the resources in their territories.

The Orang Suku Laut's network of interrelated territories adheres to an internal logic as follows. They practice a mobile economy and thus have various sites of production, which are socially identified. Their selection of production sites is based on two principles: first, which areas the different Orang Suku Laut *sukus* consider as theirs, and second, which areas can produce the best yields for the season. This parceling of resources is an important model that ensures sustainability, as some scholars have aptly argued (e.g., Djohani 1995: 122–23) that it prevents overexploitation of maritime resources via conservation.

The imposition of borders on the Orang Suku Laut's maritime world has come to mean that they can no longer traverse their domain and practice their mobile economy without impediment. They now need to cross borders in order to move around what they consider to be their home base. As borders become equipped with new technologies of surveillance, this means two things: first, they must subject themselves to the sovereignty of a recognized state in order to obtain the correct documents to legitimate their movement; and second, surveillance often requires them to carry out different forms of negotiations if they have a need or desire to make border crossings. Below is an example of how two Orang Suku Laut brothers, Boat and Den from Pulau Nanga, describe the impact of such borders and contesting sovereignties.

Boat: [Many of us] go into Singapore [to sell our sea cucumbers, crocodiles and turtles at the Pasir Panjang trading station]. However, if we meet the marine customs officers, we encounter difficulties...It is the marine customs officers from Balai [Indonesia] that we fear most. We are not afraid of the customs officers from Singapore.

Den: The officers from Balai keep a watch even at night and they will send us back to the customs officers at the jetty in Tanjung Pinang.

Boat: The officers from Balai are always asking for bribes.

Den: The customs officers from Singapore are not *jahat* (wicked). They will simply ask us if we are bringing in any drugs. If we do not have any drugs, they will not give us any trouble and let us in. They will only arrest us if we have drugs with us...[The customs officers from Balai] will ask us if we have any money. If we do not have any money, we will be arrested. They want money. If it is a big boat, they want 200 to 300 dollars.

Boat: We are talking about Singaporean currency. If it is a small boat, then they may ask for 10,000 rupiah.

Apart from the need to carry out negotiations such as described above, Den also showed me the documents that he had obtained to legitimize his mobility:

Den: I even have the cards for entry into Singapore here with me. [I had to pay] S$30 for these permit papers. [Even with these papers, the customs officers at Balai] will give trouble...if you do not give them any money, you will be arrested and taken to Balai or Blakan Padang.

The imbalance of opportunities across one or another border creates compelling reasons for the Orang Suku Laut to attempt crossing them. However, when their border crossing negotiations fail, they are immediately be categorized as illegal immigrants and arrested. Bribery has thus become a means to grease their mobility across borders. As noted by Donnan and Wilson (1999: 91), borders create "their own kinds of opportunities for informal commerce and illicit economic dealing."

Borders have divided the Orang Suku Laut's territory into zones wherein they may be, at best, permitted to remain for a stipulated time period or, at worst, prevented from entering at all. Thus, as explained by Den below, the period in which he is now allowed to remain in Singapore depends solely on what is in the paper documents issued to him by the state of Singapore.

> Den: I got these papers of permit a long time ago—a few years back. These papers are no longer valid. The permit allows us to be in Singapore for two days. If we arrive today, we will have to leave the next day.

The geopolitics of borders has significantly articulated a new horizontal and relational logic of economic, social, and cultural structures. Not only has their tenure of territory been redefined, but the Orang Suku Laut have also been relegated to the status of, at best, a minority group within the region, or at worst, outsiders or illegal intruders.

Gendering of Borders and Spaces

From the perspective of the Orang Suku Laut, the maritime world in that they inhabit is regarded as the life and living space for all—men, women, and children alike. All are seen to have shared these spaces, and to have had equitable access to all resources for their sustenance. In their work and other daily activities, there is no demarcation of male and female spaces.

The houseboat functions as a living space as well as a site of production and can be owned by men or women, or by both. The ideals and realities of the relationships between Orang Suku Laut men and women are clearly reflected in the spatial structure of their houseboats, where neither spatial barriers nor genderized spaces exist in either the home or the workplace. What we know as the "private sphere" or home and the "public sphere" or workplace merge into one single shared spatial context—the houseboat. Men and women have equal control of their houseboat; and as partners, they jointly engage in the family-oriented activity of fishing. The formation of man/woman partnerships to fish and the couple's productivity as a team are central to their identity as Orang Suku Laut.

The non-gendered and shared nature of the Orang Suku Laut spaces bears many implications, especially for the women. First, the equal right to mobility enables the women to have similar access to information and knowledge of the spaces. Second, equal access to spaces allows the women to apply their knowledge in effective ways. Third, shared spaces are intricately connected with equal advantage in the rights of ownership, inheritance, and claims. Fourth, as there is equal access to and control of income—generating activities, the women earn an equal income too.

This tradition of non-gendered spaces is now being challenged by the imposition of borders by external agendas. The Orang Suku Laut are presently caught in a web of institutionalized spatial and gendered segregation, and the impact has fallen particularly hard on women. Below are two examples that highlight this impact. The first describes the gendering of spaces within the zone that has since been demarcated by the borders to be the Province of Riau, Indonesia, and the second illustrates the problems that the Orang Suku Laut—and especially the women—are confronted with when they attempt to cross the border between Indonesia and Singapore.

The Indonesian state is aware that the Orang Suku Laut possess a different set of interpretations with respect to spatial arrangements, property ownership, and the division of labor, and wishes to prescribe a proper order for their lifestyle. In the name of "development" (*pembangunan*),[6] the state is working in partnership with the Muslim Malays of Riau to pressure the Orang Suku Laut into what is believed to be a more progressive (*maju*) lifestyle—which, as it is defined by the Malays, is to be achieved by observing Malay *adat* (code of proper conduct) guided by local interpretations of Islam. The observance of Malay *adat*, among other conditions, entails (1) building a place of worship in one's community, (2) observing regular daily prayers, (3) gendered ownership of property, and (4) gendered division of labor. These consequences bring extensive changes to the spatial alignments of Orang Suku Laut men and women. My informants explain that building a place of worship and observing the stipulated daily prayers would oblige them to be land-bound. Fishing, as they explained, involves irregular hours. It is therefore difficult for them to observe the rituals of prayer as well as carry enough fresh water for pre-prayer cleansing in their houseboats.

The Orang Suku Laut have also felt the impact of development and progress in other areas. Space, as defined by the Muslim Malays, must be genderized for progress to occur. The shared and non-gendered space of the Orang Suku Laut's maritime world and of their houseboats is regarded as "unprogressive" (*tidak maju*). Further, they must also genderize all aspects of their lifestyle: the boat and fishing gear thus fall within the domain of the men, whereas the land-based house and its maintenance are the woman's sphere. This inevitably means that all fishing activities are be carried out only by men, and it is no longer "proper" for women to be out at sea.

The impact of the genderization of space has added yet another dimension to borders between states. The maritime world of the Orang Suku Laut is no longer an open space for them to traverse, nor is it a production site accessible to both men and women. The reason is explained by Boat and Den, the Orang Suku Laut brothers from Pulau Nanga:

Den: I bring in sea cucumbers to [the Pasir Panjang Barter trading station in] Singapore. The customs officers of Singapore will stop us to ask what we bring in—sea cucumbers or marijuana. When we tell them we are bringing in sea cucumbers, they will contact our *thau-ke* in Pasir Panjang before they allow us to land. In Pasir Panjang, there are many Chinese and Indian *thau-ke.*

Boat: We bring in fish for the people of Singapore.

Den: I have cards for entry into Singapore here with me.

Cynthia: Do you have to pay for these documents?

Den: S$30…these papers of permit [to enter Singapore] were made in Singapore. Formerly, our children were allowed to accompany us into Pasir Panjang, Singapore. Now, they no longer allow our children in. Women are not allowed in…I don't know why. I got these documents a long time ago—a few years back. These papers are no longer valid. The permit allows us to be in Singapore for two days. If we arrive today, we will have to leave the next day.

Up to this day, the Singaporean port authorities will not grant Orang Suku Laut women and children the documents necessary to cross the border from Indonesia to Singapore. Iyang, Den's wife, explains the situation:

Iyang: From Blakan Padang…[we used to] enter Singapore. [Now] Den goes in on his own. I cannot enter Singapore with him so I wait in Blakan Padang for him…I have never been [to the Pasir Panjang Barter Trading Station], but I have heard Den talk about it.

Den: I row a small *sampan* (boat) into Singapore. If we were to start rowing from here, we can reach Singapore within two days. If we make our way to Singapore from Blakan Padang, it is even nearer. If we start off at ten o'clock in the morning, we can reach Singapore by 3 P.M. It takes only one day.

Iyang: We are used to rowing.

Cynthia: However, it requires three people to row the boat?

Den: Yes. If there are no strong winds, we can reach there in even faster time.

Many Orang Suku Laut bring their maritime products to the barter trading station in Singapore. A kilogram of *nabi* (a type of sea cucumber), as Den explained, would fetch S$45 in Singapore, whereas the same product would only fetch between 5,000 and 8,000 rupiah (approximately S$2 to S$4) in Indonesia. Important to note is the fact that the entire production process of harvesting the sea cucumbers (and other maritime products) is carried out by men and women together, until they reach the border between Indonesia and Singapore. At that point, their working partnership is forcibly halted by the border. Orang Suku Laut women are not allowed to cross the border to sell their products, but instead must rely on the men to negotiate the prices for their products and carry out the sale. This has substantially altered the working partnership of the Orang Suku

Laut couples as well as their incomes. In the past, the women had always participated in the marketing of their products; in fact, many Orang Suku Laut men feel that the women are better negotiators in the market and are thus able to bring in a higher income for their products. Now, as Iyang explains, the women have to wait at Blakan Padang while the men make the border crossing.

In short, the Orang Suku Laut are reclassified when they attempt to cross the border, and the women in particular are categorized as unacceptable candidates for the crossing. As noted by Donnan and Wilson (1999: 108), "all people who cross international borders must negotiate not only with the structures of state power that they encounter, ... but also with new frameworks of social status and organization with their concomitant cultural ideals and values." The border between Singapore and Indonesia has come to signify a zone of transition and gender distinctions for the Orang Suku Laut and marks the point where the women lose all access to and control over their resources.

Modification of Resources

An important aspect of the Orang Suku Laut's conception of the sea and coastal spaces is their ability to identify available and potential areas for fishing, trapping, charcoal making, worship, refuge, living, production, obtaining construction materials, hunting, gathering, and collecting. The Orang Suku Laut possess neither paper nor printed maps; instead, their abilities in resource identification are transmitted either orally or via the method of participant observation. The mental and orally transmitted maps of the Orang Suku Laut greatly reveal the discovered as well as the potential wealth of the region's resources. The historical significance of these indigenous maps of resource identification lies in the fact that they have maintained an entire socioeconomic system that has sustained the lives and living spaces of the Orang Suku Laut for centuries.

Just as significant is the fact that the Orang Suku Laut's identifications and usages of the region's resources have yet to be fully documented by anyone else. For example, the Orang Suku Laut possess vast knowledge of marine species, edible and medicinal plants, and detoxifying agents that currently have no market value. They also possess extensive knowledge of the multiple micro-environmental niches and in-depth understanding of tides, winds, currents, breeding grounds, danger zones, refuge areas, and fresh water points that are necessary for the sustenance of human and maritime life.

The one inescapable fact regarding borders is that they all secure territories, which are repositories of human and natural resources (Donnan and Wilson 1999: 15). As strategic signs of different orders of sovereignty and domain, borders also signal other orders of knowledge for the territories they have secured. The imposition of borders within the maritime world has therefore resulted in a redefinition of the resource and production spaces of the Orang Suku Laut. Local state powers, along with the multi- and transnational corporations that have penetrated the Orang Suku Laut's world, are executing agendas of standardizing population and resource maps for local and global developmental and economic programs. This has entailed, on the one hand, the codification of the individual and the com- munity, and on the other, the redefinition of spatial configurations through state-mandated forms of residence, social organization, property, and pro- duction. As aptly described by Scott (1998: 3), the aim is "to arrange its sub- jects/citizens in a manner that is increasingly legible, uniform, and hence more amenable to manipulation and control" in order to standardize mea- surement and calculation from above and achieve economic growth.

Each bounded zone within the region signifies a different order of sov- ereignty. Consequently different policies on resource identification and management are executed by the different nation-states. For example, with regard to identifying what constitutes human resources, the Orang Suku Laut do not come into consideration at all in Singapore. The Singaporean authorities are proud of having modernized and developed Singapore by either resettling communities such as the Orang Suku Laut into high-rise flats and recategorizing them as "Malays," or alternatively, by removing them from the Republic of Singapore (Mariam 2002). Within the borders of the territory defined as the Republic of Indonesia, the Indonesian govern- ment considers the Orang Suku Laut *suku-suku terasing* (isolated and alien peoples) or *suku suku terbelakang* (isolated and backward peoples), who form communities that the authorities define as "pre-villages" or "tradi- tional villages" (Colchester 1986: 89). The ultimate goal of the Indonesian government is to transform the mobile lifestyle of the Orang Suku Laut by resettling them in urban settings so that they can be integrated into the social, political, and economic mainstream of Indonesian life.

It is thus not surprising that the spatial economy of the Orang Suku Laut has consequently been extensively curtailed by borders symbolizing new orders of sovereignties within the region. Wholly new perspectives of what constitutes resources are being generated by these new sovereignties. From the viewpoint of the respective states, their aim of developing an integrated global commodity market means that their allocation of land and resources must now be determined by external international agendas designed to produce immediate and high revenues. That is to say, whatev- er is not able to yield immediate revenue is not viewed as a resource.

For example, the master plan of the Indonesian government and busi- ness entrepreneurs is to remap Riau and redefine its resources so as to pre- sent it as a global investment zone by outlining plans to develop Riau into a region for marine tourism, agribusiness, and industry (Singapore Busi- ness 1990). Within these three sectors, multinational corporations and local state institutions have been encouraged to build industrial parks. One consequence of this is that much of the region's landscape of diverse flora and fauna has been eradicated. In other words, a landscape held by Jakarta to be low-yielding, though much treasured by the Orang Suku Laut, is being re-created into production spaces for high-yielding investments.

Other resources, such as water, have also been transformed into high-yielding resources by bilateral investment projects of the states in the region. They are now locked by the state to serve what the state defines as higher state interests. For example, in view of her increasing water needs as a result of projected population growth and further industrialization, Singapore now needs alternative supplies of water apart from her traditional purchase of it from Johor, Malaysia. An agreement was therefore signed on 28 August 1990 between the Singaporean and Indonesian governments to embark on joint development of tourism, water supply, and industries in the Riau area. This agreement explicitly states, "Singapore and Indonesia will co-operate in the sourcing, supply and distribution of water to Singapore. The terms of co-operation will be set out on a separate agreement" (Straits Times 1990b: 1).

As far as is currently known, three freshwater reservoirs are to be created on the island of Bintan alone. One is specifically to serve the beach resorts on the north coast of Bintan (which has traditionally been an area inhabited by the Orang Suku Laut), another in the middle of Bintan island, and the third is a dam in Teluk Bintan (the Bay of Bintan) from which seawater is to be pumped, and into which several rivers are to pour their fresh water. The fresh water thus collected will far exceed the needs of the Orang Suku Laut and the other inhabitants of Bintan, who together form a total population of 90,000. Much of the water resource in Bintan will therefore now be channeled to meet the needs of other populations, most likely to Singapore (Straits Times 1990a). Thus, in a collusion of interests between the Singapore government, the Indonesian government, and private sector conglomerates, the local resources of the indigenous population have been greatly modified. Such modification inevitably challenges the basic fabric of the Orang Suku Laut's survival.

Conclusion

It is paradoxical that in the contemporary movement of reorganizing spatial relations to form more integrated and connected borderless worlds such as the Growth Triangle, such zones have, internally at least, become more divided and dislocated as a consequence. The development of borderless worlds does not inhibit but actually hastens the simultaneous development of ever more bordered worlds characterized by stark inequalities and divides. It seems that the concept or its practice deconstructs itself. Borderless worlds, in short, border worlds.

The maritime world of the Orang Suku Laut which has been encroached upon by the Growth Triangle, provides a case in point. First, since, as the very concept of the Growth Triangle is distinctively premised on clear border divisions between nation-states, the operation of the entire concept as agreed by the participating states rests primarily on knowing "precisely" what each member state's "respective position is" (Jakarta Post 2000: 1). Thus, second, the power to define the internal and external borders of such spaces, and the decisive power to define who will be allowed to participate in such zones still rests primarily with the decision of each participating nation state. Therefore, rather than effecting a "multinational" and "graduated" zone of sovereignty" (Ong 1999: 215) in the maritime world of the Orang Suku Laut, the Growth Triangle has, in fact, divided the maritime world of the Orang Suku Laut into different spatial polities. Each polity has come to represent a different sovereignty, knowledge, and political economy. In that order, each polity has also come to represent a different mode of resource allocation, production, and consumption. The shaping of these new spatial realities has, however, often ignored the essential features of another reality—the reality of a functioning social order that has sustained the lives and livelihoods such as that of the Orang Suku Laut, among others, for centuries.

The border is multidimensional in meaning. As Wilson and Donnan (1999: 15) elaborate, it is first the judicial border, which simultaneously separates and joins states. Second, it embodies those agents and institutions of a state that demarcate and sustain the border, and whose power and control spreads from the border into the territory of the state.

Third, as frontiers, which are territorial in nature, borders must be negotiated by people via a variety of behaviors and meanings associated with their membership in their nations and states (see also Wilson and Donnan 1998: 9). Fourth, as the interface between two systems of activity, organization, and meaning, it also forms an identity line characterized by ambiguity and danger, which marks off insiders from outsiders (see also Douglas 1970 and Wallman 1978: 206). All these issues draw attention to the relational nature of borders. On one level, they represent a symbolic zone of transition in policy shifts at the macro level; on another, they also represent the multiple repertoires of identities and realities at these significant sites of change as well as shifts in social relations at the interpersonal level, including the mental constructions of self and other.

Borderless world discourses are thus revealed to be the fantasies of the few who can dream of becoming homogeneous in a world where just "being" is a persistent struggle for so many. The contestations and conflicts in the life and living spaces of the Orang Suku Laut are one example of the impact generated by policies bolstering the interests of nation-states. The maritime world of the Orang Suku Laut constitutes a finite resource base. Competitions for its control has led to a progressive differentiation, that favors the strong and penalizes the vulnerable, and the Orang Suku Laut women and children in particular have been dealt a double blow in this situation.

Notes

1. The challenge posed by Baud and van Schendel (1997: 212) is the need to redress the imbalance of the state-centered studies, and to discover which social forces originate in borderlands and what effects they have both locally and beyond.
2. This figure was verbally communicated to me by the Kantor Sosial (Social Office) in Tanjung Pinang, Riau, 1993.
3. From the perspective of Indonesian officials, the lack of adherence to one of the five mainstream religions in Indonesia (Islam, Protestantism, Roman Catholicism, Hinduism, and Buddhism) implies that one is a communist.
4. Sassen (1995) presents the examples of supranational entities such as GATT (General Agreement on Tariffs and Trade) and NAFTA (North American Free Trade Association), which have formed a kind of "economic citizenship" that demands accountability from global firms and markets or planetary organizations such as the United Nations, but not from national governments.
5. Elsewhere (Chou 2003: 108–40), I have shown how the Orang Suku Laut understand that money is a symbol (Hart 1986) of the overarching political authority or state that is issuing it. In these terms, the Orang Suku Laut explain that a change in the currency used indicates a change in the central political body that is issuing it.
6. The official term for development in Indonesia is *pembangunan. Bangun,* "to develop or rise," with the affixes *pe-* and *-an* indicates a durative event or ongoing process. As noted by Hobart (1993: 7), this term also emphasizes "the need for guidance by those with power and knowledge, in this case the government officials who elaborated the notion in the first place."

References

Anderson, M. 1996. *Frontiers: Territory and State Formation in the Modern World.* Oxford: Polity.

Baud, M., and W. van Schendel. 1997. "Toward a Comparative History of Boderland." *Journal of World History,* 8, no. 2: 211–42.

Guide for Investors. 1991. Batam: Batam Industrial Development Authority.

Bienefeld, Manfred. 1994. "Capitalism and the Nation State in the Dog Days of the Twentieth Century." In Ralph Miliband and Leo Panitch, eds., *The Socialist Register–1994.* London: The Merlin Press.

Castells, Manuel. 1989. *The Informational City: Economic Restructuring and Urban Development.* Oxford: Blackwell.

———. 1993. "The Informational Economy and the New International Division of Labor." In M. Carnoy et al. eds. *The New Global Economy in the Information Age: Reflections on our Changing World,* University Park: Pennsylvania State University Press.

———. 1996. *The Rise of the Network Society.* Oxford: Blackwell.

Chen, Edward, and C. H. Kwan. 1997. *Asia's Borderless Economy: The Emergence of Sub-regional Zones.* St. Leonards, New South Wales: Allen & Unwin.

Chou, Cynthia. 1997. "Contesting the Tenure of Territoriality: The Orang Suku Laut." In Cynthia Chou and Wil Dirks, eds., *Riau in Transition, Bijdraden tot de Taal-, Land- en Volkenkunde* 153, no. 4: 605–29.

——. 2000. "The Orang Suku Laut of Riau, Indonesia: The Construction of Communities." Paper presented at the Maritime Worlds: Constructing Community in Coastal and Seafaring Societies Workshop at the University of Helsinki, 15–17 September 2000.

——. 2003. *Indonesian Sea Nomads: Money, Magic and Fear of the Orang Suku Laut.* London and New York: RoutledgeCurzon.

Colchester, Marcus. 1986. "Unity and Diversity: Indonesian Policy Towards Tribal Peoples." *The Ecologist* 16, no. 2/3: 89–98.

Djohani, Rili. 1995. "The Sea is My Home: The Bajau People of Bunaken Park." In Reimar Schefold, ed., *Minahasa, Past and Present: Tradition and Transition in an Outer Island of Indonesia.* Leiden: Research School Center for Non-Western Studies, Publication 28.

Donnan, Hastings, and Thomas M. Wilson, eds., 1999. *Borders: Frontiers of Identity, Nation and State.* New York: Berg.

Douglas, Mary. 1966. *Purity and Danger: An Analysis of Concepts of Pollution and Taboo.* Harmondsworth: Penguin.

Hart, Keith. 1986. "Heads or Tails? Two Sides of the Coin." *Man* 21, no. 4: 637–56.

Hobart, Mark. 1993. "Introduction: The Growth of Ignorance." In Mark Hobart, ed., *An Anthropological Critique of Development: The Growth of Ignorance.* London and New York: Routledge.

Jakarta Post. 2000. "ASEAN Troika to Cross Borders." *The Jakarta Post* 18, no. 89 (July 25): 1.

Kepulauan Riau Dalam Angka. 1987. Republic of Indonesia.

Kumar, Sree, and Lee Tsao Yuan. 1991. "A Singapore Perspective." In *Growth Triangle: The Johor-Singapore-Riau Experience,* ed. Lee Tsao Yuan. Singapore: Institute for Southeast Asian Studies.

Lee Tsao Yuan. 1997. "Growth Triangle in Singapore, Malaysia and ASEAN: Lessons for Subregional Cooperation." In *Asia's Borderless Economy: Emerging World Cities in Pacific Asia,* eds. Edward Chen and C. H. Kwan. Tokyo, New York, Paris: United Nations University Press.

Macleod, Scott, and T. G. McGee. 1996. "The Singapore-Johore-Riau Growth Triangle: An Emerging Extended Metropolitan Region." In *Emerging World Cities in Pacific Asia,* eds. Fu-chen Lo and Yue-man Yueng. Tokyo/New York/Paris: United Nations University Press.

Mariam Mohammed Ali. 2002. "Singapore's Orang Seletar, Orang Kallang, and Orang Selat: The Last Settlements." In Geoffrey Benjamin and Cynthia Chou, eds. *Tribal Communities in the Malay World: Historical,*

Cultural, and Social Perspectives. Leiden and Singapore: International Institute for Asian Studies and Institute of Southeast Asian Studies.

Matheson, Virginia. 1989. "Pulau Penyengat: Nineteenth Century Islamic Centre of Riau." *Archipel* no. 37: 153–72.

Ong, Aiwha 1999. *Flexible Citizenship: The Cultural Logics of Transnationality.* Durham, N.C.: Duke University Press.

Raja Ali Haji ibn Ahmad. 1982. *The Precious Gift (Tufat al-Nafis),* trans. Virginia Matheson and Barbara Watson Andaya. Kuala Lumpur: Oxford University Press.

Ross, J. K. 1975. "Social Borders: Definitions of Diversity." *Current Anthropology,* 16, no. 1: 53–72.

Sandbukt, Øyvind. 1982. *Duano Littoral Fishing-Adaptive Strategies within a Market Economy.* Ph.D. dissertation, Department of Social Anthropology, University of Cambridge.

Sassen, Saskia. 1995. *Losing Control? Sovereignty in an Age of Globalization.* New York: Columbia University Press.

Scott, James C. 1998. *Seeing Like a State: How Certain Schemes to Improve the Human Condition Have Failed.* New Haven: Yale University Press.

Schot, J. G. 1882. "De Battam Archipel." *De Indische Gids* 4, no. 2: 182.

Singapore Business. 1990. "Riau: An Investor's Guide to the 3,000 Island Province." *Singapore Business* 14 (December): 12.

Soh, Suzanne, and Chuang Peck Ming. 1990. "Investing in Riau: Promises and Perils." *Singapore Business,* December 14, no. 12: 31–53 [Special theme issue].

Sopher, David. 1977. *The Sea Nomads: A Study of the Maritime Boat People of Southeast Asia.* Singapore: National Museum Publication.

Straits Times. 1990a. "Singapore Team Finds Water Potential in Riau." *Straits Times* (April 10).

———. 1990b. "S'pore, Jakarta Seal Riau Deal: Accord to Develop Tourism, Water Supply and Industries." *Straits Times* (August 29), 1.

———. 2001. "New S'pore Consulate in Riau to Boost Economic Links." *Straits Times* (February 15), A1.

Thompson, J. T. 1851. "Description of the Eastern Coast of Johor and Pahang, and Adjacent Islands." *Journal of the Indian Archipelago and Eastern Asia,* 1: 341–51.

Wallman, S. 1978. "The Boundaries of 'Race': Processes of Ethnicity in England." *Man* 13, no. 2: 200–17.

Wee, Vivienne. 1985. *Melayu: Hierarchies of Being in Riau.* Ph.D. dissertation, Australian National University, Canberra.

——. 1988. "Material Dependence and Symbolic Independence: Constructions of *Melayu* Ethnicity in Island Riau." In *Ethnic Diversity and the Control of Natural Resources in Southeast Asia,* eds. A. Terry Ramboo, Kathleen Gillogly, and Karl L. Hutterer. Ann Arbor: Center for Southeast and Southeast Asian Studies, The University of Michigan.

Wee, Viviene, and Cynthia Chou. 1997. "Continuity and Discontinuity in the Multiple Realities of Riau." In Cynthia Chou and Wil Derks, eds., *Riau in Transition, Bijdragen tot de Taal-, Land- en Volkenkunde* 153, no. 4: 527–41.

Wilson, Thomas M., and Hastings Donnan. 1998. "Nation, State and Identity at International Borders." In Thomas M. Wilson and Hastings Donnan, eds., *Border Identities: Nation and State at International Frontiers,* Cambridge: Cambridge University Press.

Wolters, O. W. 1970. *The Fall of Srivijaya in Malay History.* London: Asia Major Library.

6

IN THE MARGIN OF A BORDERLAND:
THE FLORENESE COMMUNITY BETWEEN
NUNUKAN AND TAWAU

Riwanto Tirtosudarmo

Introduction

THIS IS AN ACCOUNT OF THE FLORENESE migrant community, a Catholic minority group, living in the Nunukan-Tawau area on the borderland of East Kalimantan, Indonesia and Sabah, Malaysia.[1] Nunukan is a small island located in the northeast of East Kalimantan province, whereas Tawau is a major port town in the southeastern part of Sabah. Although Nunukan and Tawau are separated by an international boundary, they constitute a transnational social space that integrates these two borderlands into a single social and economic complex. The everyday lives of peoples in this border area are linked through economic and transport networks, most evident in the boats and ships that ply the waters between Nunukan and Tawau on an almost hourly basis.

The Florenese originally moved to the area from East Flores in eastern Indonesia, partly intending to seek a better livelihood away from their agriculturally and resource poor place of origin, with its limited opportunity for social mobility. On their journey to Sabah, the island of Nunukan provided a shelter for the Florenese, and in time it became an important transit place before the border. Steadily growing in numbers since the early 1950s, the Florenese have been mostly attracted by opportunities to work as laborers for various plantations crops in Sabah, and as a result have established a "home away from home" in this borderland. (In Sabah, the Florenese are just one of several migrant groups from Indonesia.)

While many studies on the borderland communities primarily explain the marginal existence of the communities in relation to the center of the nation-states, the Florenese here cannot simply be seen as borderlanders

but are perhaps more properly characterized as a transnational community.[2] In addition, as a migrant community, the Florenese exhibit many levels of marginality. First, they constitute within a migrant community of a
national minority group, in terms of both ethnicity and religion. Second,
in terms of socioeconomic strata the Florenese rank low, being mostly
employed as plantation workers with relatively low wages. Third, as a
transnational minority group, they are generally denied citizenship, and
they are discriminated against by the host state and the dominant ethnic
groups. For the Florenese, the borderland therefore must be seen not just
as a transnational geographic space but also as transnational social and
political spaces that significantly locate them in the marginal situation.
This essay illuminates the nature of Florenese migration behavior and the
informal networks they have established which shape a remarkable and
contentious process of cross-border movement outside state control.

Florenese Migration: Broader Context and Origin

Writting just before Indonesia entered an almost unimaginable economic
and then political crisis, Hugo (1997: 100) argued that "in the second half
of the 1990s Indonesians will become even more mobile, their internal
and international movements will become more complex in their spatial
patterning and a wider spectrum of the population will become
involved." The monetary crisis that started around mid 1997 had strong
repercussions throughout the whole of Southeast Asia, and especially in
Indonesia. With around two thirds of the Southeast Asian population,
Indonesia has been the most critically affected country, both economically and politically. The crisis, particularly on its economic side, produced
mixed results with regard to population mobility in Indonesia. Cross-border movements have increased, and such movement is perceived as a
means to alternative sources of income. In addition, the patterns and volume of international mobility have been significantly affected. The dominant destinations have long been the Middle East and Malaysia. Middle
Eastern countries, unaffected by the crisis, understandably remained
more important destinations, whereas Malaysia responded by tightening
its border. This has resulted in an increasing incidence of illegal or undocumented labor migration.

From a broad regional perspective, the early 1980s showed a shift in
labor migration in Southeast Asia: the movement of migrant workers
across nation-state's borders added to the continuing in-country migration. Within Insular Southeast Asia, Malaysia in particular attracted laborers from neighboring countries as the demand for laborers began to
exceed the country's own labor supply. History apparently repeats itself,
as indentured labors were again recruited from Indonesia and South Asia,
especially Bangladesh. The labor migration from Indonesia to Malaysia is

particularly interesting because the flow of labor has increasingly overwhelmed the capacity of both sending and receiving states to control cross-border movement. Since the onset of the economic crisis, the consequences of massive, uncontrolled labor flows from Indonesia to Malaysia, resulting in a large influx of illegal and undocumented workers, have worried both Indonesian and Malaysian authorities. In Malaysia, a massive deportation, occurred from July through September 2002 based on a new immigration law forced thousands of undocumented Indonesian and Filipino migrant workers to return to their countries. In the case of the deportation of Indonesian migrants from Sabah, Nunukan has become the main shelter.[3]

More than two decades ago, the Australian human geographer Dean Forbes (1981), published an important critique of migration studies in Indonesia, clustering the existing studies into three groups: first, studies on circulation in Indonesia, notably that of Hugo based on Jakarta and West Java; second, studies on "traditional" forces and their role in mobility (mainly in West Sumatra); and third, migration studies using structural approaches to understand "uneven development" and mobility, particularly the work of Titus and Forbes himself on South Sulawesi. In the conclusion of his critique, Forbes offered his view on the relationship between migration and development. He argued that if our concern is with long-term solutions to the problems that give rise to circulation—the pitfalls of uneven development—and to which circulation also contributes, then we must turn our attention to regional development policy in Indonesia. Quoting Titus (1978: 202), he noted that New Order policies have failed to deal adequately with regional inequality, and instead have reinforced historical inequalities (Forbes 1981: 60): "The present development indicators as well as the persisting pattern of inter-regional migration point to a continued process of increasing inequality which is tied to the New Order development concept.... Only a more egalitarian and decentralized policy which benefits both peripheral regions and marginal social groups will be able to end these dilemmas."

In May 1998, twenty years after Titus wrote his analysis, Suharto's three-decade-old New Order regime collapsed after failing to revive the country's economic fortunes. Following this, one of its main features of the new rapidly developed political landscape was the devolution and decentralization of power and authority to the regional-level governments. In January 2001 a new regional autonomy law was formally implemented, full of promises to become (in Titus' words) a "more egalitarian and decentralized policy" benefiting both peripheral regions and marginal groups. In fact, inequality cannot be isolated within Indonesia's borders, and the movement of Florenese laborers to Sabah since the 1950s indicates that economic inequality has strong roots at the regional level.

The Florenese who migrated to Sabah are known there as *Orang Timor* ("people from the east" in Malay) or Timorese, in English.[4] These people originally came from various places in the district (*kabupaten*) of East Flores, in the East Nusatenggara Province (NTT) of eastern Indonesia. The district capital of East Flores is Larantuka, an old port town, home of the Catholic bishop and the center of social and economic activities in East Flores and the surrounding islands. As a port town, Larantuka constitutes an insular transportation hub that connects its surrounding islands, such as Adonara, Solor, and Lembata. This complex of islands is a major source of Florenese labor migrants to Sabah. Before the government introduced the K.M. Awu, a national shipping (PELNI) vessel that takes Florenese directly to Nunukan,[5] the final port before the port of Tawau in Sabah, smaller private ships enabled the Florenese to go to Malaysia. In the early 1950s, the Florenese needed at least a month to travel to Nunukan, as they had to change vessels and stay in several ports, such as Maumere (Flores), Surabaya (East Java), Makassar, Pare-Pare (both in South Sulawesi), and Tarakan (East Kalimantan). Today the Florenese need only four days to reach Nunukan on the K.M. Awu, which plies the seas between Maumere and Nunukan every two weeks.

In East Flores District, population increase since 1961 has been variable. Although population pressure has been felt as the number of people per square kilometer continues to increase (Table 6.1.), the rate of population growth since 1961 has been generally declining (Table 6.2.) and shows a drastic drop between 1971–80 and 1980–90, even experiencing negative growth in the period 1990–2000. The latter negative growth is most likely due to the separation of Lembata, which became a new district in 2000.

Table 1. Population Size, Density and Sex Ratio, 1961–2000

Year	Total	Density per km^2	Sex ratio
1961	194,203	63.1	88.3
1971	229,789	74.6	87.3[b]
1980	257,689	83.7	79.8
1990	265,759[a]	86.3	77.7
2000	197,241	108.8	88.9

[a]Population of Lembata = 84,875 persons (32 percent of the East Flores population).
[b]Kantor Statistik Propinsi NTT (1991).

Table 2. Population Growth, 1961–2000

Year	Percent Growth
1961–1971	1.71
1971–1980	1.27
1980–1990	0.31
1990–2000	-2.94

The generally low population growth in East Flores resulted mainly from low levels of fertility and high rates of out-migration. Another demographic characteristic of the region is the unbalanced sex ratio, which reflects high out-migration rates for the male population (BPS 1981, 2001).

The geographic orientation of the Florenese who migrated to Sabah through Nunukan seems to have been strongly influenced by their daily experiences in their place of origin. Interestingly, the geographic image of the Nunukan-Tawau area, for the Florenese, resembles their geographic experiences at home—islands surrounding the port of Larantuka. Frequent sea transportation between Larantuka and the other small towns, such as Weiwerang in Adonara and Lewoleba in Lembata, have strengthened their association with Nunukan and Tawau. Psychologically, perhaps, this could also explain the relatively ease of adjustment for Florenese in the Nunukan-Tawau area.

The people of East Flores, often known in Flores as Larantuka people, are considered apart from the other peoples in the rest of Flores as they are influenced by the migrants from various cultural backgrounds who have resided in Larantuka. Ethnically, however, people in East Flores belong to the more generic Lamaholot ethnic group, who all speak Lamaholot. Geographically, Lamaholot is used by people on the eastern part of the island of Flores, as well as on Adonara, Solor, and Lembata. This region is therefore known as the Lamaholot region. The only distinctive group within this region considered to have a different language are the Kedang, who live on the northern part of Lembata.[6]

According to Barnes (1974), the Lamaholot region comprises an area that is linguistically and culturally distinct from the Sikka region. In general terms, one can speak of a coherent Lamaholot culture. At the same time, though, the notion of coherence has to be qualified. The Lamaholot language is spoken on the East Flores mainland and on Solor, Adonara, and Lembata, along with Kedang, which is linguistically independent although culturally related. There are three distinct Lamaholot dialects, with further linguistic subgroups. Although people can understand each other throughout the region, words and intonation vary greatly, often from village to village. This diversity is also reflected in the interpretations of similar customs, beliefs, and manifestations of material culture (Barnes 1994).

Based on the result of its 2000 Population Census, the Indonesian Central Bureau of Statistics classified the population of East Flores into several ethnic groups. The largest group (156,257 persons or 79.2 percent) is represented by the Lamaholot, Lamah, and Lamaloko. The second group (22,066 persons or 11.2 percent) comprises the Solor and Solot ethnic communities. The Larantuka people account for 7,526 persons (3.8 percent), and the rest belong to minority groups such as the Sikka, Ende, Bajau, Javanese, and generic "Florenese."[7] According to the 2000 Population Census, the majority of people in East Flores (79.3 percent) are Catholic. Approximately 20 percent of the East Flores population is Muslim. The Muslim population resides mainly in the coastal areas of East Adonara District on Adonara Island. Protestants represent another minority in East Flores.

Although Christianity and Islam have been adopted by people for hundreds of years, Lamaholot local beliefs are apparently still alive and widely practiced by the people. The people of East Flores worship their ancestors through a practice known as *Lerawulan*. The customary rituals and festivities are in many cases related to daily activities of agriculture and the life cycle. The *sambut baru* ceremonies, for example, are often lavish affairs conducted locally as religious rituals in which a child is baptized or receives the first sacrament. The rituals and festivities are well entrenched despite past government attempts to abolish them. The success of the Florenese migration is often reflected in the grand scale of their rituals and ceremonies back home.

A particular local tradition that strongly affects the lives of the Florenese is related to the marriage arrangement and ceremony. According to customary law, the bridegroom is obliged to provide an elephant tusk, and the bride must reciprocate with a traditional woven cotton cloth. Although this practice is merely symbolic, it has created a heavy burden for young Florenese who wish to marry. A study by Graham (n.d.) in the 1980s shows that these difficulties, as perceived by young Florenese, have strongly influenced their propensity to migrate—first to avoid the burden of tradition, and second to arrange marriages outside their home villages, where customary marriage laws can be ignored.[8]

The continuing existence of traditional beliefs is also strongly related to the social system and structure of the Florenese communities, which are dominated by several major clans such as the *Koten, Kelen, Hurit,* and *Marang* (believed to be the legitimate authority of the Lamaholot people). These clans control the land ownership as well as Florenese leadership positions. The heavily hierarchical social structure of the Florenese also results in the people at the lower end of the social strata perceiving outmigration as the only alternative to improve their socioeconomic status.

The dry climate and the poor natural resources in most parts of East Flores have a significant bearing on the economic life of the Florenese. Their main agricultural activity is dryland farming, such crops as corn, rice, and cassava. Their farmland often consists of very small plots brought under traditional farming techniques and yielding little more than subsistence. According to the 2000 population census, 73 percent of the population engages in agriculture, slightly less than in 1990 (77 percent). Nonagricultural activity has therefore risen slightly from 5 to 7 percent within the last 10 years, while the service sector has also increased from 9 to 10 percent.

In 2000, the level of education in East Flores was still very low, with approximately half of the population either possessing no schooling or not having graduated from elementary school; only around 35 percent of the population has graduated from elementary school. The paucity of natural resources and economic opportunities, in addition to limited access to land, has always been a strong factor pushing the population to migrate in search of better lives.

Nunukan, Tawau, and the Catholic Missionaries[9]

Nunukan and Tawau face each other and represent two neighboring countries, Indonesia and Malaysia, respectively. The two localities are separated only by water, an international boundary, and a ninety-minute speedboat or three-hour passenger boat trip. Only recently Nunukan was a mere subdistrict within-Bulungan district, but it is now a small port town developing into the capital city of a newly created district—a result of post–Suharto decentralization policy. Nunukan, as an administrative and bureaucratic space in itself, has therefore emerged as a new force on the political scene of the East Kalimantan-Sabah borderland.[10]

In the context of economic development in the border zone between East Kalimantan and Sabah, Nunukan's role is crucial due to the recent, intensified social and economic interface with Tawau. The strong dynamic between Nunukan and Tawau is a reflection of the high levels of trade between not only the two localities, but also the much more extensive areas of the East Kalimantan, Sulawesi, Java, and Nusatenggara provinces directed toward the demographically smaller Sabah on the other side of the border. Underlying the seemingly purely economic development are strong social and cultural ties that link the peoples of the two localities. The migrant communities in these two areas, such as the Bugis and the Florenese, represent transnational communities that interconnect not only through economic activities but, more importantly, through social and cultural networks.

In 1999 (the first year of the so-called *reformasi* or reformation period), the former Bulungan District of East Kalimantan was divided into two new districts: Nunukan and Malinau. These new districts are located in the border zone with Sabah: its border with Malinau is entirely on land, while that with Nunukan is on both land and sea. The inland border in fact, is not only with Sabah but also (more remotely) with Sarawak, though almost 70 percent of its length defines the borderlands with Sabah. The population of Nunukan District in 2000 was 82,754. Nunukan has five subdistricts: Nunukan, Sebatik, Krayan, Sembakung, and Lumbis, of which the first three lie in the borderland.

Krayan, with a population of 9,349, is the third-largest subdistrict and is mostly inhabited by Londaye Dayak and relatively small numbers of migrants. Economic interaction is directly conducted across the land border, particularly at Ba Kakalan, with both Sarawak and Sabah. Traditional trading relationships probably existed between the partitioned Londaye Dayak, from both Indonesia and Malaysia. More recently, the Indonesian government has provided PLBs (*pas lintas batas* or border crossing passes) for those residents.[11] Unfortunately, there is not yet any developed transportation infrastructure in the area: So people have to walk around four hours, or drive one and a half hours by motorcycle (except in the rainy season) from Ba Kakalan in Krayan to Limbang in Sarawak. There is also an eight-passenger DAS air flight that services a route from Tarakan or Nunukan to Long Bawan in Krayan.

Sebatik is the second-largest subdistrict with a population of 22,034. Located on an island that is shared with Sabah (with the Malaysian side under the Tawau administration), it boasts three important villages—Bambangan in the west, and Sungai Pancang and Sungai Nyamuk in the east. As in other subdistricts in the border area, the government provides PLBs for residents. Nunukan, which comprises Nunukan Island and a portion of the mainland, is the largest subdistrict, with a population of 36,065. scattered in five villages—on the eastern coast of Kalimantan. Four villages on Nunukan Island—West Nunukan, East Nunukan, North Nunukan, and Sebuku—are inhabited by 27,874 people, and the rest reside in around twenty scattered hamlets in Sebuku, including two UPTs (*unit pemukiman transmigrasi* or transmigration settlement units), Sanur and Makmur, with 3,691 inhabitants (Population Profile 2000). Just as the population of Krayan (the Dayak Londaye) maintains a traditional relation with their kin in Limbang, Sarawak, the inhabitants of Sebatik and Nunukan have a similar relationship with the inhabitants of Tawau, Sabah. However, the relationship of the Bugis in Nunukan and Sebatik and the Bugis in Tawau is relatively recent compared to that of the Dayak Londaye. The government provision of PLBs has been a particularly effective means of strengthening these ties.

The most important agent sustaining the Florenese border community is the Catholic Church. The churches in Tawau (*Gereja Katolik Holy Trinity*) and in Nunukan (*Paroki Santo Gabriel*) are actively involved in helping resolve various problems facing the migrant communities. The first Catholic mission in Sabah was opened in early 1883 in Sandakan, but it lasted for only two years. Later in 1914, missionaries first visited Tawau and found some Catholic adherents living there. Further development of coal mining around Tawau attracted more Catholic attention, particularly among the many Chinese and Filipinos who worked in the mining industry. Facing demand from its growing Catholic population, Fr. A. Stotter, a former rector of St. Mary's Sandakan mission and founder of the Tawau mission, started paying more attention to conducting a ministry at Tawau and its outstations, such as Kudat and Marudu Bay. One report noted that after his first two years of work between 1920 and 1922, the fruits of Fr. Sotter's initial pastoral care were spectacular, even though he still resided in Sandakan but often visited Tawau by boat during this period. The process of obtaining land, collecting funds, and increasing contact with people led to quite successful development of the Catholic mission in Tawau.

The mission faced various problems as well as opportunities to keep its mission sustainable. Immediately prior to the coming of the Japanese during World War II, the British had destroyed bridges and other facilities, then during the Japanese Occupation, mission property was destroyed, the mission bank accounts frozen, and missionaries detained. Nonetheless Mass and Church activities continued to be performed. After the end of the war in August 1945, Fr. Mulders, rector of Tawau, was released from internment and launched the rebuilding of the mission.

The paramount mission of the Catholic Church actually is to minister not only to people within the Church but also throughout the wider community. Another important effort is to confront the problems of such people as refugees, illegal residents, and the disabled. One group among other "lost sheep" comprises those, classified as illegal workers or undocumented residents, who originally came from Indonesia (mostly Flores) and the Philippines. For the local church, it is like standing at a crossroads, facing two paths simultaneously—defending those who are under threat of being expelled from their homes, and striving to comply with the state law that does not permit illegal residents to stay in the country. Standing firmly to provide humanitarian assistance and support its members' right to live, the Church has, for instance, approached several institutions responsible for foreign migrants, to resolve the uncertainty of illegal migrants' status while respecting the existing law implemented in the country.

The first pioneering migrants from Flores arrived in Tawau during the early 1950s after a journey that took several weeks or a month. Before arriving in Sabah, they had to evade the coastal security forces guarding the coast. Having successfully entered Sabah, those Florenese waited to be hired by rubber plantation owners, who were mostly British. Working throughout the week on the plantations, the migrant workers would visit Tawau parish regularly on Sundays.

In later developments, particularly in the 1970s, more migrants from Flores (Adonara, East Flores) came for reunions with family members living in Tawau and places surrounding it. Many were accepted for work in the domestic and construction sectors as well as on plantations, particularly oil palm. Simultaneously with these developments, problems arose, and the latest recent round of expulsions has pushed the Church to pay more attention to undocumented migrants. To prove its commitment to its members, the Holy Trinity Church established a ministry called Kesatuan Kebajikan Katolik Indonesia (KKKI or the Indonesian Catholic Association for Goodness) of Tawau in 1992. The initial idea to establish this fellowship came from Mgr. Antonius Pain Ratu, who was visiting Tawau at the time. His chief motive was to "bring all Catholic people closer together, which would enable them to help one another." Thus, members of the ministry would consist of people from different Indonesian ethnic backgrounds, the majority being the Florenese.

This ministry has had two major purposes, spiritual and nonspiritual. In spiritual or pastoral care, members of the community receive attention while they are experiencing problems or sickness, either at home or in the hospital. This arm of the ministry also raises funds to help families with funeral expenses. In the nonspiritual sector, the ministry has the responsibility for collecting money and clothing, as well as preparing accommodation and other necessities for the needy.

Under Church leadership, a Florenese community organization (KKI or Keluarga Katolik Indonesia, the Indonesian Catholic Association, formerly Keluarga Kebajikan Katolik Indonesia) was formed in Tawau whose leaders work closely with the priests to provide social and religious services to the Florenese community. The leaders of this organization also act as a medium of communication between the Tawau and Nunukan churches. The social services provided by the Church are primarily centered on the needs of the Florenese as a religious community, for example, such events as marriages and christenings. In reality this also includes helping migrants find relief from their economic difficulties and social hardships. The Catholic Church in Tawau plays an important role in mediating between Florenese migrants and state officials in cases related to the improper documentation and immigration status of migrants and their families. The Church in Nunukan sheltered hundreds of Florenese families deported by the Malaysian government during August and September 2002.[12] In a situation in which both states are generally ignorant of, and in many instances exploitative and discriminative toward, Florenese migrants, the Church is a pivotal protector of this marginal community.[13]

In both Nunukan and Tawau, Florenese community members maintain relations with their kin in East Flores through social and familial networks. Their cultural commitment as Florenese has influenced their strong traditional belief system as well as their adherence to the Catholic religion. This social and cultural background, in addition to their place in the labor market, has significantly distinguished Florenese identity in relation to other ethnic groups and states. For the Florenese, in both Nunukan and Tawau, the Catholic Church has played an important role in shaping identity and easing the hardships of their migrations. As for the Church, the presence of the Florenese provides it with a *raison d'être* for its presence in the borderlands.

The Making of a Marginal, Transnational Community

The development of the Florenese community in Sabah paralleled the establishment of Sabah in the 1950s as a frontier area for various extractive activities and plantation estates. Although few Florenese migrated before the 1950s, the rate of Florenese migration increased as of the early 1950s, reaching its peak in the 1980s. It appears to have dropped during Confrontation in the early 1960s but escalated thereafter.

Florenese migration to Sabah is a typical chain migration, operating through familial and kinship networks. It is therefore a form of labor mobility outside of formal recruitment processes.[14] In the context of migration studies in Indonesia, Florenese migration constitutes a new type of migration that combines traditional/ethnic migration and the international movement of labor. From a different perspective, Florenese migration also can be classified as labor migration beyond state control. In this context, Forbes' (1981) classification of population mobility based on studies conducted in Indonesia during the 1970s and 1980s overlooks the phenomen of international migration, which has in fact been steadily increasing since the 1970s, particularly to Malaysia.[15]

Geographically, Sabah has become the hub of the BIMP-EAGA (Brunei Indonesia Malaysia Philippine—East Asian Growth Association) system, which consists of Brunei, northern provinces of Indonesia and, East Malaysia (namely Sarawak and Sabah), and the southeastern Philippine provinces.[16] The sultanate of Brunei is the only nation member of the configuration, the rest being subregions of the other member countries. Irregular migration is a noteworthy feature of this system.[17] Brunei recognizes that migrant workers are and will be an essential component of its labor force, and has adopted pragmatic migration policies to suit its needs. For example, Brunei has significantly influenced irregular migration in the region by providing an exit point for "social visit" pass holders in Sabah and Sarawak. (To avoid overstaying their visas, "social visit" pass holders exit to Brunei before or at the time of their visas' expiration, and return to Sabah and Sarawak with a new "chop.") In this context, irregular migration to Sabah (and perhaps to Malaysia as a whole) is illustrative of the tensions between economic and political concerns. On the one hand, the state of Sabah is very much dependent on migrant labor, and its plantation, construction, and service sectors rely heavily on irregular migrant workers. On the other hand, concerns over ethnic balance and fears that migrants are affecting the future of the state have contributed to the formation of negative views toward migrants.

In the Nunukan-Tawau area, the Bugis from South Sulawesi represent the largest migrant group. In Nunukan, besides Bugis and Florenese, one finds Javanese, Torajans (also from South Sulawesi), and Tidungs who are held to be the indigenous population. In Tawau, apart from the Bugis, are Malays (who dominate politics), Chinese (who dominate the economic sector), and other minority groups, including the indigenous "Kadazan-Dusun" and migrant groups such as the Bajaus and the Tausugs originally from the southern Philippines. Ethnic identity and categorization in Sabah, as in Malaysia as a whole, is highly contested and constructed according to the interest of the ruling elites and changing political contexts. Sabah in particular provides an example of a very dynamic system of ethnic politics, where political alliances are constantly reconfigured (through ethnic inclusion or exclusion) following changes in the ethnic categorizations in the population census. The Kadazan-Dusun category, for example, is a bureaucratic construction that makes little sense ethnographically. Meanwhile, the Bajau may be migrants to the Tawau area, but they are not migrants to eastern Sabah as the Jolo-Sabah corridor is well documented as their place of origin, going back at least 200 years.[18]

The Florenese migrated from East Flores and entered Sabah to take on various unskilled jobs, mostly on plantations. While some succeeded in settling in Sabah, many who failed decided to stay and work in Nunukan. The Florenese community, in both Tawau (as well as in other places in Sabah) and Nunukan, maintained their ethnic identity—their mother tongue, Catholic religion, and links to their homeland in East Flores. The Florenese are a borderland community, with elements of a transnational community. As such, they represent a new dimension to the existing knowledge of borderland communities in Southeast Asia, which is dominated by studies on purely indigenous communities.[19] Borderland communities are generally perceived as prone to tensions within their own nation-states, but the Florenese are at the same time exposed to local, national, and international quandaries. In this regard, the conventional approach to borderland communities should be adjusted for the study of such communities as the Florenese in Nunukan-Tawau. Research on transnational communities, as argued by Portes et al. (1999: 218), is in its infancy and still highly fragmented, lacking both a well-defined theoretical framework and analytical rigor. Existing studies often use disparate units of analysis (i.e., individuals, groups, organizations, and local states) and mix diverse levels of abstraction.

In her study of Dominicans in Boston, Levitt (1999) describes the transnational community as "[a] group that is formed by migrants and non-migrants who are strongly connected to a particular place. Transnational communities arise from the strong, interpersonal networks through which migration begins. As these networks strengthen and spread, they develop into larger communities of individuals who are more loosely tied to one another." The Florenese community in Nunukan-Tawau may be seen as the embryonic phase of such a transnational community.

The literature on transnational communities is strongly dominated by studies in the U.S., mostly dealing with Mexican communities, and the subject matter has often not been clearly demarcated between borderlands and transnational communities. Studies of transnational communities generally point to the impact of globalization and contextualize transnational communities within various contending transnational actors and agencies (see Portes et al. 1999, Wadley 2002). In this sense, transnational Florenese communities can be seen as a manifestation of globalization in the peripheral areas of Southeast Asia. Whatever the perspective adopted, the Florenese community in Nunukan-Tawau is clearly a transnational ethnic minority group that has been discriminated against, both economically and politically. The discrimination experienced by the Florenese is partly rooted in their social place in the labor market hierarchy and their identification as Catholics in predominantly Muslim societies.

Now numbering in the thousands, the Florenese are scattered throughout Sabah, but most reside in enclaves surrounding oil palm, cocoa, and tobacco plantation estates. Their main function as unskilled migrant workers (a modern euphemism for "coolies") who mostly engage in plantation work have made this community rather distinct and easy to identify. The physical appearance of Florenese is also distinct in that their skin tends to be darker and their hair curlier than the Malay or indigenous "Sabahan" peoples. Their devout Catholicism marks them as a distinct religious community, just as Islam is becoming the dominant religion in Malaysia.

The Florenese who migrated to Sabah in the early 1950s eventually created a sustained sense of community based on familial and relational networks. Several informants from the first generation of migrants—now in their late sixties—apparently succeeded in their professional careers and now enjoy their roles as the informal leaders of the Florenese community. These respected elders reside in both Tawau and Nunukan, with close communication being maintained across the border. Two of the most prominent community leaders are Tuan Azam in Tawau and Om Franky in Nunukan.[20] Both Tuan Azam and Om Franky came to Sabah in their teens in the late 1950s, attracted by success stories of other Florenese who had returned from Sabah. The story of their attempt to enter Sabah generally constitutes the typical migrant narrative, though it differs in some respects. The main relevant differences between Tuan Azam and Om Franky are their final destinations and nationalities. Tuan Azam, who converted to Islam, decided to become a Malaysian citizen and stay in Tawau; Om Franky, who joined the Indonesian militia during Confrontation, remained an Indonesian citizen and lives in Nunukan. These two informal leaders have maintained their friendship and function as "godfathers" to the Florenese community in Nunukan-Tawau.

The role both Tuan Azam and Om Franky play in nurturing the Florenese migrant community is an outgrowth of their shared sense of belonging and strong connection to their origins—East Flores. As leaders of a transnational community, these two geographically and nationally separated men have apparently transcended their formal national citizenships. In this regard, their business involvement in transporting and recruiting Florenese labor from East Flores for work in Sabah may also explain the strength of their involvement in guarding the Florenese migrant community. Tuan Azam, who retired as a police colonel, has now opened a passport service that essentially operates as a labor recruitment or employment agency. His extensive connections with Malaysian authorities, particularly immigration officials, in Tawau as well as Kota Kinabalu, combined with his vast knowledge of and access to the plantation business network in Sabah, facilitates "good business" with migrant workers.

While Tuan Azam is actively involved in providing services for labor recruiters and suppliers in Sabah, Om Franky, having retired from a leading post in the Indonesian militia, joined the shipping company that operates twice a year between Nunukan and East Flores. His experience in the militia is instrumental in controlling Florenese port laborers in Nunukan when they become restless. Owing to their physical presence and perceived authority derived from their previous experiences and careers, Tuan Azam and Om Franky are able to exercise a critical function as patrons for the Florenese transnational community.

The perception people in other ethnic groups have of Florenese migrants as *Orang Timor,* strongly identifying them as people with particular physical and sociocultural characteristics, has strengthened Florenese self-perception and ethnic identity. Furthermore, the employment of the Florenese majority as plantation laborers has strengthened their social and economic status identification in Sabah as the "low working class" within the strongly ethnicized social and economic hierarchy of Sabah society. The Catholicism of most Florenese has meanwhile established them in a particular sociopolitical niche as a minority group within a society where Islam is increasingly the politically dominant majority. Muslim migrant groups, particularly the Bugis from South Sulawesi, are easily accommodated within the Malay-Muslim political alliances that represent the dominant group in Sabah. The same cannot be said of the Florenese.

Notes

1. The author thanks Koji Miyazaki, Director of Research Institute for Language and Culture of Asia and Africa (ILCAA), Tokyo University of Foreign Studies and Coordinator of Sabah Research Project, for allowing the author to be part of his organized study. Fieldwork was conducted in East Flores by the author and Bayu Setiawan in February 2002 and in Sabah with John Haba in July 2002 and June 2003. The author thanks both of these researchers for their assistance and companionship. The preliminary findings, entitled "The Florenese Migration to Sabah, East Malaysia: Socio-Demographic Background and Socio-Cultural Adaptation" by Riwanto Tirtosudarmo and John Haba, were presented at the workshop Culture and Development in and Around Sabah at the ILCAA, 23–24 January 2003. The author also thanks Reed L. Wadley and Michèle Ford for their useful and insightful suggestions for the revision of earlier versions of this paper, which was presented at the Third International Convention of Asian Studies (ICAS3) in Singapore, 18–22 August 2003.
2. On the contentious relations of borderland communities and states in the Southeast Asian context, see the review article by Horstmann (2002).
3. For discussion of cross-border Indonesian migrant workers and the "Nunukan Tragedy," see Tirtosudarmo (2004).
4. See Hugo (2002) for a map of migration routes from Flores.
5. See www.pelni.com/pelni_awu_schedule.htm.
6. According to Barnes (1980), the Kedang are characterized not only by their different language but also by their physical environment and administrative boundaries.
7. This shows that, using the Indonesian Central Bureau of Statistics ethnic classification, several different names are used for identifying Florenese ethnic groups.

8. Graham (n.d.) notes that "institutional interests at different levels of church and state also generate divergent views and conflicting policies based on what officials in particular hierarchical settings perceive as the hidden dangers of and/or the benefits that accrue to such transnational labour migration. Whatever the policies formulated at the national level in Indonesia, the two most prominent institutional discourses that are promulgated locally place themselves for quite complex reasons firmly against the patterns of labour migration established early on." Graham argues that a longstanding anxiety over competing codes of sexual morality underlies the Catholic Church's expressed concern about the adverse effects of labor migration on Christian family life in Flores. Graham suspects that a range of political issues concerning the desire for order and control inform the discourse of Indonesian officials of the East Flores regency about unregulated labor migration undermining local attempts at economic development.

9. Catholic activities reported here are largely based on John Haba's draft paper entitled "Catholic Church and Incoming Migrants: A Preliminary Investigation."

10. Nunukan as a new district—granted autonomous administrative power under the new regional autonomy law—could also become a new economic and political force in the context of the BIMP-EAGA framework. For more detailed information on Nunukan, see Tirtosudarmo and Haba, (2005).

11. Indonesian citizens officially residing in the districts located at the border areas are entitled to *pas lintas batas* (border crossing passes). With this pass a resident is allowed to enter Malaysia and stay within the border area for a month.

12. Around 300 Florenese children (6–17 years of age), left by their parents who are working in Sabah, currently remain under Church guardianship in Nunukan.

13. In Nunukan, an organization (KEKARNUSA—Kerukunan Keluarga Nusatenggara or the Association of the Nusatenggara Brotherhood) has been formed by people hailing from East Nusatenggara. It was established to serve the needs of the migrant families from all places in the eastern part of Indonesia. During the "Nunukan crisis" of August and September 2002, according to its leaders, it successfully mobilized funds for migrant workers expelled from Sabah. It also formed a cooperative that provides services to the local administration, such as cleaning the city roads. At the time of the fieldwork, the leaders of this organization were also considering mobilizing its members to join a particular political party in the next general election of 2004.

14. In the first half of the twentieth century, the Dutch colonial state recruited mostly Javanese for export to Sabah as indentured labor for the British North Borneo Company. For a fuller discussion on Javanese labor in Sabah, see Miyazaki (2003).

15. Cross-border migration and transnational communities, while not recent phenomena, are clearly under-researched and neglected by social scientists in Southeast Asia. Cross-border migration and transnational communities emerged as nation-states became entrenched. Yet, as in the cases of the Florenese in Sabah, the Sangirese in the southern Philippines, and the Minangkabaus of East Malaysia, boundaries of nation-states seem irrelevant when migrants are continuously interacting with their relatives in their place of origin. For discussion of contemporary issues of cross-border movement in Indonesia, see Tirtosudarmo and Haba (2005).

16. On labor migration in BIMP-EAGA, particularly Sabah, see Kurus et al. (1998).

17. The term "irregular migration" in this paper is interchangable with "undocumented" and "illegal" migration. On this issue in Southeast Asia, see Asis (2004).

18. For a discussion on this issue, see Stephen (2000) and Uesugi (2000).

19. In Southeast Asia, studies of borderland communities have mostly concentrated on indigenous populations, such as Wadley's (2000) on Iban transna-

tional circular labor migration in northwestern Borneo, Horstmann's (in this volume) on Thai-speaking Muslims from the west coast of southern Thailand and Buddist Thais from northeast Malaysia, and Uchibori's (2002) study of Iban cultural citizenship in Sarawak and Brunei.

20. Tuan Azam and Om Franky are not their real names. *Tuan* is a Malay word meaning mister, and *Om* is originally a Dutch word meaning uncle.

References

Asis, Maruja M. B. 2004. "Borders, Globalization and Irregular Migration in Southeast Asia." In A. Ananta and E. Nurvidya Arifin, eds. *International Migration in Southeast Asia*. Singapore: ISEAS.

Barnes, Robert H. 1974. *Kedang: A Study of the Collective Thought of an Eastern Indonesian People*. Oxford: Clarendon Press.

Barnes, Ruth. 1994. "East Flores Regency." In Roy W. Hamilton, ed. *Gift of the Cotton Maiden: Textiles of Flores and the Solor Islands*. Los Angeles: Fowler Museum of Cultural History.

BPS. 1981. "Penduduk Nusa Tenggara, Maluku, dan Irian Jaya Menurut Propinsi dan Kabupaten/Kotamadya" (*Population of Nusa Tenggara, Maluku and Irian Jaya*). Seri L No.7. Hasil Pencacahan Lengkap Sensus Penduduk 1980.

———. 2001. "Karakteristik Penduduk Kabupaten Flores Timur" (Population Characteristics of East Flores District). Hasil Sensus Penduduk 2000, Kabupaten Flores Timur.

Forbes, Dean. 1981. "Mobility and Uneven Development in Indonesia: A Critique of Explanations of Migration and Circular Migration." In G. W. Jones and H. V. Richter, eds., *Population Mobility and Development: Southeast Asia and the Pacific*. Canberra: Development Studies Centre Monograph no. 27, Australian National University.

Horstmann, Alexander. 2002. "Incorporation and Resistance: Border-Crossings and Social Transformation in Southeast Asia." *Antropologi Indonesia*, 26, no. 67: 12–29.

Hugo, Graeme. 1997. "Changing Patterns and Processes in Population Mobility." In Gavin W. Jones and Terence H. Hull, eds., *Indonesia Assessment: Population and Human Resources*, Canberra and Singapore: Australian National University and Institute of Southeast Asian Studies.

———. 2002. "Indonesia's Look Abroad: Country Profile." Migration Information Source, Migration Policy Institute.

Kantor Statistik Propinsi NTT. 1991. "Indikator Kesejahteraan Masyarakat NTT 1990" (Social Welfare Indicators of East Nusa Tenggara 1990. Kantor Statistik Propinsi NTT.

Kurus, Bilson, et al. 1998. „Migrant Labor Flows in the East ASEAN Region: Prospects and Challenges." *Borneo Review* 9, no. 2: 156–86.

Levitt, Peggy. 1999. "Towards an Understanding of Transnational Community Forms and Their Impact on Immigrant Incorporations." Paper presented at the Comparative Immigration and Integration Program Winter Workshop, University of California, San Diego, 19 February.

Miyazaki, Koji. 2001. "Socio-cultural Processes of Development: Sabah and BIMP-EAGA." Paper presented at the workshop "Social-Cultural Processes of Development: Sabah and BIMP-EAGA, Tokyo University of Foreign Studies and Institute for Development Studies, Kota Kinibalu, Sabah, 28 August.

——. 2003. "Migrants across the Colonial Border: Javanese Labourers to North Borneo." Paper presented at the workshop "Culture and Development in and around Sabah," Tokyo University for Foreign Studies, Tokyo, 23–24 January.

Graham, Penelope. n.d. *"Widows" at Home, Workers Abroad: Florenese Women and Labour Migration.* Unpublished ms. Monash University, Melbourne, Australia.

Population Profile. 2000. *Population Profile of Nunukan District.* Kabupaten Nunukan.

Portes, Alejandro, Luis E. Guarnizo, and Patricia Landolt, eds., 1999. *Transnational Communities.* Special issue of *Ethnic and Racial Studies* 22, no. 2.

Stephen, Jeannet. 2000. "The Value of Ethnic Labels in Relation to Ethnic Identity in Sabah: The Case of Kadazandusuns." Paper presented at the Borneo Research Conference, Kuching, Sarawak.

Tirtosudarmo, Riwanto. 2004. "Cross-Border Migration in Indonesia and the Nunukan Tragedy." In A. Ananta and E. Nurvidya Arifin, eds., *International Migration in Southeast Asia.* Singapore: ISEAS.

Tirtosudarmo, Riwanto, and John Haba, eds., 2005. *From Entikong to Nunukan: The Dynamics of the Borderland Area of Indonesia's Kalimantan and East Malaysia.* Jakarta: Penerbit Sinar Harapan.

Titus, M. J. 1978. "Interregional Migration in Southeast Asia as a Reflection of Social and Regional Inequalities." *Tijdschrift voor Economische en sociale Geografie* 69, no. 4: 194–204.

Uchibori, Motomitzu. 2002. "In the Two States: Cultural Citizenship of the Iban in Sarawak and Brunei." *Sabah Museum Monograph* 7: 111–27.

Uesugi, Tomiyuki. 2000. "Migration and Ethnic Categorization at International Frontier: The Case of Sabah, East Malaysia." In *Population Movement in Southeast Asia: Changing Identities and Strategies for Survival,* eds. Abe Ken-ichi and Ishii Masako. Osaka: The Japan Center for Area Studies, National Museum of Ethnology.

Wadley, Reed L. 2000. "Transnational Circular Labour Migration in Northwestern Borneo." *Revue europeene des Migrations Internationales* no. 16 : 127–49.

——. 2002. "Border Studies Beyond Indonesia: A Comparative Perspective." *Antropologi Indonesia* 26, no. 67: 1–11.

Centering the Margin III: Political Economy of Southeast Asian Borderlands

7

Deconstructing Citizenship from the Border: Dual Ethnic Minorities and Local Reworking of Citizenship at the Thai-Malaysian Frontier

Alexander Horstmann

The impasse is the inevitable exclusiveness of citizenship which distinguishes those who have it from those who don't. (Patton and Caserio 2000: 1)

Introduction

FOR THAI-SPEAKING MUSLIMS in Satun on the west coast of southern Thailand and Thai Buddhist monks in Kelantan on the east coast of northern Malaysia, the local reworking of citizenship constitutes an important strategy to deal with the constraints that have been designed by the state to control the populations at the border. Holders of dual citizenship on the Thai-Malaysian border use state documents to their personal advantage. This essay examines border crossing practices as a way of life for ethnic minorities partitioned between two or more countries. Border communities resent their inferior position within the nation-state. By joining Buddhist or Muslim networks across the border, border people counter the effects of citizenship as an instrument of control. This essay explores the tension between personal and national identity and examines ambiguous identities and identity shifts in the spaces between the Thai and Malay worlds. These new spaces in-between Thailand and Malaysia are not only limiting, but also liberating and empowering for the lives of the communities on each side of the border.[1]

These networks of border people are changing and reworking the meaning of citizenship.[2] In many discourses of the state, holders of dual citizenship are seen and treated as troublemakers whose participation in more than one national polity violates the concept of sovereignty. Migration and

Endnotes for this chapter begin on page 174.

religious movements and the resulting border-crossing networks have established firm routes, crisscrossing political boundaries. Let me make clear from the beginning that the aim of this chapter is not to celebrate the reworking of citizenship, but to show some of the ways in which it is appropriated and used in people's struggles in the Thai-Malaysian borderland.

One of my most puzzling findings when conducting ethnographic research on border crossings on the Thai-Malaysian border was the acquisition of dual citizenship by members of transnational ethnic minorities. Thai-speaking Muslims from the west coast of southern Thailand and Buddhist Thais from northern Malaysia acquire multiple citizenship rights through various means: by registering the birth of their children just across the border, by marriage, by making use of kinship relations or inventing them, and by applying for naturalization. In the course of my fieldwork, I became conscious that the adoption of dual citizenship not only reflects a pluri-local social life, it is also embedded in long-lasting social relations that encompass Thailand and Malaysia, relations in which distinctions of national identity are rendered increasingly meaningless. Dual citizenship constitutes an important strategy to deal with the constraints that have been designed by the state. Members of ethnic minorities use state documents to their personal advantage, producing identity cards to facilitate their border crossings.[3] Ethnic minorities on the Thai-Malaysian border have generally been seen as peripheral and inferior by governments and dominant ethnic groups in both Malaysia and Thailand. The Patani Malays, the Thai-speaking Muslims in Satun in Thailand, and the Kelantan Thais in Malaysia constitute minorities who are "trapped" on the national border between a hostile state that offers them citizenship reluctantly, and a mother country that offers them little by way of support (e.g., Rabinowitz 1998: 156).

To be sure, daily raids on the border aimed at "illegal" migrants, and reports of beatings in prisons to prevent illegal reentry, are brutal reminders of the presence of the nation-state. But although the state remains the single most powerful form of political organization in the region, its inability to purge the practice of dual citizenship shows that postnational forms of belonging are a reality. In fact, the flexible use of citizenship seems to be a characteristic strategy of enclave cultures in the borderland. Moreover, I observed that ethnic minorities do not renounce their citizenship rights after acquiring new ones; on the contrary, they carefully keep their old identity cards.[4]

While people ignore as far as possible the bureaucratic implications of moving across a modern international frontier, they are keenly aware of the differences between Thai and Malay society and of their position in each. The Patani Malays on the east coast of southern Thailand, the Sam-Sam on the west coast of southern Thailand, and the Kelantan Thais on the east coast of northeast Malaysia have a marginal status similar to that of the Palestinian citizens of Israel.[5]

Cut off from their parent group by national borders, ethnic minorities are partitioned between a hostile state that gives them citizenship (but withholds state resources and certain rights from them) and an ambiguous position within their parent group. In the consolidation of the Thai-Malaysian border (in 1911 and 1949), Siam had to reconcile its territorial ambitions with British colonial interests. Siam ceded the tributary provinces of Kedah, Kelantan, and Terengganu, but kept control of Pattani, Naratiwat, and Songkhla on the east coast, and Satun on the west coast. The loosely organized hierarchical arrangement of overlapping tiers of tributary states typical of the pre-colonial period, in which small states functioned as umbrellas under the protection of larger and higher umbrellas, gave way to the more recent Western arrangement of sovereign states with defined and mutually exclusive national boundaries.

Double citizenship is a "hidden transcript," in Scott's (1990) terminology, which results from social, economic, and political forces pushing and pulling border peoples in multiple directions.[6] Centuries-old struggles between the Siamese monarchy and the Malay sultanate produced a rebellious Malay minority on the Thai frontier. The Patani Malays on the east coast maintain well-established kinship and Islamic networks across the border to Kelantan and Trengganu. The villagers perceive the other side of the border very much as part of their social world (Carsten 1998). Border crossing was until very recently very simple, and for the local people, there was effectively no border. Well into the early twentieth century, people used to cross the international border by foot, by ferry, or by boat without worrying about the border police. The inland massifs, the forests, and the many small islands along the Andaman Sea provided space for refuge and hiding places for indigenous peoples, dissidents, and social bandits alike. Thai Buddhists and Malay Muslims used to cross the border as part of their everyday life to participate in marriages and funerals. In much of their daily life even today, the local practices of people living on the border contradict and even render absurd the nation-state concept of sovereignty.

Muslim villagers from Thailand work in the fisheries and factories, and specialize in *tom yum* (sour hot soup) restaurants that can be found all over Malaysia, in order to escape poverty and unemployment in southern Thailand (Dorairajoo 2002). While people living in provinces adjunct to the border benefit from border passes, many of the people crossing the international border become illegal migrants. On the other hand, political dissidents are hiding in Kelantanese villages that have been established by Patani Malays. They benefit from sympathies of the Patani nobility and *ulama* who have become Malaysian citizens and operate from Malaysia and Saudi Arabia. In sharp contrast, the Thai-speaking Muslims from the west coastal province of Satun are more vulnerable to arrest (Horstmann 2002b). During my fieldwork in Langkawi, I witnessed the exploitation of Thai-speaking villagers at the hands of brokers, who promised them valuable residency permits in exchange for indentured labor. Likewise, Thai Muslim women who marry Malaysian men are ready to submit themselves to the authority of their partners in order to stay in Malaysia and eventually become Malaysian citizens. Thai-speaking villagers are called *orang Siam* (Siamese people) by Malay villagers and not *orang Islam* (Muslim people), a term that separates rather than includes them. Thai-speaking villagers are believed to be "polluted" by the consumption of Thai foods and Thai language, and to be lax in their Islamic practice.

The Buddhist networks linking Thai Buddhist villagers in Kelantan and Kedah with the Thailand Sangha have also intensified. Thus, Thai monks from the Buddhist Mahachulalongkorn University in Bangkok stay in Kedah's *wat* (monastery) on a temporary basis. The exchanges and contacts with Thai monasteries are also increasing. The assistant to the chief monk in Kelantan Phra Buntham at Wat Utamara in Bangsae receives his regalia from the Thai Buddhist order. Officials from the Department of Religion in Bangkok supervise funeral rituals in Kelantan. The Theravada monasteries have developed a special relation with the Malaysian Chinese. In search of salvation, the urban Chinese sponsor the Buddhist temple, whose clergy is entirely comprised of Kelantanese Thais. This is yet another aspect of the ethnic specialization of the Kelantan Thais: offering religious services to their Malay neighbors, the Buddhist clergy in Kelantan is sought for merit making at Buddhist monasteries. The Thai Kelantanese villages attract Chinese visitors from as far as Johor and Singapore.

Reflections on Citizenship

Citizenship has become a newly popular topic for public discussion in Thailand and in the world at large. As Patton and Caserio (2000: 1–14) argue, multiple disciplines with multiple motives have converged on this term. Recent work in political philosophy and social history by Fraser (1997) and Tilly (1995) addresses not only the notion of citizenship, its genesis, and its reworking in historical, social, political, and legal practice, but also the possibilities of recovering it in order to escape the impasse in which our traditional ideas of citizenship have landed us.

Instead of seeing it from a state perspective, I shall treat citizenship as a practice that is situated in social and cultural relations and negotiated in relations of power, domination, and resistance. Instead of taking for granted citizenship as a concept entailing universal rights, we should enquire about the work citizenship does, the problems citizenship creates, and the impasses or damage to which a failure to rethink the concept could lead.

Postcolonial theory, which reexamines the use and meaning of citizenship in the wake of the nationalist projects that imperialism left behind, helps us to liberate the concept of citizenship from its static, almost mystical character, by overcoming the straightjacket of the nation-state to which it has been inevitably attached. Breaking through the impasse of citizenship will require a subversive approach to citizenship that looks into the ways in which different categories of citizen and noncitizen are produced and inspects the sites where the boundaries of membership are historically contested.[7]

I join the efforts of other authors who have looked at ethnic minorities in the Southeast Asian borderlands (see, for example, Tapp 1989; Walker 1997; Evans, Hutton, and Eng 2000). In this works, citizenship has been liberated from its mystical character, and its significance in everyday life is applied to a wider discussion about the transformation of livelihood in the borderlands, the increasing control the state holds over people's lives, the location of ethnic minorities in the nation-state space, and the strategies followed by border people.[8]

I argue that dual citizenship is embedded in border-crossing networks, which reflect the inability of the state to purge dual citizenship, indicating that forms of postnational belonging have become a social reality. The analysis of border-crossing structures and their dynamic of change, practices of dual citizenship, and of the transformation of state-centered concepts within that framework, leads me to conclude that state sovereignty may never have been fully achieved, and that the people themselves play an important role in shaping the negotiation and practical use of citizenship.

This essay seeks to contribute to the anthropology of the state from the local level of the border from a fresh angle. The double identity-card holders are both making use of the border and contesting their incorporation in the host state. Their local reworking of citizenship is tailored to the practical needs of the border people through revival of multiple contacts and relations across the border. The intensification of labor migration and the revival of religious movements result in the transnationalization of the everyday life of migrants and travelers. People move across the border almost despite the regulations of the state. Borders are also discursively constructed in narratives of the Self and the Other, with very material consequences. The practices of people at the border question much of our assumed knowledge about the nature of the state. As it stands, citizenship ideologies are heavily deconstructed from the border in multiple directions.

In the Malaysian discourse, Thailand is associated with criminality, disorder, and sex tourism. This discourse justifies the construction of a wall separating the Malay from the Thai world. The Thai government complains that Malaysia is a haven for Islamic fundamentalist movements. The escalation of the cultural competition results in the construction of various stereotypes and pejorative connotations of the Other (Horstmann 2002b).

Border people make use of the border and their ethnic-religious networks as a resource. In doing so, they benefit from the compliance of the state, whose agents cooperate in border trade and in the trade in identity cards and working permits. Most important, the states may see their partitioned minorities across the border as a sort of extension of their cultural territory and hence turn a blind eye to the practice of dual citizenship. The Malaysian government has a very ambiguous relationship to the Muslim population in Thailand. While it tolerates transnationalism from Patani to a certain extent, control of citizenship has become much tighter in recent years.

The Sam-Sam on the Thai-Malaysian Border

While the Sam-Sam are a historical category (meaning mixed, half-race Thai-speaking Muslims on the west coast of South Thailand in the spaces in-between Theravada Buddhism and Islam), the Malays in present-day Langkawi distinguish themselves from the *orang Siam*. It is alleged that Thai-speaking Muslims do not pray properly, or observe Islamic rules of diet and hygiene. During the golden age of banditry from 1900 to 1920, the Sam-Sam are said to have provided the most notorious gang leaders (Cheah Boon Kheng 1988). The Sam-Sam, mostly involved in the agrarian sector of the economy as sharecroppers or laborers represented the lowest social stratum in Kedah, Perlis, and Satun: "They constituted a social class which had to bear almost unlimited demands on its services during the pre-colonial period, and later as main targets of the various taxes, land tax, land rent, unpaid services, etc., imposed by British and Thai administrations. When faced with the problems of poor land, occasional disasters such as drought, poor harvests, or other natural disasters, these peasants were left with only one recourse for their survival, namely theft" (Cheah Boon Kheng 1988: 44).

Nishii examines the process of emergence and transformation of their peripheral ethnicity (2000: 180ff.). They were regarded by the Siamese rulers as *chao pa*, uncivilized criminals living in the forest and kept at arm's length by the Malays who wanted to defend the Islamic Malay world from invasion by Thai animist and Thai Buddhist elements. While the younger generation of the Sam-Sam in Malaysia, being ashamed of the practices of its ancestors, has abandoned the Thai language, Muslims in Thailand find themselves having to adjust to the presence of the Thai state. The identity of the Sam-Sam integrates elements from the Thai and Malay worlds, playing on the ambiguities between cultural boundaries. Refusing an essentialized national identity has advantages for the Thai-speaking Muslim migrants who establish social networks in Thailand and in Malaysia that sometimes include government officials.

The borderland, scene 1:
The gendering of citizenship in border-crossing marriage

Habibah lives with Hazemi in a small, one-story house in Kampung Temoyong, near Hazemi's mother's house. Habibah comes from Ban Ko Sarai, a small island near Amphor Muang Satun in southern Thailand. She began to work in Malaysia at the age of fourteen, refusing an offer from her well-to-do brother in Saudi Arabia to continue her education in Thailand.

Habibah recalls that she often was beaten in school by her Thai Buddhist headmaster and felt discriminated against. Offers of jobs from kin, who recruited labor in Sarai, brought her to Kuala Lumpur, Penang, and Langkawi. Habibah's experiences have included poor living conditions, poor wages, and sexual harassment. She regularly returned home to Sarai and maintained close relationships with kin and friends. During her last job, was in a souvenir shop at the international airport of Langkawi where she met Hazemi, her present husband. Habibah is among 2,400 Thai women from Muslim communities in southern Thailand who are married to Malaysian men and registered with the Islamic office in Kuah, Langkawi.

A male fantasy is projected onto the daughters of Thai-speaking Muslims of the west coast of southern Thailand, who are imagined (and desired) to be submissive housewives. It is men from the lower social strata who are inclined to seek Thai wives, because they have problems marrying Malay women, who are more self-confident and freer in their relationships and who have much better life chances than their Thai counterparts. A pattern is emerging on the Thai-Malaysian border in which Malay men, especially from Langkawi, by virtue of their citizenship, have the power to ask for Sam-Sam daughters.[9] The pattern of marriage reflects the gendering of cross-border relations in Thailand and Malaysia and maps of power relations within which Malaysian men marry Thai women and unequal gender relationships are reproduced. Habibah uses a border pass as an inhabitant of one of the five border provinces in southern Thailand (Satun). She has been applying for a Malaysian passport, in vain so far.9 She is therefore forced to return to Thailand to renew her border pass. Without an identity card, Habibah has to live a migrant's life with irregular employment and lower wages. Her movements in Langkawi and in Malaysia are very careful, restricted, and vulnerable. She is even subject to occasional control or harassment by border police. Habibah has established close ties with other women from Thailand in Kampung Temoyong and in Langkawi, such as Jamila, with whom she can exchange information about work opportunities and news in Thailand.

On the other hand, Malaysian women tend to avoid and ignore her, contributing to her humiliation and marginal position in the village. Habibah suffers from loneliness and the fact that she is not integrated into the daily life of the village. She is certain, however, that she never wants to return to Sarai or southern Thailand, which from her perspective is underdeveloped (*mai pattana*), neglected, and dirty. Hazemi, on the other hand, enjoys traveling to Thailand. Habibah concentrates on her marriage with Hazemi and on raising their son, who is learning Arabic and Malay crafts. In addition, she prepares lunches for a hotel, to help the family budget. Having children has stabilized her relationship, and helped improve her status in the village.

Her insistence on a formal Islamic marriage in the town of Kuah was motivated by her aspiration for more security in her relationship with Hazemi. She felt especially depressed about Hazemi's unfaithfulness and his relationship with yet another Malay woman. Worse still was having to do the washing and cleaning for a household of five persons, while being ill-treated and humiliated by her mother-in-law. Many women from Thailand become the victims of discrimination, sexual violence, or confinement to the house. Habibah told me about underage minor wives who have been dropped by their Malay husbands, and who are confined to the house with no means to support themselves.

Some women are crippled by their hardships. In the end, Habibah decided to endure the hardships, afraid to return to Thailand empty-handed. Habibah's story illustrates how women from southern Thailand are vulnerable to exploitation and unequal gender relations. It is common for such binational families to have members on both sides of the border, like Jamila's daughter from her first marriage, who is attending the Thai school in Ban Sarai to be educated in the Thai way. As a foreigner without certain rights and without claim to state resources, Habibah felt that her precarious status was being used against her.

Overall, the transformation of citizenship among Thai-speaking Muslim communities on Malaysia's west coast has an important gender dimension. The women from Thailand are not easily integrated into village society, but face hostility from the husband's family as well as from other Malay women, who feel that the availability of submissive Thai women is a threat to their own status and independence. While Carsten (1997, 1998) shows that southern Thailand is very much on the cultural map of Langkawi villagers, who themselves have migrant backgrounds, unequal gender relations are reproduced in marriage migration on the Thai-Malaysian border, and subtle differences between women keep Thai Muslim women outside Malay women's circles.

The pattern of border-crossing marriage reflects a power regime that is further transforming citizenship. Women adjust to the Malay life, which includes the Islamization of their lifestyles. Their children grow up in a Malay way. Resistance to marginalization includes close social ties with other Thai women at home as well as in Langkawi. While the women suppress the Thai language in Malaysia, they use their southern Thai dialect in conversation with fellow Thai women. Thus, married women are at home in both languages, moving back and forth between the home in Thailand and the home in Malaysia. Through their Malaysian partner, they have access to Malaysian citizenship, the Langkawi labor market, and certain state resources—in short, to a better life. But they do not leave their homes in Thailand behind. Instead, they keep the old identity card for convenience and maintain close contact with family networks in Thailand and in the Islamic world at large.

Fig. 7.1. Malay men and Thai women in Langkawi (photo A. Horstmann).

The borderland, scene 2:
Fishing illegally in Malaysian waters

After five days at sea they are tired, thirsty, and hungry. The fishermen secure the fish, wash the boat, and repair the net. The catch is washed, sorted, and weighed. The fishermen are paid immediately. After bathing carefully, the men sit at the table to drink sweet tea and to smoke. Their gossip focuses on increasing police controls, and strategies for outwitting them, and on related experiences with Malaysian police. Depending on the weather, the young men fish in Langkawi for a tour of fourteen days. They use the money to pay for the maintenance of the boat and to finance Islamic education in Pattani province for themselves and for their three sisters. Nearly every young man from Ban Sarai in southern Thailand has experienced being arrested, imprisoned, and fined on Malaysian soil. Stories of being humiliated in prison by the Malaysian authorities circulate. When they are not able to pay the fine, their small boats, their means of existence, are burnt.

In Sarai, the rapid depletion of natural resources is threatening the subsistence of people who simply do not have enough income to pay for the maintenance of their boats. Big trawlers use spotlights and thick nets that catch not just fish, crab, and shrimp, but all kinds of sea life. The small fishermen in Sarai are afraid to talk about the local mafia, who own the trawlers and are also involved in illegal, border-crossing trade. Powerful gangsters, who combine legal and illegal forms of accumulation—trading, smuggling, and prostitution—and cooperate with local politicians and bureaucrats, kill opponents easily. The diminishing prospects, especially for young people, make for a depressing atmosphere in the village. Drug addiction among youth is rampant, with young people dying of overdoses or drug-related health hazards at an early age. There are parents who have lost their sons at their most productive age.

In the process of the emergence of a transnational space, life in Sarai and Langkawi is fundamentally changing. The division between the people who migrate and those who are bound to home is exacerbating social differentiation, competition for resources, and bitter divisions in the village. Diminishing prospects necessitate survival tactics, among which crossing the border to Langkawi is by far the most significant. Most households in Ban Sarai have family members in Langkawi, either daughters married to Malaysian men or sons fishing illegally in Malaysian waters or taking up casual jobs. Although fishermen from Thailand are fully aware of the risks involved, they develop strategies in order to get a foothold in Langkawi and to survive in a basically hostile environment. Key among these is to build social ties with people in Langkawi—with villagers, kin, and even the lower-ranked police. For any of the fisher folk from Thailand, a patron-client relationship with a middleman is crucial to future border crossings. In parallel, Muslim fishermen from Thailand claim solidarities with distant kin in Langkawi on the basis of Muslim identity and kinship relations.

According to Malaysian regulations, work permits for fishing in Langkawi can be issued on condition that the owner of the boat is a Malaysian citizen. However, it is well known that the papers that document Malaysian ownership can be bought on the black market, for boats on which Thai fishermen may be temporally employed. The illegal fishermen benefit from the fact that it is impossible to distinguish them physically from the Malay villagers. Yet, as already noted in the case of Habibah, the newcomers are not fully integrated into Malay society, and do not join the Malaysians in their Friday prayers, local mosque associations, festivals, and ceremonies. Being most vulnerable to arrest and deportation, fishermen try to keep a low profile in Langkawi. The relationship of fishermen from Thailand to the Malaysian middleman underlines the extremely vulnerable status of Thai citizens fishing in Malaysian waters. In order to achieve a reciprocal relationship, fishermen from Thailand demonstrate their loyalty to their chosen patron by giving all their catch to him.

Obviously, this is very beneficial to the middleman, who can then rely on hardworking, faithful clients. In exchange for their loyalty, the illegal fishermen expect some form of protection. But like the kinship ties and common faith that are invoked to garner solidarity and help, the superficially harmonious relationship with the middleman masks exploitation. Such jobs are taken by fishermen from Thailand, because only they are satisfied with lower wages, higher interest rates, and insecure, temporary employment. It is true that Malay middlemen provide at least some sort of security for the fishermen who can land and sell their catch on Malay shores. However, this space is a vulnerable one that can change from one day to the next.

The borderland, scene 3:
Longing for Malaysian citizenship in Langkawi

The pioneer settlers in Sarai remembers when they fled the Japanese occupation in Langkawi to Sarai. Then there were only a handful of families making a livelihood from fishing and planting coconut trees. Plentiful fish and crab were found in the sea, and tigers and snakes were the only dangers. The grandmother migrated from Perlis and did not speak a word of Thai, while the grandfather, who settled in Setul, had once been a *nakleng*, a local strongman. They have nine children who shuttle between Sarai and Langkawi. The grandfather recalls that fishermen were once dependent only on the forces of nature, but now the cultural crisis in Ban Sarai has hit the family and two of the sons have died in their twenties, probably from drug addiction. Most of the more than four hundred families who try to make a living in Ban Sarai live a hand-to-mouth existence and do not know how to pay the rising costs for their motorized boats. As members and citizens of the Thai state, their children are registered in Thailand, attend Thai primary school, and are eligible for military service. Their daughters and sons move back and forth between Ban Sarai and Langkawi, benefiting from the uncertain, ambiguous space in the sea and the geographical proximity of Langkawi, lying just south of the Thai border.

One of the striking features of Muslims from Thailand is their effort to become as Malay as possible by emphasizing kinship ties, emotional bonds, language, and religion. But in a move for a better life, Muslims from Thailand aim first to become Malaysian citizens in order to settle down in Langkawi and make a livelihood from fishing. In the last decade or so, Muslims from Thailand have begun to settle on the periphery of Langkawi. In Kampung Serat on the island of Pulau Dayang Bunting at the back of Langkawi the wooden shacks of the new settlers are easily detectable, hastily constructed either on the coast or in the water, fully exposed to the intense heat of the sun. The established Malaysian rubber tappers' households occupy ancient stone houses on the hill whose fenced gardens on carefully prepared roads with street names all point to state-led local development. On closer inspection, many established families in Serat trace their origin to southern Thailand. In between the established members and the newcomers to the village, settlers try to assimilate by building stone houses to resemble the villagers' ancient ones.

The most recent wave of outsiders has been confronted by a strict immigration regime. One Thai Muslim broker, having obtained Malaysian citizenship rights early on and established a close relationship with the local district officer, is alleged to have exploited the precarious position of the new arrivals. This broker used his privileged position to apply for permission for forty fictitious relatives and their households from Ko Bulon in Amphor Muang Satun to settle down in Kampung Serat. He has also bought a dozen used Thai motorized fishing boats from Krabi and registered them in Malaysia; he now lends them to new labor recruits who work without wages and are in debt to him. In the process of applying for new documents, the newcomers are heavily dependent on the good will of their broker, who uses his position in the borderland to recruit cheap labor, thereby accumulating wealth through their efforts.

Communication between the newcomers and the established families in Kampung is minimal, in part because some newcomers are not able to converse freely in the Malay language. Due to their precarious position, parents neither register their children nor send them to primary school and the children grow up as illiterates in a highly literate Malaysian society. Disobedient clients are easily deported back to Thailand. The newcomers take on odd jobs in the village, including cleaning the school, gardening in the established houses, laboring tapping rubber, and minding children. The broker meanwhile invests his profits in a resort hotel in Bulon Island back in southern Thailand. For the construction, the maintenance and the management of the resort, he again makes use of his relatives' cheap labor. In fact, the roles played by this broker strikingly exemplify the changing role of kinship relations as the borderlands become subject to rural poverty and socioeconomic inequality—a context in which kinship relations are sometimes used for exploitative purposes. The example illustrates the rules that characterize movement on the Thai-Malaysian border.

In places such as Ko Sarai or Ko Bulon, it is not difficult to trace kinship relations. While Malaysian regulations require a kin connection to obtain a local identity card, the bilingual broker who prepares the papers has ample room to invent kinship relations and to make up relatives. The newcomers are ill at ease with Malay culture, Malay language, Malay bureaucrats, and Malay teachers. The only characteristics that they share with Malaysian villagers are fishing skills and Muslim identity. Nonetheless, the prospect of rich fishing grounds and a sustainable income is sufficient motivation for impoverished households to take on the role of "aliens." Settlement in Langkawi, even in an inferior social position, is a rare and precious opportunity for social mobility not to be missed by marginal fishermen. Once settled, the Thai households can benefit from shuttling between Thailand and Malaysia, trading Thai nets and fishing equipment, or smuggling Thai merchandise. They may even act as brokers for other fishermen who want to fish illegally in Malaysian territory. And the game goes on.

The Ethnic Thais in Northwest and Northeast Malaysia

The Thai minority in Kelantan has long interested cultural anthropologists (Golomb 1978; Kershaw 1969, 1980, 1982, 1984; Yusoff 1993). Ismail Yusoff's (1993) study of the social organization and cultural reproduction of a Buddhist temple in Kelantan illustrates how Thai-Malaysian villagers are strongly attached to, and deeply involved in Theravada Buddhism. Yusoff, who prefers the English term "Siamese" (from the Malay word *orang Siam*), shows that Theravada Buddhism is essential to guarantee the persistence of Thai ethnicity in an Islamic stronghold, and that the continuing regulation and management of Theravada Buddhism serves as an ethnic boundary marker to other ethnic groups. He argues that the Buddhist temple in Kelantan acquires special meanings and orders, which distinguishes it from temples in Thailand.

Golomb's published dissertation (1978) concludes that the ethnic Thais in Kelantan occupied a cultural niche, and had become brokers of morality in relation to the rural Malays. He argues that the Kelantan Thais were accentuating such cultural and ethnic boundary markers as Theravada Buddhism, their role as healers, their practice of magic, gambling, and raising pigs. Kershaw's (1969, 1980, 1982, 1984) research on local politics complements this perspective on the ethnic niche of the Kelantan Thais, who balance their alliances between the rural and urban Chinese and the rural Malays to cope with fears of economic dispossession and growing Islamization. Since these studies were carried out, the growing racial tensions on the east coast of northern Malaysia, though heightened, have not resulted in an assault on Theravada Buddhism.

Border crossing trips to Thailand by Thai residents of Malaysia are associated with much joy and excitement. Young women and men use the border passes to cross the Thai-Malaysian border without much bureaucratic effort. Although owners of border passes are allowed to stay in Thailand for up to six months, young people seldom stay longer than a few days and sometimes return on the same evening. Young people cross the border to Thailand to participate in entertainment, to eat Thai food, or Thai beer. They return with cheap Thai merchandise, pop music, and magazines.

The Thai in Malaysia have long been regarded as an inferior race, just like the Sam-Sam discussed earlier. In contemporary Malaysia, Thais have a reputation for being alcoholic, criminal, poor, illiterate, and stubborn. In addition, in the context of the rapid Islamization of Kelantan, the Thai environment is seen as ritually dirty and religiously polluted. Thus, dogs, which can come from Thai Buddhist villages into Malay spaces, are chased away. This has not always been the case. The Thais consider themselves indigenous settlers, sons of the soil. The first prime minister of Malaysia, Tonku Abdulrahman, was a product of Siamese marriage politics in Kedah. His mother, a daughter of King Rama IV, was a Thai, and the first wife of Chayo Praya of Saiburee, Sultan Abdulhammed of Kedah. She donated land for a Buddhist temple, which bears her name and symbolizes Malay-Siamese relations in the old days.

Thai citizenship can be acquired in a number of ways if birth is registered in Thailand. Not least because so many Thai prostitutes are married to local Thai-Malaysian men, Thai citizenship can be arranged in neighboring Narathiwat province. As large numbers of Kelantanese Thai have kinship ties with Takbai Thais, Thai citizenship can be acquired by registering birth in Thailand or by inventing kinship ties. In addition, Kelantanese Thai who worked on the Nikhom state schemes in the neighboring province of Naratiwat have obtained citizenship rights. While the acquisition of citizenship in Malaysia is increasingly out of reach for the Sam-Sam, the Kelantanese Thai use the fuzzy enforcement of the Thai border to their advantage.

The borderland, scene 4:
Teaching Thai cultural identity in Malaysia

We meet at a checkpoint on the Thai-Malaysian border in Sungai Golok with a Thai teacher, a Thai official, and a Thai-Malaysian student from Kampung Bang Sae in Kelantan who is studying Thai in a program of the Songkhla Foundation. We are heading for Wat Utamara in Bang Sae, which houses the chief abbot of Kelantan. In Bang Sae, we begin to talk with Thai youth about Thai identity in Kelantan. The foundation supports the reproduction of Theravada Buddhism and Thai traditions in Malaysia, targeting Thai youth in particular. The Thai teacher (from Isan), who volunteers for the foundation, is on good terms with the village youth and engages the boys in Thai boxing. In the evening, the girls perform a *manohra* dance for which they had several weeks of training.

The visitors are welcomed with a Thai Wai (traditional Thai greeting) and some enthusiasm. The girls ask the visitors for their opinion of the *manohra* dance, especially its authenticity. They tell us that they are collecting money for the Kelantanese Thai-Malaysian association from wealthy temples to buy *manohra* costumes instead of borrowing them from southern Thailand. Buddhist monks play a special role in northern Malaysia. In addition to taking care of the religious matters of the community, they teach the Thai language.

Because teachers, materials and books are lacking in the region; the Thai community depends on the temple not only for religious purposes, but also for the reproduction of Thai cultural identity at large. In addition to religion and language, monks teach Thai customs and Thai manners. The reliance on the monks is a consequence of the fact that few people outside Thailand are educated to become Thai teachers. Little money from the Thai consulate is forthcoming. In Bang Sae, the Thai school is linked to the training center for Thai-Malaysian youth. As attendance at Thai lessons is low and limited to children and youth, the graduates' Thai literacy does not extend beyond the elementary level. But not only does the Kelantan Thai community lack Thai teachers; it also increasingly lacks its most important cultural capital-Buddhist monks. The solution to the dilemma is to bring in monks from Thailand, which further intensifies border-crossing networks. It is not uncommon in contemporary Kelantan to find hundred-year-old temples deserted because there are simply not enough monks to staff the vacant temple positions.

There are meanwhile some very well-sponsored, well-staffed temples, supported by the Thailand Sangha. Bang Sae is. Bang Sae, a big village near the Golok checkpoint, hosts the spectacular temple of Wat Utamara, a postmodern bricolage that integrates architectural styles and symbols from the Thai, Chinese, and Indian worlds and beliefs. Wat Utamara houses the chief abbot of Kelantan. The temple has visitors from Thailand and Khota Baru, as well as from Johor and Singapore, and the dormitory can easily accommodate fifty guests at a time.

Fig. 7.2. Two charismatic monks in Kelantan, Malaysia (photo A. Horstmann).

Rupture and Disjuncture in Everyday Thai Life

The factors that produce the fragmentation of everyday life are the isolation of Thai villagers in the Malay World, especially the youth, and the lengthy periods spent outside the village. Young people are increasingly dissatisfied with the monotonous and hard labor in the fields, the low earnings, and, most of all the boredom of village life. Migration to Singapore is increasingly attractive to Thai village youngsters. But border crossings to Singapore are highly regulated, and immigrants are subject to massive government discipline that includes health checks and skill examinations. On Kelantan, young men who are engaged in physical, stressful labor are often addicted to drugs, which are readily available in Thai villages there. Although they try to participate in the *Sonkran* or *Loykratong* festivals where possible in order to share the excitement or to find a Thai spouse, young men spend much of their life outside the village.

Lately, Thai youth have become the subject of discourse on the moral values of the Thai in Malaysia. Parents complain about their sons' refusal to robe as monks even for the shortest Lenten period, which is seen as the rite of passage to adulthood. Refusal to submit to the regime of the temple is seen as a threat to the reproduction of Thai ethnicity. Thus, the young men who focus their lifestyles on desire and consumption are seen as jeopardizing Thai traditions. Their habits of drinking, sex with prostitutes, and drug use add to the stigmatization of Thai youth. Inspired by these anxieties, a new generation of Buddhist monks in Kelantan has started a campaign, focused on the spiritual state of Thai youth. Phra Buntam and Phra Plian present themselves as modern, knowledgeable monks who want to develop the spiritual knowledge of the lay people by targeting Thai youth. They believe that they have a special responsibility to educate stubborn villagers, especially young people, who are said to be losing touch with Buddhism. These monks emphasize new ways of teaching Buddhism as a form of self-development, and mobilize transnational cultural capital to incorporate the Thai-Malaysian youth into their circles. In Bang Sae, a Thai-Malaysian youth center integrates traditional Thai drums (which are unused) and modern stereo-karaoke equipment, for which is extremely popular with Thai youth. In addition, women organize *manohra* classes and the monks teach computer and Internet classes.

Phra Buntam and Phra Plian distinguish themselves from the traditional monks who only stay in the temple and rely on folk knowledge. Instead, they stress the importance of the text, the teaching of the Buddha (*Dharma*), meditation practice, ascetic values and bodily discipline, and the rules of the Buddhist canon. In short, they understand study of the *Dharma* as cultural work on the self. This campaign to develop Thai-Malaysian youth is integrated into networks with Buddhist foundations in Bangkok and Songkhla, which select young men to participate in a program to study Thai language at Thaksin University in Songkhla in hopes that they will in turn promote Buddhist values and Thai ethnic identity. In parallel to religious practices and cultural work in rural Kelantan, Buntam and Plian are integrated into the cosmological order of the Thai Buddhist Sangha. Ajarn Buntam has been nominated as Phra Choi Petsuwan and has received his insignia from the Thai king. He is a potential successor of the chief monk in Kelantan.

In a context in which the institutions of cultural life are fragmented, and in which the ethnic Thais are increasingly marginalized, a new generation of intellectuals is targeting Thai-Malaysian youth as a symbol of Thai ethnic identity in Malaysia. The fact that indigenous monks are disappearing apparently does not weaken the central role of the religious sphere in the revitalization of Thai ethnic identity.

Since the rise of Islam after the PAS-ulama took over local government in Kelantan in 1990 and its Islamist discourse, which dominates the everyday communication of the Kelantanese Thais, the revitalization of Buddhism has a particular relevance for the personal identity of the Kelantan Thai. Thai villagers are skeptical about the help and representation from the Thai consul, other diplomats, the senator and politicians who appear at festivals, as they have no dealings with the everyday realities of the villagers.

Buddhist Networks

The Buddhist grassroots movement extends from Bangkok to Singapore via Kuala Lumpur, and on the way encompasses a handful of Kelantan villages, which are considered sacred. Exemplary temples in northwest and northeastern Malaysia, such as Wat Utamara, have extensive links with the Thai Sangha as well as wealthy Chinese patrons in Thailand, Malaysia, and Singapore who are ready to sponsor the spectacular renovation of an entire temple in the hope of acquiring merit (*tambun*). The Thai religious elite in Kelantan nurtures networks of communication and support with Buddhist foundations in Singapore. In this way, Malaysian Chinese patrons from Johor Baru or Singapore are bound to particular Buddhist temples in Kelantan where the bones of their ancestors are interred. On the occasion of prayers for their ancestors, wealthy Chinese patrons drive their families in Mercedes-Benzes from Johor to the sleepy rural villages of Kelantan. The village provides only junior monks and a small hall (*sala*) for the funeral ritual, underlining the minor importance of the ritual which is performed solely for the Chinese visitors. The chief abbot of Kelantan is known to spend lengthy periods in Singapore.

As shown above, young men from Tumpat and Pasir Puteh are migrating to Singapore. This pattern of movement involves all young men. Some wealthy temples in Kedah have established formal agreements with the Buddhist University, Mahachula Mahavitayalai, under which young graduates can be recruited to Mahachula to occupy vacant positions in some Malaysian temples in Kedah. In a context of diminishing staff, educated Thai monks are gradually replacing indigenous monks. Buddhist pilgrimage routes between southern Thailand and Singapore encompass Kelantanese villages whose temples are considered sacred and which become tourist spots as a result.

The revitalized exchange is greatly supported by the diplomatic representations of the Thai kingdom in Malaysia, such as the Thai consulate in Khota Bharu. The Thai consul has an interesting function in the Thai borderland. He not only shows up on important ceremonial occasions, but also mediates between the Thai state and the Thai-Malaysian Sangha. If necessary, a large Buddha image will cross the border in a diplomatic car so as to avoid any spot checks from the border custom officials.

Using terms of kinship and racial assumptions of common blood, government officials from the Thai consulate claim a common destiny with Thailand across the border. The presence and overseeing of Thai officials at a funeral ceremony in Kelantan has changed the character of the ritual, transforming it from a local ritual into a performance of Thai statecraft. The Buddhist foundation in Songkhla plays a conspicuous role in training selected Kelantanese Thais to lead in political seminars, meditation courses, and Thai studies programs.

Border Crossing Networks and the Thai State

The politics of Thai ethnic identity in northeast Malaysia involves many players who claim to represent Thai-Malaysian peasants. Anthropologists have seldom commented on the political perspective of the ethnic Thais and their relationship with neighboring Thailand (but see Kershaw 1984). The Thais are too few in number and too domesticated to present any threat to the Malaysian state. The manifold cultural interactions with the rural Malays and the symbolic patronage of the sultan prevent any violent assault on Thai communities. The impoverished Thai villages in Kelantan and Kedah have seen a revival of Buddhist culture, supported in part by the Thai state. In this revival of Thai identity, Buddhist monks play a leading role. As a religious elite, Buddhist monks are the gatekeepers of Thai language and Thai traditions, which are now being accentuated anew. The Thai cultural association is mobilized to buy *manohra* costumes, which had hitherto to be borrowed from southern Thailand, dusty music ensembles are unpacked, and many Buddhist stupas and all kinds of Buddhist goods are imported. Numerous Buddhist temples are being built on the model of Bangkok temples, thriving on the money flooding in from wealthy Chinese patrons in Johor, Singapore, and Thailand eager to make merit, and on the growing integration of the Malaysian monks into the Thai sangha. Kelantan villages acquire a new role in the process as sacred sites on a reimagined pilgrimage route from Nakhorn Sri Thammarat's Wat Mahathat to Singapore that crisscrosses political boundaries for Chinese patrons and Thai pilgrimage tourists. Thai monks, who come from the Buddhist University (*Mahachulalongkorn*) in Bangkok or the Buddhist foundation in Songkhla with the mission of reviving Thai traditions and modeling them according to Thai rules, subvert the national idea of citizenship and transform Buddhist monks in Malaysia into agents with double citizenship. Through the Wat, as the central pillar of Thai culture, this reorganization of local religious concepts of meditation along national models also captures the attention of villagers—especially of young people.

Border Cultures and Citizenship on the Thai-Malaysian Frontier

The revival of Thai culture and Buddhism on the Thai-Malaysian border, although minuscule, parallels the resurgence of Islam. The resurgence of Islam on the Thai-Malaysian border parallels the spread of Islamic networks across the Malaysian, Indonesian, and Philippine borders. The revivalism of Buddhism in turn parallels the reawakening of Buddhist networks in Thailand, Burma, Yunnan, and Laos (Cohen 2000). The networks are not limited to the border, but are part of a larger process of globalization and the intensification of border crossings. The most important transnational social spaces, constructed through border-crossing migration, marriage, trade, and conflict, are visible in the borderlands. The enclave populations on the Thai-Malaysian border are transnational communities for whom border crossing is a way of life. Recent years have witnessed a shift of emphasis from the concrete interaction of minorities and the state on the ground to the local reworking and filtering of national and global scripts in the local context in the work of borderland scholars (Horstmann 2002a). This interaction of ethnic minorities who find themselves subject to national citizenship regimes in which the state defines them as the Other, is crucial to the social transformation of the Thai-Malaysian border. It is important to start with citizenship as a focal point. This essay has presented some findings on the practical, silent reworking of citizenship rules by border people for their own purpose. The practical reworking of citizenship occurs in response to the real needs of border people in everyday life. In the marginal space where one nation-state ends and another begins, local communities play on the ambiguity of identity in the borderland and make use of their networks across the border as a resource.

Carsten (1998) argues that the local perception of the borderland differs substantially from that of the center, and that border people avoid as much as possible the legal hurdles that crossing an international border implies. Carsten compares the local perception of the border with kinship relations. However, the relations across the border are far from unproblematic, since regimes of citizenship produce social differentiation along nationality lines. Thai- and Malay-speaking Muslims in southern Thailand resent their inferior position in Thai and in Malay society. By joining Buddhist or Muslim networks across the border, and by seeking niches in the host society (Miyazaki 2000), border people counter the disciplinary effects of citizenship regimes.

Double citizenship seems to be one of the patterns in the political ecology of the borderland in which border people are reworking the government rules according to their own interests. Pursuit of this status relies on the implicit or explicit compliance on at least one side of the border. Indeed, these assumed blood ties seem to be an essential element of citizenship ideology on the Thai-Malaysian border. This essay has explored the terrain of tension between personal and national identity. Instead of assuming a definite landscape of the borderland, it emphasizes the ambiguity and shifts between the Thai and Malay worlds. The new spaces of migrants and monks not only limit, but also empower the lives of the respective ethnic minorities. This shows how people can develop means to circumvent national imaginaries of the modern nation-state. But while the case of Thai-speaking Muslims from the west coast showcases migrants' vulnerability to state persecution as well as their creativity in reacting to it, the case of the Thai monks in Kelantan perhaps better illustrates the role of border people in changing the state and contributing to its ideology.

Notes

1. The author would like to acknowledge the financial support of the Fritz Thyssen Research Foundation, the German Research Foundation (DFG), and the German Academic Exchange Service (DAAD), and the assistance in the form of the inspiring questions from the faculties of the Centre of Southeast Asian Studies (CSEAS) in Kyoto and ILCAA, TUFS, in Tokyo where this paper was presented. Special thanks are due to Koji Miyazaki (ILCAA) and Yoko Hayami (CSEAS, Kyoto). Thanks are also extended to Reed L. Wadley for his helpful reading of this chapter.
2. The study of border crossing also necessitates a multi-sited fieldwork approach that adapts to the lifestyle of border-crossing people.
3. Ong (1999) makes an invaluable contribution to the anthropology of citizenship under global conditions. She introduces the label "flexible citizenship" to underline the flexible use of the passport in global business and family networks.
4. The Palestinian citizens of Israel are marginalized twice over. As citizens of Israel, they are members of a racialized minority perceived by many Israelis as potentially disloyal and subversive. Meanwhile, implicated by their residence and citizenship in Israel, and by their growing acculturation into Israeli life, they tend to be suspected and marginalized by Palestinians elsewhere and by Arabs generally (Rabinowitz 1998).
5. Scott (1990) distinguishes "hidden transcripts" from "public transcripts" in the relation of dominance and the subaltern. Scott explains that as open resistance in most cases would be suicidal, transcripts behind the stage provide a space for the subaltern to criticize the master. "Hidden transcripts" are not only rhetorical, but include practices of resistance, which Scott aptly calls "infrapolitics" of subordinate groups.
6. Anderson ([1983] 1991) and Thongchai (1994), whose works on the formation of the modern nation-state give insights into the genesis and formation of citizenship in Southeast Asia, suggest such an approach. State borders play a crucial role in that analysis. That the borders of the pre-colonial Southeast Asian state (negeri) were qualitatively different from those of the modern nation-

state was a crucial aspect of Anderson's theory. Thongchai argues that the border implies a hierarchical organization of the territorial state from the very beginning, not only in terms of class and status, but also in terms of an ethnogeography that puts its subjects in an inferior relation to Bangkok space.

7. See Wadley (2003) for a case study from Kalimantan that questions this assumption.

8. Note that the Langkawi Malay men who marry women from Thailand are at the bottom of the local social ladder.

9. As the wife of a Malaysian citizen, Habibah is eligible for Malaysian citizenship after five years of residence and employment.

References

Anderson, Benedict. 1991 (1983). *Imagined Communities: Reflections on the Origin and Spread of Nationalism.* 2nd ed. London: Verso.

Carsten, Janet. 1997. *The Heat of the Hearth. The Process of Kinship in a Malay Fishing Community.* Oxford: Clarendon Press.

——. 1998 "Borders, Boundaries, Tradition and State on the Malaysian Periphery." In Thomas M. Wilson and Hastings Donnan, eds., *Border Identities: Nation and State at International Frontiers,.* Cambridge: Cambridge University Press.

Cheah Boon Kheng. 1988. *The Peasant Robbers of Kedah, 1900–1929: Historical and Folk Perceptions.* Singapore: Oxford University Press.

Cohen, Paul. 2000. "A Buddhist Kingdom in the Golden Triangle: Buddhist Revivalism and the Charismatic Monk Khruba Bunchum." *Australian Journal of Anthropology* 11, no. 2: 141–54.

Evans, Grant, Christopher Hutton, and Kuah Khun Eng, eds. 2000. *Where China Meets Southeast Asia: Social and Cultural Change in the Border Regions.* Singapore: Institute of Southeast Asian Studies.

Fraser, Nancy. 1997. *Justice Interruptus: Critical Reflections on the Postsocialist Condition.* New York: Routledge.

Golomb, Louis. 1978. *Brokers of Morality: Thai Ethnic Adaptation in a Rural Malaysian Setting.* Honolulu: University Press of Hawaii.

Goody, Jack. 1990. *The Oriental, the Ancient and the Primitive : Systems of Marriage and the Family in the Pre-industrial Societies of Eurasia.* Cambridge: Cambridge Univ. Pr.

Horstmann, Alexander. 2002a. "Incorporation and Resistance: Borderlands, Transnational Communities and Social Change in Southeast Asia." *Working Paper Series WPTC-02-04, Transnational Communities,* ESRC Research Programme, University of Oxford.

——. 2002b. *Class, Culture, and Space: The Construction and Shaping of Communal Space in South Thailand.* London and New Brunswick: Transaction Publishers.

Kershaw, Roger. 1969. *The Thais of Kelantan: A Socio-Political Study of an Ethnic Outpost*. Ph.D. thesis, University of London.

———. 1980. "Frontiers within Frontiers: The Persistence of Thai ethnicity in Kelantan, Malaysia" (Review Article). *Journal of the Siam Society* no. 69: 145–58.

———. 1982. "A Little Drama of Ethnicity: Some Sociological Aspects of the Kelantan Manora." *Southeast Asian Journal of Social Science* no. 10: 69–95.

———. 1984. "Native but Not Bumiputra: Crisis and Complexity in the Political Status of the Kelantan Thais after Independence." *Contributions to Southeast Asian Ethnography* no. 3: 46–71.

Miyazaki, Koji. 2000. "Javanese-Malay: Between Adaptation and Alienation." *Sojourn*, 15, no. 1: 76–99.

Nishii, Ryoko. 2000. "Emergence and Transformation of Peripheral Ethnicity: Sam-Sam on the Thai-Malaysian Border." In Andrew Turton, ed., *Civility and Savagery: Social Identity in Tai States*, Richmond, Surrey: Curzon.

Ong, Aihwa. 1999. *Flexible Citizenship: The Cultural Logics of Transnationality*. Durham and London: Duke University Press.

Patton, Cindy, and Robert L. Caserio. 2000. "Introduction Citizenship 2000." *Cultural Studies* 14, no. 1: 1–14.

Rabinowitz, Dan. 1998. "National Identity on the Frontier: Palestinians in the Israeli Education System." In Thomas M. Wilson and Hastings Donnan, eds. *Border Identities: Nation and State at International Frontiers*. Cambridge: Cambridge University Press.

Scott, James C. 1990. *Domination and the Arts of Resistance: Hidden Transcripts*. New Haven and London: Yale University Press.

Tapp, Nicholas. 1989. *Sovereignty and Rebellion: The White Hmong of Southern Thailand*. Singapore: Oxford University Press.

Thongchai Winichakul. 1994. *Siam Mapped: A History of the Geo-body of a Nation*. Honolulu: University of Hawaii Press.

Tilly, Charles, ed. 1995. "Citizenship, Identity and Social History." *International Review of Social History* no. 40, Supplement 3.

Wadley, Reed L. 2003. "Lines in the Forest: Internal Territorialization and Local Accommodation in West Kalimantan, Indonesia (1865–1979)." *South East Asia Research* 11, no. 1: 91–112.

Walker, Andrew. 1997. *The Legend of the Golden Boat: Regulation, Transport and Trade in North-Western Laos*. Ph.D. thesis. Canberra: Australian National University.

Yusoff, Ismail Mohamed. 1993. *Buddhism and Ethnicity: Social Organization of a Buddhist Temple in Kelantan*. Singapore: Institute of Southeast Asian Studies.

8

SEX AND THE SACRED: SOJOURNERS AND VISITORS IN THE MAKING OF THE SOUTHERN THAI BORDERLAND

Marc Askew

Approaching the Borderland of Lower South Thailand

EACH DAY, THE BORDER ENTRY POINTS of Thailand's southernmost provinces at Sadao, Pedang Besar, Betong, and Sungai-Kolok witness a continuous flow of people and goods moving across the frontier check points bordering the Malaysian states of Perlis, Kedah, Perak, and Kelantan.[1] By far the greater number of these people are Malaysians crossing into Thailand on short-term visits. For people of the Chinese and Malay Muslim communities of neighboring localities, such border crossing is a routine that has been incorporated into the patterns of their everyday lives. The formal borders inscribed less than a century ago by British imperial authorities (with the reluctant cooperation of the Siamese state, in 1908) across the settlement spaces of Malay Muslims, Chinese, and Thai have little social meaning (see, e.g., Carsten 1998). On evenings and particularly on weekends, this flow of people intensifies, with thousands of men and women from farther afield entering Thailand—from Kuala Lumpur, Penang, Johor, and Singapore—for short periods of shopping, shrine visiting, and indulgence in the renowned entertainment and commercial sex industry of the towns of the Lower South. Since the 1970s, flows of visitors from Malaysia and Singapore to Thailand's Lower South have played a significant role in diversifying the image of this region from one of a dangerous space associated with communist insurgency and militant Muslim separatism, to one also associated with pleasure, recreation, and religious visitation.[2]

Endnotes for this chapter begin on page 201.

To be sure, this borderland remains highly problematic for the Thai state. It is a site that hosts numerous illicit activities ranging from drug running to people and arms smuggling. These activities are tied to Malaysian and Thai crime syndicates and networks of Thai bureaucrats, and they are fueled by official corruption on both sides of the border. The sporadic attempts of the Thai state to regulate illicit cross-border movements and transactions are themselves undermined by powerful groups of "influential figures" whose interests lie in keeping the border porous and malleable. The recent resurgence of assertive and violent Muslim separatism (over the years 2003 and 2004) has also shown the sensitivity of this borderland to global ideological movements and conflicts. The borderland of the Lower South is, however, multilayered: it is an ethnically and economically diverse territory, and despite its common identification with the Malay Muslim majority population of four of its border provinces (Narathiwat, Pattani, Satun, and Yala), strong contrasts prevail between its predominantly rubber- and rice-growing agrarian regions and its commercial and market towns, where Thai Buddhists and the Sino-Thai predominate. My aim here is to isolate and explore the generally neglected processes of visitation (more conventionally labelled "tourism") that have helped shape a complex and multilayered space in Lower South Thailand, extending from its core in Songkhla province across a variety of sites in Yala and Pattani (Figure 8.1).

The sites and activities of a variagated tourist system intimately linked to Malaysia and Singapore form one of the most conspicuous features of Lower South Thailand's borderland. It is a space that has been shaped, and continues to be reproduced, by interaction between a number of groups, including local inhabitants, a Thai-tourist oriented work force, and Malaysian-Singaporean tourists/sojourners. This borderland and its intimate relationship to the distinctive patterns of movement and motivation among Malaysians and Singaporean visitors can be characterized in terms of a combination of two dimensions, the "sacred" and the "sexual." Malaysian and Singaporean visitation to the Lower South is focused not so much on visiting natural attractions or vacationing, but rather on three key activities: shopping, visits to temple and shrine sites, and involvement in activities that are illicit, expensive, or prohibited in their own countries—predominantly the use of prostitution services and gambling. The motivations and dispositions underlying this dominant triad of activities may be summarized as "consumption," "blessing," and "catharsis," respectively. Although shopping is a major activity and attraction for many visitors, shrine visitation and engagement in sex-related recreation are an essential part of the total complex of their activities, and they are the focus of this exploration.

In this discussion I treat cross-border "tourism" of Singaporeans and Malaysians as a cultural practice involving differentiated patterns of visitation and engagement. I argue here that these patterns of visitation by

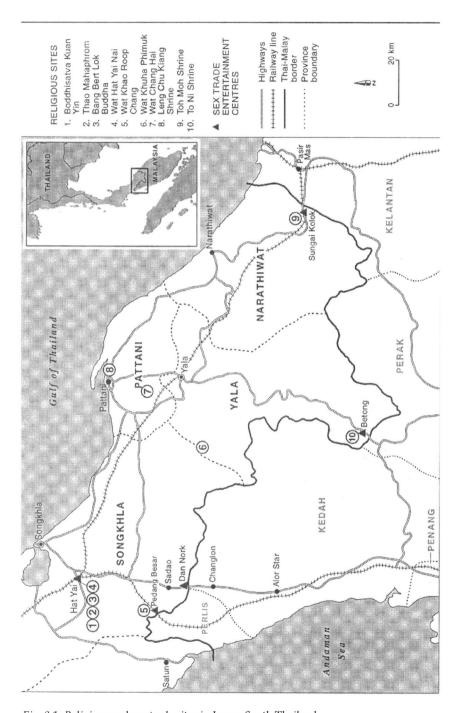

Fig. 8.1. *Religious and sex trade sites in Lower South Thailand.*

Malaysians and Singaporeans are characterized by an emic perception of Thailand's simultaneous "difference" and "familiarity." The "difference," aside from price differentials, is represented by the contrast between the legal/moral regimes distinguishing visitors' countries and Thailand, which encompass sexual behaviors as well as ethnic and religious expression, the latter being particularly important among the Sino-Malaysians. Thailand, perceived as a place of powerful monks and ancient magic, has long been regarded as a source of sacred potency in Malaysia and Singapore. In the mode of its difference, then, the borderland of the Lower South functions as a space of permissiveness for both religious expression and sexual desire. "Familiarity" is also a key dimension marking the perceptions and practices of Malaysians and Singaporeans. For the Chinese of these two countries, the towns of the Lower South represent a shared recognizable ethnic identity, common dialects, and diasporic heritage, together with a syncretic religious culture and symbolism. These similarities are reinforced by a long history of routine border-crossing practices, and by business and kinship interconnections in the peninsular (see, e.g., Cushman 1991). Multiple language competencies in the borderland enable many individuals of different ethnicities and nationalities to interact. Aside from this generally hospitable linguistic environment, the familiarity of the borderland is enhanced by numerous and varied long-term connections between Malaysians, Singaporeans, and Thais, connections that have been reinforced by regular contact through visits for business or relaxation. This juxtaposition of difference and familiarity in the Lower South borderland means that tourists' border crossings are not driven solely by the pragmatic attractions of the price differences prevailing between countries: When considered as cultural practices, these border crossing movements can be interpreted ethnographically as transgressive and affirming practices for Malaysians and Singaporeans in various ways.

My emphasis in this discussion coincides with other anthropological, geographical, and cultural studies approaches in viewing "borderlands" as sites that expose patterns of transgression against forms of state- and center-defined identity (Dube 1999; Gupta and Ferguson 1992; Kalra and Prewal 1999). The borderland discussed here is constituted by people, their movement, perceptions, and experiences. It is not simply a geographical space inscribed by state agencies (a "zone"), nor is it the possession of one quintessentially "local" community. In the "anthropology of frontiers," there is a danger of reifying the idea of "border cultures" and "border communities" and in so doing reproducing a very traditional anthropology with a focus on "local communities" (i.e., those long resident) and their negotiation of identity and survival. While this does remain a vital concern for researchers in many areas, attention also needs to be given to more complex cultural configurations emerging in Southeast Asian borderlands. In the case of Thailand's Lower South, the bor-

derland can be seen as ambivalent, dynamic, and heterogeneous, constituting, in a sense, a "third country" (see, e.g., Anzaldúa 1999: 25). This borderland is being shaped by patterns of movement and engagement
between groups of people who are, in many cases, not quintessentially
"local," yet nor are they totally "foreign": they are mobile "communities"
of visitation and sojourn that are central to the reproduction of the Lower
South Thailand borderland as both a sexualized and a sacred space.

Touring a Sacred Borderland: Big Buddhas, Blessings, and Magic
Thailand, the Happy Frontier of Holiday Merit Making

"If you want happy, you go Thailand." Such a statement might at first be
expected to have come from a hedonistic tourist in search of profane pleasures. But it did not: The speaker was a Chinese-Malaysian man, Mr. Lee,
who runs a small minibus business in a town in Kedah state. On this occasion he was bringing middle-aged housewives to temples and shrines in
Hat Yai and its vicinity for a one-day visit. The first stop was the Bodhisattva Kuan Yin statue (in Thai pronunciation the name is rendered
"Kuan Im"), erected on the Kho Hong hills overlooking the city of Hat Yai.
As Mr. Lee spoke to me about his business, his passengers rushed to a stall
to purchase incense before mounting the steps of the pavilion, which supported the white jade statue of the Chinese goddess. This statue of Kuan
Yin is one among an increasing number of monumental religious sites
and shrines that have been erected in the border provinces of South Thailand over the last decade. Officials and business organizations in Hat Yai
note that tourists' shrine visits generate relatively low average expenditure—estimated at roughly 10 per cent of direct tourist per capita spending—but they also stress that it is a core element in visitor's itineraries, so
much so that temple- and shrine-related festivals have received considerable official promotion in the past decade (Author's interviews with
Deputy Secretary of the Hat Yai Chamber of Commerce, and the President, Hat Yai Federation of Tourist Organizations, February 2003). This
average estimation of expenditure also masks a wide variation in the levels at which Malaysians and Singaporeans engage with religious sites and
practitioners in the borderland. Notably, Malay Muslims are not part of
this conspicuous phenomenon of shrine and sacred site visitation.
Although the Lower South does feature many mosques, they are not particularly exceptional to Malays.

Mr. Lee summarized the motivations and experience of his Sino-
Malaysian passengers in terms of "happiness," a simple summation of a
cluster of dispositions and feelings that other shrine visitors express in more
specific terms. These terms all center on the aims of gaining blessing, good
fortune, safety, and good health through giving offerings and affirming religious commitment by paying respect to sacred images. Thai shrine visitors

express the motivations and benefits in terms of the "merit" (*bun*) they seek for another lifetime, and the comfort (*khwansabai chai*) that they derive from the rituals of offering. Showing respect (*nap theu*) to sacred images through customary routines of obeisance (*wai phra*) is an expected and usually necessary activity in Thai traditional travel. These dispositions are compatible with long-held Chinese practices and beliefs connected with showing respect to spirits (*bai shen*), seeking help from deities (*qin shen*), and accumulating merit (*ji de*). It is not only the more purely Chinese shrines and monuments that attract Chinese Malaysians and Singaporeans, but also Thai temples and monuments. Forms of Theravada Buddhism, Thai and Sinhalese, are not entirely foreign; indeed, Thai temples and monks have been established in Penang and Singapore since at least the 1930s, and longer in the case of the established Thai communities in Kedah, Kelantan, Perak, Perlis, and Ipoh (see, e.g., McDougall 1956: 45–50). The juxtaposition of different but complementary religious sites in the Lower South accommodates the essentially syncretic nature of Chinese religious beliefs, which combine Buddhism and Taoism and a reverence for objects assigned sanctity through association with legend and miracles. Further, this accommodation of syncretic Nanyang Chinese religious impulses in the Lower South is extended and crystallized in certain places where the sacred objects and deities associated with Mahayana and Theravada Buddhism and Taoism are all concentrated in the same site. But the religious culture of these visitors is not simply a continuation of older forms of Chinese folk religion common in the region: reform and lay-oriented Buddhist movements with a strong emphasis on meditation and Dharma study have also strongly influenced and informed the dispositions of many shrine and temple visitors (see, e.g., Clammer 1993). Malaysian and Singaporean visitors to Lower South Thailand engage with religious sites at various levels and approach such visitations with a range of dispositions. Most commonly, visitors encounter shrines, temples, and monuments as part of a general sightseeing travel itinerary in a package tour or one-day tour program, usually in family groups transported in coaches and minibuses. Another subset of visitors comprises those who travel as devotees of particular shrines or sanctuaries, or special tour groups who attend at temples for meditation practices. At another level there are individuals who have specific objectives in connection with particular monks, individual temples, shamans, and specialists in magic tattoos.

It might be considered highly questionable to label as "pilgrims" the thousands of Sino-Malaysian and Singaporean visitors to the shrines, religious monuments, and temple festivals of Lower South Thailand. After all, for most visitors attendance at these sites constitutes just one experience in a cluster of activities that include shopping and eating at restaurants. Nonetheless, such visits are an indispensable activity in their itineraries: prayers at shrines and monuments, although relatively brief, are taken seriously, even if for Western observers the behavior may appear highly mechanical and perfunctory. The profane/sacred mix in contemporary Asian pilgrimage is no exception to a worldwide historical pattern that has seen an increasing convergence between travel for devotional purposes and vacationing travel that incorporates religious activity (see, e.g., Cohen 1992; Grayburn 1983; Turner 1973; Tomasi 2002; Reader 1987). But it is hazardous to posit an ideal "true" form of the pilgrim and pilgrimage practice against which more apparently touristic forms can be dismissed as simply profane, superficial, and devoid of religious meaning. With reference to Chinese popular religious traditions in general and Malaysia in particular, Jean De Bernardi has stressed that "the sacred" is widely dispersed in everyday life and space, and thus modernist Western attributions of clear and isolated dichotomies between "sacred" and "profane" realms are not applicable in interpreting what De Bernardi denotes as "Chinese religious culture"—a syncretic blend of Taoism, Buddhism, and traditional beliefs expressed not through formal canonical doctrine but in popular worship and calendrical festivals (De Bernardi 1992: 252–54). This has importance in interpreting Chinese travel behavior, because it helps us comprehend the ease with which auspicious objects and sites are accommodated in the context of apparently profane holiday activities such as shopping and sightseeing. I suggest in this context that the Chinese Malaysians and Singaporeans who visit the religious monuments of Lower South Thailand do indeed act as pilgrims, at least in those moments where they encounter deity images, pay their respects, donate money, and pray for good health and good fortune. This is also consistent with common Thai patterns of travel, where *pai thieo* (literally "going around," an expression denoting a range of travel behaviors) invariably involves visits to temples and where, conversely, specific journeys devoted to temple-based worship (as in Thot Phapha) generally include shopping as an integral part of the overall travel occasion.

The particular appeals of the Lower South to Singaporeans and Malaysians, and the varying levels of their engagement with religious sites and institutions of the borderland, lie in the ways that they facilitate a form of ethno-religious identification. This may not approximate fully to Victor Turner's depiction of the pilgrim's experience as "communitas"—a deeply felt sense of religious "oneness" generated by the shared liminality of journeys to, and encounters with, sacred "centers out there" (Turner 1973). Nonetheless, at a variety of levels we can see that different engagements among visitors to sites in the Lower South evoke broader communities formed around ethno-religious markers and devotional practice. I suggest that "cultural communion" (rather than communitas) is a more appropriate phrase to characterize this process of collective identification. For the Nanyang Chinese, Lower South Thailand acts in a sense as a hinterland of diaspora identity, functioning as a haven for affirming and expressing shared elements of culture with a freedom not entirely possible in Malaysia or Singapore. The religious accommodations represented by numerous sites and practitioners in the borderland of the Lower South make it a fertile space in Southeast Asia where communities of affiliation are evoked and generated.

Tourists and local Thais alike frequently affirm the benefits and inherent goodness of Thailand's accommodation of religious expression, and believe that it is this accommodation that draws people to visit the Lower South from Malaysia and Singapore. To this dimension of "accommodation" in the Thai religious sphere as a factor for attraction, we should also add "proliferation" to highlight the number and variety of sacred sites and religious and magical practitioners that are concentrated in the provinces of the Lower South. Consideration of a selection of these helps to highlight the cultural and economic processes and interactions at play in the production and reproduction of the borderland and its role as a sacralized space.

The Familiar

The Chinese shrines of the Lower South are sites that are clearly familiar to Chinese visitors from Malaysia and Singapore: they have recognizable functions and rituals of respect, and their histories and deities are easily accessible by recourse to Chinese language literature or shrine attendants who can communicate in Chinese dialects and Mandarin. In an important sense, these sites affirm to their visitors the shared character of Nanyang Chinese identity through religion. Like other Nanyang Chinese, the Sino-Thai of the Lower South have adapted to the customs of their new homeland but maintain ethnic continuity and collective cohesion through widely shared religious practices (Raybeck 1983: 17). Notable among these has been the veneration of gods and deities of southern China, as well as of local pioneer gods and deities representing the collective settlement experience of the Chinese trading diaspora (Tadao 1981). The popularity of worship of the female deity Lim Ko Niao at the Leng Chu Kiang shrine in Thailand's southern coastal town of Pattani assumes significance in this context of collective Nanyang Chinese memory, and its popularization through tourism visitation and promotion. The divine status of Lim Ko Niao has been traced to a local legend: Sometime during the seventeenth century, a Chinese woman by this name sailed from Fujian province in southern China to the Malay seaport of Pattani in order to find her only brother, who had settled there. The legend has it that her brother had converted to Islam and married a princess of the royal house of Pattani. He had been given the task of constructing the mosque of Kerisik for the Sultan. Apparently in protest at her brother's conversion, the sister committed suicide. Prior to this she laid a curse on the mosque, and as a result it was never completed. Some time after her death, Lim Ko Niao's spirit reputedly showed itself to seafarers and travelers and successfully protected them from danger. An image was fashioned from the wood of the cashew tree on which she had hanged herself and was later enshrined in the Leng Chu Kiang shrine in the center of Pattani town (Wyatt and Teeuw 1970: 224). Over the years an annual ceremony evolved whereby the sacred image of Lim Ko Niao, together with effigies of nineteen other gods and deities, is transported across the Bang Nara River and through a barrier of fire back to the shrine. The fame of the deity was formerly largely confined to the Sino-Thai of the region, but over the past decade, encouraged by publicity from the shrine's organizing association and the Tourist Authority of Thailand, the shrine and its dramatic ceremony now attracts thousands of visitors, especially Chinese from Malaysia (Vipasai 2002).

The Remote

In attending the Chinese shrines in places such as Betong, Hat Yai, Pattani, and Sungai-Kolok, visitors encounter little that is strange, mysterious, or remote to their religious experience. There are, however, sites in the Lower South that embody something of the character of pilgrimage places dubbed by Victor Turner as "centers out there"—places that are geographically remote and associated with auspiciousness, power, and mystery (Turner 1973). Such a place is the cave sanctuary of Wat Khao Roop Chang ('The Temple of the Elephant-shaped Mountain').

Wat Khao Roop Chang is located in Sadao District of Songkhla province, some twelve kilometers from the Thai border town of Pedang Besar. Two key features characterize this as a site that taps both Chinese Mahayana and Thai Theravada Buddhist traditions, and endow it with sacredness and miraculous power: first, as a cave and a mountain sanctuary, it evokes long-held associations between remote places and spiritual power; and second, the special character of the place is reinforced by its intimate connection with a charismatic monk and his revelatory visions (see, e.g., Tambiah 1984; Yü 1992). At first sight there is little about this site that suggests it is a remote and wild place traditionally connected with the lives of pious wandering monks. Rather, it resembles a monumental and syncretic religious theme park. The sanctuary incorporates statues of Chinese Mahayana deities (such as Kuan Yin and a host of other Bodhisattvas), Thai-style Bhuddha images, a Brahma image and a huge replica of an Indian temple, together with numerous Chinese-style embellishments including a dragon balustrade flanking the steps leading to the cave, and an elaborate Chinese-style entrance gate. Whereas the cave sanctuary was certainly remote at the time of its first occupation, it is now easily accessible by sealed road. Nonetheless, the temple's reputation is directly connected to its evolution as a highly potent site through the activities of the Chinese monk Meng San and the sacrifices he has made in the name of the Bodhisattva Kuan Yin.

The story of the abbot of Wat Khao Roop Chang is recorded in a guide published by a Mahayana Buddhist foundation based in Singapore. Printed in the Thai, Chinese, and English languages, the guide relates how the Chinese-born Meng San settled in Singapore and later studied with a Ch'an (Zen) master. Traveling to Taiwan in 1967, Meng San was ordained as a Mahayana Buddhist monk. In the following year he returned to Singapore and joined a pilgrimage to holy sites in Sri Lanka and India. While visiting Bodhagaya he undertook his first trial of faith by burning off one of his fingers. On his return from India he went to Penang, Malaysia, where he met a prominent Thai Buddhist and joined him in meditation practice in a cave at the foot of the mountain known as Khao Roop Chang, after which Meng San was ordained into the Theravadan monkhood. His solitary meditation in the cave sanctuary was graced by a number of visions of Mahayana deities, and Meng San pledged to build statues in their honor. He then set out on a rigorous, solitary walk to Singapore and soon attracted a following of devotees. With the aid of donations and volunteer assistance, he began excavation of the Khao Roop Chang cave and added a number of facilities, such as water tanks and generators for lighting the cave (Prawat Wat Khao Roop Chang 2001). The subsequent development of the cave temple over the past several decades has been generated by a self-reinforcing process, or cycle: Meng San began with self-mutilation—having cut off both his ears and burned another finger—and pledges to the deities, then fulfilled these pledges by erecting holy images with the aid of funds solicited from a growing body of devotees in southern Thailand, Singapore, and Malaysia. Meng San's ascetic journeying, his visions while meditating, and his self-mutilation are both recognizable and complementary expressions of faith in the traditions of the Ch'an (Zen) and the Pure Land schools that dominate Chinese Mahayana Buddhism (Chen 1973: 268–70; Cleary 1994: 1–21; Reichelt 1934: 273–74).

Visitors attend Wat Khao Roop Chang as individuals, in family groups, or as members of organized bus tours. Activity at the cave sanctuary is punctuated by various ceremonies devoted to the dedication of new monuments and structures or the calendrical celebrations associated with particular deities. People's level of engagement with the temple and its activities varies, depending on whether visitors are weekend tourists, devotees of Meng San, members of Buddhist organizations, or monks. Although the site incorporates images associated with Thai Theravada Buddhism and is officially registered as a temple under Thai Sangha law, its statuary and decoration are overwhelmingly Chinese in their characteristically syncretic blend of Mahayana Buddhist and Taoist imagery. Critical to reinforcing the prominence of this site is the association of the Thai-Malaysian borderland with potency and power. The story of Meng San reinforces a widely shared view in Malaysia and Singapore that Thailand is a particularly ancient and sacred place imbued with spiritual potency, while at the same time the narrative is consistent with the founding myths of more ancient pilgrimage sites in China (see, e.g., Yü 1992).

The Monumental

Large images of the Buddha, Boddhisatvas, and other sacred images have become a prominent feature of the sites attracting visitors to Lower South Thailand. They are typically promoted in tourist brochures (and on placards at the sites themselves) as being unique by virtue of their size—the "biggest" reclining Buddha in southern Thailand, for example, or the "tallest" Kuan Yin statue in the county. This proliferation of gigantic monuments is conspicuously on the rise in the broader Asian region, extending from India to China, and it is hardly unique to Thailand (see, e.g., Reina 2000). Most obviously this phenomenon has emerged in connection with the economic prosperity of the region over the last two decades of the twentieth century and an associated surge in the erection of highly visible landmarks on the part of particular religious groups, state agencies, or both of these in combination. I suggest that we can conceptualize this as a "symbolic economy" of religious sites, a system driven by a cultural imperative among both local people and visitors to materialize devotion in monumental form and attract spiritual investment through popular patronage. This system, at its most obvious level, involves the production and marketing of objects and places for forms of "consumption" such as mass tourism, a process widely theorized by Western urbanists and geographers in terms of commodification, embodied in the phrase "the selling of places" (Urry 1995; Zukin 1991). But for Thailand and the Asian region in general, it is not adequate to explain or understand the significance of religious monument-building only in terms of the material imperatives surrounding the fabrication of spectacles and places for profit making.[3] As Richard O'Connor has emphasized, "merit" and the "market" have always been inextricably linked in the Thai religious system, and this is also an abiding nexus in Chinese religious culture (O'Connor 1986). Within Theravada and Mahayana Buddhist traditions (and those of other world religions), religious sites and monumental statues, whether new or old, are objects with a special kind of valency—that is, they are widely acknowledged as being endowed with spiritual and magic agency (Davis 1998). Their valency is founded on a widely shared and longstanding cultural disposition—embraced on both sides of the border—to sacralize sites and spaces (see, e.g., Askew 2003).

The visual featurism associated with this explosion of monument-oriented piety finds historical resonance in the large Buddha images produced by premodern societies throughout the region, and as such might be assumed simply to be a traditional expression of faith. But the contemporary impulse toward constructing large religious monuments is distinguished from motives for earlier monument building by its high level of competitiveness and featurism, characteristics that reflect the commercialism and market-oriented nature of contemporary religions in Asia and throughout the world (Lee 1993). The creation of religious landmarks is also critically connected to the production of landscapes for tourism and the competition between locales over status and income. Hat Yai's promotion of monument building over recent years may hence be at least partly attributable to the need to keep visitors in the vicinity of the city for longer periods, and thereby compete with Bangkok for pilgrim-tourists, by introducing powerful images that were once exclusive to Bangkok (e.g., the Thao Mahaphrom in Hat Yai, erected to compete with the Erawan Brahma shrine in the capital) (see Figure 8.2). Although it is multifaceted in its mix of Chinese and Thai symbolic elements, this symbolic economy of the Lower South highlights the affirmation (or at least the conspicuous rearticulation) of a coextensive Chinese ethno-religious identity straddling the national borders of Malaysia and Thailand and extending through to Singapore. Aihwa Ong has explored the varied ways that "diasporan-Chinese subjects" have sought to affirm identity through accumulating the symbolic capital of modernity in the contemporary period (Ong 1999). The borderland of the Lower South might be treated as a field for this diaspora's investment in symbolic capital of a more traditional kind dependent on, rather than detached from places.

Fig. 8.2. *Malaysian Chinese visitors paying respect to the Thao Mahaphrom image in Hat Yai. (photo M. Askew).*

The present complex of monumental religious sites popular among Malaysian and Singaporean visitors to the Lower South incorporates old images, renovated and transformed old sites, and completely new sites. The older monuments of Buddha images sited in Thai Theravada temples (*wat*). Itineraries are normally included in the one-day package tour marketed by the many small tourist agencies in Hat Yai. But the older Buddha images of the region are being overshadowed (literally and in terms of popularity) by monuments constructed little more than a decade ago, and in many cases less. These new images share a number of distinctive features. First, with only a few exceptions, they represent Chinese Mahayana Buddhist deities, or they are syncretic in religious expression. Second, the most popular of these sites stand out as individual monuments and are usually not associated with any temple complex or community of monks. These two characteristics are tied to the conditions that surround the images' construction; that is, the conscious building of landmarks by local authorities and organizations, and a symbolic orientation toward a local and visitor population that shares a common Chinese and Sino-Thai syncretic religious worldview. Third, many of the more popular new sites are located not in remote areas, but in the vicinity of Hat Yai, the region's tourist and business hub. The most prominent of these new monuments around Hat Yai are the Kuan Yin statue, the Brahma Shrine (Thao Mahaphrom), and a golden image of the "world conquering Buddha" (Phra Phuttha Bang Bert Lok). Here I will discuss the Kuan Yin statue as an exemplar.

On the hill next to the Thao Mahaphrom, a 9.9-meter statue of the Chinese Boddhisatva Kuan Yin stands on a lotus-flower pedestal, benevolently overlooking the city. It attracts an even larger number of visitors than the Thao Mahaphrom, including both Thais and tourists. They arrive in private cars, taxis, minibuses, and large tour coaches. The distinctiveness of this image, as reiterated by tourist guides, brochures, and ceremonial plaques at the site, is deemed to lie not in its size alone—after all, this statue can hardly compete with the indisputably tallest Kuan Yin in the South, a 19-meter-high statue built outside the city of Nakhon Sri Thammarat—but rather in its preciousness, as revealed through the rare and expensive materials of its construction and craftsmanship. The goddess and the images of the devotees that surround her have been carved from white jadeite stones specially obtained from China, and the designer, a skilled maker of monuments was also from China. Thus the significance of this Kuan Yin image, registered in its height, is reinforced by its association with material value, preciousness, and authenticity. Kuan Yin is popularly known as a goddess of mercy in the Mahayana Buddhist tradition. Visitors attending the image emphasize that they make obeisance to the image in order to seek protection from misfortune and relief from suffering, in contrast to the more pecuniary requests directed to the Brahma image on the adjacent hill.

Kuan Yin is very familiar to visitors from Malaysia, Singapore, and others from East Asian countries—notably the Taiwanese—who travel to Hat Yai and the Lower South. And it is just as significant that this Chinese Mahayana deity has been incorporated into the popular religion of Thai Buddhists in general over the past two decades. Depicted as a slender, white-robed female (either standing or seated) in Chinese Buddhist iconography, Kuan Yin is a feminized form of the Boddhisatva Avalokitesvara, whose avowed mission it is to help mortals escape the eternal cycle of suffering and rebirth (Martin and Ramsay 1995: 5–21). The various southern Chinese speech groups who settled in peninsular and mainland Southeast Asia in increasing numbers from the nineteenth century recognized Kuan Yin as one of their numerous important deities and maintained images of her in their shrines (Hamilton 1999: 3; McDougall 1956: 20). Since the 1980s, Kuan Yin has come to be widely embraced as a popular deity among both Sino-Thais and Thais with no Chinese ancestry. Scholars have associated this phenomenon with the growth of prosperity-oriented cults that have accompanied economic growth in Thailand (see e.g., Jackson 1999: 268–73). The growing popularity of Kuan Yin has also been a Southeast Asian regional phenomenon, visible in neighboring Malaysia as well as Singapore (Lee and Ackerman 1997: 68–71). Given such contemporary trends, the construction of a spectacular monument to the goddess Kuan Yin on the hills outside Hat Yai is not particularly surprising, nor is it in any way alien to the syncretic religious landscape of Thailand.

The project of building an impressive monument to the Boddhistava Kuan Yin might perhaps be read simply as a local story of pride and place making. The project was devised and planned by the Hat Yai municipal authorities together with the city's thirteen Chinese shrine foundations. But this was far more than a local project. When viewed in the context of Hat Yai's reliance on tourist income, the monument's landmark value becomes immediately apparent. Even before its official unveiling, the Kuan Yin statue was incorporated into the list of Hat Yai's tourist attractions, an expanding ensemble of monumental sacred sites in Songkhla province, and particularly in the vicinity of the city. The statue symbolizes the dedication of the local Chinese of Hat Yai to the precepts of eclectic Buddhism, but more than this, its whole design and the widely publicized character of its construction also label the monument as Chinese in a very transnational sense. The Kuan Yin statue, though also patronized by Thai domestic tourists, gains most of its donations from Malaysian and Singaporean visitors. The names of these donors are conspicuously displayed on the marbled benches that congest the area surrounding the statue. The president of Hat Yai's Tourist Federation divulged to me that although there are Thai visitors who donate benches to the site, officials remove these and distribute them to local schools and temples. By contrast, most of the benches donated by Malaysians and Singaporians are retained to encourage their compatriots to donate money and gain blessings.

Magic and Monks

Although the continuous stream of coaches and minibuses bearing visitors to shrines, temples, and monuments is the most prominent sign of religious-oriented tourism in the Lower South, there is a less publicly visible, but nonetheless significant level of engagement occurring between visitors from Malaysia and Singapore, and Thai monks and practitioners of magic. In Hat Yai and other parts of the Lower South, individuals and small groups of friends seek out wise men (*achan*) and Theravada Buddhist monks who specialize in magic spells, fortune telling, and the application of magic tattoos. These seekers after magical power are distinguishable from the bulk of shrine goers on a number of counts: notably, they are almost exclusively male (in contrast to the families that dominate the visitor groups to the shrines and sanctuaries), and they include Singaporeans and Malaysians of Indian background as well as Chinese. Their knowledge about Thai monks and the *achan* has been gained not from official and commercial tourist sources, but from informal information networks in their own countries and in particular through local Thai taxi drivers, with whom they often cultivate enduring connections and friendship.

Achan Bom[4] is one of the most renowned practitioners of sacred tattoos and magic in Hat Yai. His activities and networks aptly illustrate the significance of the informal dynamics that sustain the encounters between Malaysians, Singaporeans, and the Lower South borderland. Achan Bom practices a range of magic crafts in a small shrine in a suburb of Hat Yai. The altar of his shrine exhibits the standard features of Thai spirit mediums, featuring a syncretic assemblage of images of revered Thai monks, King Chulalongkorn, and Chinese deities, as well as the obligatory image of a *rusi,* or hermit. It is to this shrine that many taxi drivers escort regular customers who indicate an interest in gaining advice or protection in the form of tattoos. Achan Bom's reputation is spread by word of mouth and attested to by stories of his satisfied customers. Sunthorn and Don, taxi drivers who ply their trade from outside two of Hat Yai's many tourist hotels, related to me how one Malaysian man attributed his miraculous survival in a severe car accident to the protective power of Achan Bom's tattoo. They reinforced this evidence of magical efficacy with stories of men who had used the auspicious numbers given them by Achan Bom to win large sums in the Malaysian government lottery. The walls of his shrine are covered with the names of Malaysians who have visited him and the amounts of money they have donated; so numerous are they that he erected a board outside his shrine with many more names of donors.

Practitioners of magic like Achan Bom attract a steady flow of Singaporean and Malaysian men who see in his tattoos and his divination a means of gaining protection from danger and ill health, as well as potency in the form of good luck to aid them in accumulating wealth and good fortune. Among his clients are also men who are drawn to study the arcane practices of magic, and he has several *luksit* (disciples) who have established shrines in their homes in Malaysia. Like other Thai magic practitioners, Achan Bom is frequently invited to visit his *luksit* in Malaysia and Singapore and dispense magic to his disciples' friends and acquaintances.

The Sexualized Borderland
A Permissive Space

The "sexualized" character of the borderland of the Lower South is expressed in and generated by a number of interacting processes, the two most obvious being large-scale movement of women from other parts of Thailand and neighboring regions to Hat Yai and the border towns to enter the various modes of sex and entertainment work, and their engagement in the gendered division of labor in the tourist-oriented work force. It is also expressed in the prominence of sexual desire among men visiting the borderland and the popular identification of the towns of the Lower South with the availability of sexual pleasure.[5] The sites of the Lower South's sex and entertainment sector constitute a permissive zone for thousands of Malaysian and Singaporean men to engage in forms of sexual and recreational behavior with a freedom and abandon impossible in their own countries. Behavioral sanctions imposed by legal/religious regimes as well as social and economic constraints in Malaysia and Singapore were frequent complaints among the male tourists—including those of Chinese, Malay, and Indian ethnicity—whom I encountered in the sex-trade sites along the border. For these men, Thailand represented an escape, albeit briefly, from the daily round of life in their own countries. The cathartic nature of the experience—which essentially involves drinking, involvement with sex workers, and often gambling—was succinctly expressed by Manu, an Indian Malaysian businessman from Ipoh, who proclaimed: "When we come to Thailand, we forget everything." For men like Manu, trips to the border are a seasonal event, a chance to escape with friends from the obligations of family life (including their wives) and the daily grind of work. For many others, who frequent the border weekly or every day, the borderland is an indispensable context for a permanent lifestyle of sojourn, one that often involves the maintenance of a Thai mistress or legal wife.

The varied practices and dispositions of the men traveling from across the border intersect with the movement of thousands of Thai women (and a smaller number of men) who move from the North and Northeast of Thailand into the tourist-oriented entertainment sector of the Lower South. Particularly in Hat Yai, this group also includes women from the provinces of the Lower South, Burma, and mainland China. They engage with the entertainment sector and its patrons in a range of modes, including direct sex work (as employees in small karaoke parlors and massage establishments), freelance prostitution (in pubs and discotheques), karaoke singing, and therapeutic massage (known as "ancient massage"). Although a pragmatic concern for income generation unites women's different styles of work, their own orientation to this work and their customers is varied, multifaceted, and mutable. The borderland is a dynamic, yet permanent, site for the convergence of mobile male and female bodies, whose interactions are shaped by the economy and infrastructure of border tourism and visitation.

The centrality of the sex trade to the Lower South's tourist economy has been noted since the early 1970s, particularly in connection with the region's main city of Hat Yai. In that decade, despite the fact that the countryside of the border provinces was considered dangerous owing to bandits, communist insurgents, and Muslim separatists, Hat Yai's tourist-based nightlife industry boomed and expanded (Wells 1973; Theh 1979). The gender sex ratio of tourists to the region provides one general background indicator of the continuing importance of sex-oriented tourism: two thirds of Malaysian and Singaporean tourists entering the Lower South as "international tourists" are male, and although the very high proportion of men recorded in the 1970s (around 90 percent) has declined (to 62.3 percent and 63.9 percent respectively for 1990 and 2000), men still outnumber women in tourist flows from these countries (TAT 1990: 22–23; TAT 2000: 33). Public comments by Malaysian and Singaporean governments on sex-oriented tourism in Thailand's Lower South have been generally subdued. The most explicit public acknowledgement of Malaysian sex tourism occurred in May 2000 when Prime Minister Mahathir openly warned Malaysian Muslim men of the risk of contracting AIDS by patronizing Thai prostitutes in Hat Yai and Songkhla (Deutsche Presse-Agentur 2000). Despite Mahathir's advice that men curb their sexual desires when in Thailand and thereby uphold the importance of the family and marriage (in particular he was stressing Muslim marriage), his statements have had little or no impact: the behavior of Malaysian men (Chinese, Indian, and Malay) in the borderland continues to contest and contradict the moral strictures of the Malaysian state. Local Thai tourism officials claim that sex-oriented tourism "nightlife" has declined at the expense of more wholesome enjoyments focusing on family-based tourism. But representatives of the hotel trade in Hat Yai point out that the sex and entertainment sector remains just as central in the preferences of visitors as it ever did (Author's interviews, TAT officials in Hat Yai, Head of Tourist Promotion Division, Hat Yai City, and President and Secretary of the Hat Yai Hotel Federation, January–February 2003).

The Sites and Infrastructure of the System

The sex-trade infrastructure of the lower south incorporates a range of interconnected services including transport, accommodation, eating establishments, and entertainment venues centered in Sino-Thai dominated settlements. The geographical hub of the tourist-oriented sex trade is the city of Hat Yai, in Songkhla province. As the largest urban center in South Thailand (with a population of over 150,000), the city maintains an overwhelming dominance in tourist accommodation when compared to the other principal Lower South urban settlements of Betong, Sungai-Kolok, and Ban Dan Nok. Not surprisingly, Hat Yai also hosts the greatest density and variety of sex-related entertainent venues (an estimated two-hundred) in all the border provinces. Sex-trade related venues span the gamut of types, ranging from cheap brothels and motels to karaoke bars of various types and sizes, massage parlors, and discotheques. Most of the larger hotels maintain a range of these venues within their premises. There are also homosexual and transvestite clubs catering to the more specialized desires of the tourist population. In the year 2000 it was estimated by one newspaper reporter that Hat Yai's commercial sex worker population numbered at least ten thousand (Charoon 2000). The other key sites of the sex trade in the Lower South are located directly on border crossings and maintain a more limited range of entertainment and sex-related venues. In the well established border trading towns of Betong (in Yala province opposite Kedah), Pedang Besar (in Songkhla province, opposite Perlis), and Sungai-Kolok (in Narathiwat Province, opposite Kelantan), the sex-related economy is articulated through the hotel accommodation facilities and service infrastructure. Prostitution-related venues in these settlements cluster inside hotels (pubs, singing cafes, and discotheques) or tend to concentrate along particular streets. Venues associated with the supply of tourist-related commercial sex services number approximately 71 in Betong, 50 in Sungai-Kolok, and 15 in Pedang Besar (author's field surveys, December 2001, June 2002).

In striking contrast to these market towns is the settlement of Ban Dan Nok ("Village of the outer side") in Sadao district of Songkhla province, which borders on Malaysia's Kedah state. This settlement has developed an almost exclusively sex trade-centered economy. Since the mid 1980s, due partly at least to the building of Malaysia's superhighway system, Dan Nok was transformed from a border crossing point with a small marketplace to a settlement of over 30 brothels and karaoke bars and a sex worker population numbering over 1,000 women (Chayanoot 1991: 41; Scott 1995). Throughout the 1990s Dan Nok continued to grow, and by the end of 2001 there were over 140 sex-related establishments with a sex worker population of at least 2,000 (author's field survey, December 2001).

Supply and Access to Commercial Sex Services

Malaysian and Singaporean men access prostitution services in a variety of settings, including those that are specifically connected with the sex act, such as massage parlors, brothels, or men's own hotel rooms, as well as entertainment venues featuring music (karaoke lounges), dancing (discotheques), and drinking (pubs and music cafes). Women's sex work correspondingly spans a range of modes: full time employment in establishments devoted to commercial sex supply, such as brothels (thinly disguised as "karaoke bars") and "modern" massage parlors; work as "ancient" masseuses or singers in karaoke lounges and "cafes" where sex is negotiable and separate from the establishment's charges; or work as freelance prostitutes (*phuying chap khaek*) who attend discotheques and encounter tourists independently in hotel lobbies (this latter mode is almost exclusively concentrated in Hat Yai). A certain measure of this variety is present in most of the border settlements; however, it is the system of "booking" that is the predominant means by which women's services are engaged. This booking system is one of the key features differentiating Malaysian/Singaporean customer-prostitute transactions from those in the Western-oriented sex-trade zones of Thailand, and it is common to other sex-trade districts in the regions of Southeast Asia dominated by the Chinese, including Malaysia and Singapore (see e.g., Brazil 1998: 89–93). According to this system, a customer "books" a woman for a specified amount of time, generally but not exclusively with the "captain," an employee of an establishment who is responsible for attracting customers and selecting women for them (Figure 8.3). The period of time for which a woman is booked may be short (for the sole purpose of sex), several hours, or a whole day. Under the booking sys-

Figure 8.3. A captain and bar worker sitting outside a karaoke lounge.

tem the full payment for the woman's sexual services and time is paid in advance to the management, with this income split between sex workers and employees. Women usually obtain extra income from tips customarily given them by customers.

The booking system applies to a range of establishments, even to those that seem, by their appearance, to be "closed"—that is, those businesses that are set up for the sole purpose of providing sexual services, with minimal allowance for any social interaction between client and sex worker. Sino-Malaysian tourists who prefer to sit in karaoke lounges and pay women singers to sit with them (generally 100 Thai Baht per hour) sometimes denigrate the more basic establishments as "f--ng shops," despite their euphemistic designation as "karaoke bars" (a measure employed by owners simply to reduce direct police harassment). Here we can distinguish these "direct" commercial sex supply establishments from the "indirect" singing karoke lounges by calling the former places "sex-karaoke." Although such establishments might be simply described as "brothels," they are far more flexible than the term implies, because they act literally as bases for escort services. Most sex workers in these establishments conduct their work outside the venues: indeed, most sex-karaoke are so small that they can not accommodate sex between customers and sex workers. They are, in fact, founded on the assumption that customers have sex with the women in their hotel rooms. The booking system, and its sliding scale of fees based on time duration and type of service, is employed by many Malaysian and Singaporean tourists to develop companionships with women. The system, ostensibly restrictive, actually ensures that men who have a particular liking for certain women, may spend time with them outside the employer's establishment. This system contrasts strikingly with Western-oriented venues such as beer bars and go-go bars, where much of the entertainment and interaction takes place in the establishment. Women who are booked for an evening or longer customarily accompany their customers to the large karaoke bars, restaurants, and discotheques, and sometimes on a weekend holiday (for example, to Samilla beach near Songkhla township). In Dan Nok, one role of the captains is to escort the women to men's hotel rooms, where they also collect booking fees in advance should customers choose any of the women brought for their perusal. Hotel bellboys, taxi drivers, and motorcycle taxi drivers act as intermediaries in booking women for customers in hotels. The widespread and varied use of the booking system among cross-border visitors highlights the difficulty of strictly separating tourists according to clear categories. Thus we find that ostensibly respectable tourists entering the Lower South on coach tours devoted to shopping and shrine visiting with their families also engage in commercial sex through the use of the booking system.

Relationships

Thousands of Malaysian and Singaporean men travel to the sex-trade sites of the Lower South for the supremely practical end of brief relaxation and sexual release. Nonetheless, the transactions that take place between many of these men and the women sex workers often develop in various ways beyond the basic exchange of sex for money. The ability of the Thai women sex workers to act as companions and become "girlfriends" is emphasized strongly on one of the major Singaporean websites devoted to sex-based tourism for men. Paradoxically, this dimension of the industry is also a source of considerable confusion for many men who find it difficult to disentangle the emotional from the material bonds in their relationships (Sammyboy.com). This mirrors the dilemmas faced there by western men, as recorded in both popular and more scholarly literature (see, e.g., Cohen 1982). In its simplest form, the highly personalized dimension of sex worker-customer encounters can be seen in the relationships of familiarity that evolve between women and their regular customers. These types of relationships are generated easily because a large proportion of the male tourists are return visitors. Connections are also easy to maintain because of the ease of cross-border communication by mobile telephone across the border. In fact, in their workplaces women are frequently occupied speaking to their *khaek pracham* (regular customers) or *faen* (boyfriends) on their mobile telephones. Like their counterparts in the Western-oriented sex trade, these women stand to benefit financially from cultivating regular customers (see, e.g., Askew 1999). Women who are in the sex-trade work force for lengthy periods are adept at learning the Malay language and elements of Chinese dialects, particularly Hokkien, which enhances their appeal to men of these speech groups, particularly older generation men who have never learned English.

At stage beyond the sex worker's role as a regular companion, a women leaves her place of work with the financial support of a male companion to become his mistress. This is a frequent occurrence. This form of relationship, as elsewhere, combines a mix of emotional and pragmatic bonds between men and women. On the part of men, particularly Chinese men who are already married, keeping of a mistress gives them the benefit of a permanent companion across the border, and it is also an option that many men recommend as an apparent safeguard against the danger of contracting AIDS. Among Chinese men in particular, the mistress serves an important role as a marker of masculine status and potency (see, e.g., Bao 1994). I suggest that maintaining cross-border mistresses by Chinese men is a continuation (albeit in transmuted and attenuated form) of a once widely practiced tradition of polygyny in the peninsular (for which see Clammer 2002: 215–51). Malay Muslim men sometimes legitimize the maintenance of a permanent sexual companion across the border is sometimes legitimized by the contracting temporary *mut'a* marriages with Thai women whom they have met at sex and other entertainment venues. The practice of *mut'a* marriage is frowned upon by Sunni Muslims, but it is accepted among Shi'ites.[6] It is commonly known that Muslim Malays arrange to take mistresses under the guise of *mut'a* marriages in Thailand by employing Shi'ite imams to authorize the arrangement (personal communication with Hashim Abdulhammid, June 2002). This seems to be a practice favored by older Malay men with religious scruples. A number of men I encountered in this research emphasized the importance of maintaining Thai mistresses across the border because Thailand represented a haven for them, a place to feel content and free of the stresses of their everyday lives at home. This highlights the important function of the tourist border space of the Lower South as a critical sexual and recreational hinterland for Malaysia and Singapore. Women benefit from these alliances at various levels. Formal marriage between Malaysian men (Chinese, Indian, and Malay) and the Thai sex workers to whom they form attachments is a common occurrence. The numerous women in Dan Nok with whom I discussed the issue of marriage and Malaysian men expressed no qualms about the necessity to convert to Islam in the event of formal marriage to a Malay Muslim, as long as the partnership was deemed a true commitment. This highlights the persistent characteristic of Thai prostitution as "open ended," that is, as a practice where the meaning of transactions is both multifaceted and mutable (see, e.g., Cohen 1993).

Border Lifestyles

The tourist-related infrastructure in the Lower South supports a space that functions as a tolerance zone for Malaysian and Singaporean men. It incorporates dimensions that are both "familiar" and "different" to these visitors. The familiarity is generated by certain cultural and linguistic similarities between visitor's societies and the host societies of the Sino-Thai township enclaves, and it is enhanced by the geographical proximity of this zone to the visitors' countries of origin and the frequency with which they engage with its key sites. Particularly at the border crossings such as Dan Nok, the settlements have developed as virtual colonies of Malaysian men, who visit weekly or even stay in Thailand every evening, simply commuting to their workplaces across the border in Malaysia. The borderland functions as a haven for this non-native "community" of men together with their Thai wives, mistresses, and lovers.

The critical "differences" that also imbue the sites of this border zone, and continue to draw an intensive circulation of visiting males, are represented by the legal/social regime of Thailand, which contrasts markedly with those of Malaysia and Singapore in that it permits behaviors that are illicit and illegal in visitor's countries of origin.[7] Hat Yai and the border towns of Lower South Thailand share similar functions with other borderland "pleasure peripheries" in the Asian region, such as the Indonesian islands of Batam and Bintan for Singaporean men, and Guangdong province for denizens of Hong Kong (for which see Brazil 1998: 77–78; Grundy-Warr and Perry 2001; Lau and Thomas 2001; Lindquist 2002).

The sexualized borderland of Lower South Thailand is a site for the expression of traditional masculinity and potency through a range of characteristically male rituals and symbols, incorporating social bonding behaviors, sexual release, and especially the acquisition of power and status through the maintenance of mistresses. In short, the borderland functions as a space of catharsis. This is expressed succinctly in the words of Mr. Yo, a Malaysian businessman who travels regularly into Thailand to visit his Thai mistress (a former masseuse in an ancient massage establishment), and to gamble and drink with his Malaysian and Thai male friends: "This [Thailand] is the place where I release tension." A married man, Mr Yo was broadly representative of many other Chinese-Malaysians with whom I conducted conversations in Dan Nok, Hat Yai, and elsewhere: he maintained a Chinese wife and family in Malaysia and a mistress in Thailand. It is not too farfetched to propose that this practice represents an adaptive form of traditional Chinese polygyny, one that is no longer practical or feasible in modern Malaysian society, yet remains entirely possible, both logistically and financially, on the borderland.

Crossing between Sex and the Sacred

I have used the themes of "sex" and "the sacred" in this paper to characterize two prominent forms of behavior engaged in by cross-border visitors, organized around particular clusters of sites in the landscape of the Lower South. In general we can analyze these as two distinct systems, with distinguishable constituencies. However, it would be a mistake to strictly separate tourists according to clear categories, for we find that men visiting the Lower South in mixed groups on coach tour also use commercial sex workers surreptitiously. To my initial surprise, I learned through a number of Thai taxi driver informants that Malay Muslim and Sino-Malaysian men visiting Hat Yai with their families frequently use them to book prostitutes in the rooms of nearby hotels for short periods of sex without the knowledge of their spouses. And just as men can incorporate sexual indulgence into an ostensibly innocent family holiday of shopping and sacred site visitation, so too do many men, traveling singly or in all-male groups take time out from their hedonistic sojourns to attend shrines and other sacred sites, purchase Buddhist amulets, and visit monks to obtain auspicious tattoos. There is no apparent sequence in these men's activities, such as seeking purification before or after indulgence in bodily pleasures. I suggest that this intimate connection between the blessing and physical catharsis that men seek in the Lower South can be framed in terms of a search for complementary virility and power—a potency for which holy men, shrines, and women act as the practical vehicles.

Conclusion

The borderland of Lower South Thailand has emerged largely as a product of border-crossing travel and visiting practices that have become integrated into an increasingly organized, but also multilayered tourist system, operating at formal and informal levels and involving different relationships connecting people to sites, activities, and patterns of movement. Viewed from an economic perspective of supply and demand, the key sex- and religious-oriented tourism sectors of Lower South Thailand might be viewed respectively as providing a passive field of supply of female bodies for the outlet of masculine sexual energies and an ensemble of variously picturesque and monumental religious sites for the diversion of families seeking respite from shopping expeditions. An ethnographic focus on the people engaged in border-crossing visitation reveals, however, that the borderland functions at a range of levels and accommodates varied patterns of movement and engagement between people.

As proposed in the introduction to this volume, borderlands offer a vantage point from which to view cultural processes and the negotiation of identities among people and communities in relation to the ideological constructs and identity discourses of the nation-state. Animated by features representing both difference and familiarity to its visitors, the Southern Thai borderland acts as a critical site for a number of processes that reveal forms of transgression and affirmation on the part of people crossing national frontiers. For instance, I have suggested that for Malaysian Chinese, religious sites on this borderland facilitate the affirmation of a transnational Chinese ethno-religious identity, encouraging a mode of cultural communion that is untrammelled by the surveillance of the Malay Islamic state. For both Chinese Singaporeans and Malaysians, the southern Thai borderland has enduring appeal as an extensive field for Buddhist merit making, one where their donations have had a tangible effect on the landscape. In this—albeit fabricated and featuristic—landscape, the generating of a symbolic economy of monumental symbols around Hat Yai and other sites represents more than simply a mechanism for drawing tourists to consume goods and spend their holidays; it is also symbolic of a shared concern with religious merit whereby visitors establish bonds with these sites. Others form enduring relationships with temples and religious practitioners. As a sexual space, the borderland accommodates the transgressive behaviors of Malaysians and Singaporeans escaping constraints and restrictions on commercial sex and entertainment in their natal homelands. Yet here too, there are variations in the meanings and modes of encounters between Malaysian and Singaporean men—Chinese, Indian, and Malay—

and the Thai women engaged in the entertainment industry. In particular we have seen that large numbers of men and women either marry or otherwise maintain enduring partnerships, often leading to men becoming semi-permanent sojourners on the borderland.

I have suggested that the distinctive patterns of movement, interaction, and motivation of visitors and sojourners in this borderland are summarized by the twin dimensions of "sex" and the "sacred." Yet, viewed as clusters of activities around particular sites, these two dimensions are not entirely mutually exclusive, more precisely, shrine attendance does not necessarily preclude engagement in hedonistic pleasures. It is in this way that we can portray the borderland in general terms as a cathartic space, open to various forms of transgression among visitors who, in various ways, are escaping the modernity of their own states, whether it be the regulatory environment and secularism of Singapore or the restrictive regime of Islamic Malaysia. But this should not be taken to imply that the borderland functions simply, or only, as a place of pleasure consumption or temporary escape for tense and overworked Malaysians and Singaporeans. This borderland is in many ways a space-in-between, a place where a variety of international "communities"—ranging from devotees and their religious/magic practitioners to men, wives, and mistresses—are continually being generated by modes of religious involvement and cross-border encounters.

Notes

1. For discussion of field observations and comments on earlier drafts of this chapter, I wish to thank Erik Cohen, Michael Herzfeld, Mark Stevenson, and Tom Wilson.
2. Over a million Malaysians and over 650,000 Singaporeans visited Thailand in the year 2000; of these, eight out of every ten Malaysians entered Thailand via the border crossing points of three Thai provinces of Songkhla, Yala, and Narathiwat, while 22 percent of all Singaporean tourists entered via the Lower South (TAT 2000: 23; Immigration Bureau, Police Department 2000a). Approximately 90 percent of visitors entering the Lower South border crossings are Malaysians, many using short-term border passes, and most traveling across the border by car. The majority of these visitors confine their activities to the Thai border provinces (TAT 2000: 28; Immigration Bureau, Police Department 2000b).
3. Note that I apply "symbolic economy" here in a rather different way from that of Sharon Zukin (1995), who uses this expression to portray the symbolic fashioning of public space by corporate capital in urban North America. While the process of production and marketing of images in her system may be broadly comparable to the process I describe in southern Thailand and Asia in general, the dimension of popular identification with religious objects is not part of her conceptual scheme.
4. I have disguised the *achan's* true identity here by using an invented name.
5. In using this characterization I draw on the work of Ursula Biemann (2000).
6. For a discussion of the disputes over the relevance and legitimacy of the mut'a marriage in contemporary Islam, see *A Shi'ite Encyclopedia*, Gale Publishing, 1995, Chapter 6A [Version 2.0, Internet Edition].

7. In Malaysia, the strict enforcement of legal sanctions against the sex industry and the application of the strict *shariah* law in some states contrasts strikingly with the openness and ease of access to sex workers in Thailand across the border (Nagaraj and Yahya 1998). In Singapore, access to sex workers is easier for men, but restricted by high prices and the limited size of the trade. Thus, many Singaporean men travel outside their country's borders to access prostitutes' services.

References

Anzaldúa, Gloria. 1999. *Borderlands/La Frontera.* 2nd ed. San Francisco: Aunt Lute Books.

Askew, Marc. 1998. "City of Women, City of Foreign Men: Working Spaces and Re-working Identities among Female Sex Workers in Bangkok's Tourist Zone." *Singapore Journal of Tropical Geography* 19, no. 2: 130–50.

——. 2003. "Transformations and Continuities: Sacralization, Space and Memory in Contemporary Bangkok." In Ronald Lukens-Bull, ed., *Sacred Places and "Modern" Landscapes: Sacred Geography in South and Southeast Asia.* Tempe, Arizona: Monograph Series Press, Program for Southeast Asian Studies, Arizona State University.

Bao, Jiemin. 1994. *Marriage among Ethnic Chinese in Bangkok: An Ethnography of Gender, Sexuality, and Ethnicity over Two Generations.* Ph.D. dissertation, University of California, Berkeley.

Biemann, Ursula. 2000. *Been There and Back to Nowhere: Gender in Transnational Spaces, Postproduction Documents 1988–2000.* Berlin: B Books.

Brazil, David. 1998. *No Money, No Honey: A Candid Look at Sex for Sale in Singapore.* 4th ed. Singapore: Angsana Books.

Carsten, Janet. 1998. "Borders, Boundaries, Tradition and State on the Malaysian Periphery." In Thomas M. Wilson and Hastings Donnan, eds., *Border Identities: Nation and State at International Frontiers.* Cambridge: Cambridge University Press.

Chayanoot Khlongsangson. 1991. *Khwamchu dan sukhaphap kap phritikam anamai khong sopheni nai kanbongkan rok ed. Koroni suksa thi Ban Dan Nork, Amphur Sadao, Changwat Songkhla* [Health Beliefs and Health Behaviour of Prostitutes in Aids Prevention: A Case Study of Ban Dan Nok, Amphur Sadao, Songkhla Province], M.Ed. thesis, Prince of Songkhla University.

Che'n, Kenneth K. S. 1973. *The Chinese Transformation of Buddhism.* New Jersey: Princeton University Press.

Clammer, John. 1993. "Religious Pluralism and Chinese Beliefs in Singapore." In Cheu Hock Tong ed., *Chinese Beliefs and Practices in Southeast Asia.* Petaling Jaya: Pelanduk Publications.

——. 2002. *Diaspora and Identity: The Sociology of Culture in Southeast Asia.* Subang Jaya, Selangor: Pelanduk Publications.

Cleary, Jonathan C., transl. 1994. *Pure Land Pure Mind: The Buddhism of Masters Chu-hung and Tsung-pen.* New York: Sutra Translation Committee of the United States and Canada.

Cohen, Erik. 1982. "Thai Girls and Farang Men: The Edge of Ambiguity." *Annals of Tourism Research* 9, no. 3: 403–28.

——. 1992. "Pilgrimage and Tourism: Convergence and Divergence." In Alan Morinis, ed., *Sacred Places: The Anthropology of Pilgrimage,* Westport, Conn.: Greenwood Press.

——. 1993. "Open-ended Prostitution as a Skilful Game of Luck: Opportunity, Risk and Security among Tourist-orientated Prostitutes in a Bangkok Soi." In Michael Hitchcock, Victor T. King, and Michael. J. G. Parnwell, eds., *Tourism in Southeast Asia.* London: Routledge.

Cushman, Jennifer W. 1991. *Family and State: The Formation of a Sino-Thai Tin-Mining Dynasty 1797–1932.* Singapore: Oxford University Press.

Davis, Richard H., ed. 1998. *Images, Miracles, and Authority in Asian Religious Traditions.* Boulder, Colo.: Westview Press.

De Bernardi, Jean. 1992. "Space and Time in Chinese Religious Culture." *History of Religions* 31, no. 2: 247–68.

Deutsche Presse-Agentur. 2000. "Mahathir Chides Malaysian Men who Indulge in Unsafe Sex Abroad." *Deutche Presse-Agentur,* 26 May Internet Edition.

Donnan, Hastings, and Thomas M. Wilson. 1994. "An Anthropology of Frontiers." In Hastings Donnan and Thomas M. Wilson, eds., *Border Approaches: Anthropological Perspectives on Frontiers.* Lanham, md: University Press of America.

Dube, Saurabh. 1999. "Traveling Light: Missionary Musings, Colonial Cultures and Anthropological Anxieties." In Raminder Kaur and John Hutnyk, eds., *Travel Worlds: Journeys in Contemporary Cultural Politics.* London: Verso.

Grayburn, Nelson H. H. 1983. *To Pray, Pay and Play: The Cultural Structure of Japanese Tourism.* Aix-en-Provence: Centre des Hautes Etudes Touristiques.

Grundy-Warr, Carl, and K. Perry. 2001. "Tourism in an Inter-state Borderland: The Case of the Indonesian-Singapore Cooperation." In Peggy Teo, T. C. Chang, and K. C. Ho, eds., *Interconnected Worlds: Tourism in Southeast Asia.* Oxford: Pergamon.

Gupta, Akhil, and James Ferguson. 1992. "Beyond 'Culture': Space, Identity and the Politics of Difference." *Cultural Anthropology* 7, no. 1: 63–79.

Hamilton, Annette. 1999. "Kwan Im, Nine Emperor Gods, and Chinese 'Spirit' in Southern Thailand." Paper presented at the 7th International Conference on Thai Studies, Amsterdam, 4–8 July.

Hewison, Kevin. 1985. "Sex Industry in Thailand: an Intimate Exploitation." *Inside Asia* (Nov–Dec): 33–35.

Immigration Bureau, Police Department. 2000a. *International Tourist Arrivals to Thailand by Nationality at Southern Ports of Entry, January–December 2000.* Bangkok: Police Department.

———. 2000b. *International Tourist Arrivals to Thailand by Mode of Transport at Southern Ports of Entry, January–December 2000.* Bangkok: Police Department.

Jackson, Peter. 1999. "Royal Spirits, Chinese Gods, and Magic Monks: Thailand's Boom-time Religions of Prosperity." *South East Asia Research* 7, no. 3: 245–320.

Kalra, Virinder S., and Navtej K. Prewal. 1999. "The Strut of the Peacocks: Partition, Travel and the Indo-Pak Border." In Raminder Kaur and John Hutnyk, eds., *Travel Worlds: Journeys in Contemporary Cultural Politics.* London: Verso.

Lau, Joseph T. F., and J. Thomas. 2001. "Risk Behaviors of Hong Kong Male Residents Traveling to Mainland China: A Potential Bridge Population for HIV Infection." *AIDS Care* 13, no. 1: 71–81.

Lee, Raymond L. M. 1993. "The Globalization of Religious Markets: International Innovations, Malaysian Consumption." *Sojourn* 8, no. 1: 35–61.

Lee, Raymond L. M., and Susan E. Ackerman. 1997. *Sacred Tensions: Modernity and Religious Transformation in Malaysia.* Columbia: University of South Carolina Press.

Lindquist, Johan. 2002. *The Anxieties of Mobility: Development, Migration and Tourism in the Indonesian Borderlands.* Ph.D. dissertation, Stockholm University.

McDougall, Colin. 1956. *Buddhism in Malaya.* Singapore: Donald Moore.

Nagaraj, Shyamala, and Siti Rohani Yahya. 1998. "Prostitution in Malaysia." In Lin Lean Lim, ed., *The Sex Sector: The Economic and Social Bases of Prostitution in Southeast Asia.* Geneva: International Labour Office.

Noi, Quek Pek. 1998. *Religious Suicide: Thought and Ritual in Mahayana Buddhism.* M.A. thesis, National University of Singapore.

O'Connor, Richard. 1986. "Merit and the Market: Thai Symbolizations of Self-Interest." *Journal of the Siam Society* No. 74: 62–82.

Ong, Aihwa. 1998. *Flexible Citizenship: The Cultural Logics of Transnationality.* Durham, NC: Duke University Press.

Ong-at Rungchantharachai. 1990. *Sopheni Khu Lok: Slok Haeng Chiwit Mut* [Eternal Prostitutes: Odyssey of Dark Lives]. Bangkok: Matichon.

Palmer, Martin, and Jay Ramsay. 1995. *Kuan Yin: Myths and Prophesies of the Chinese Goddess of Compassion*. London: Thorsons.

Prawat Wat Khao Roop Chang. 2001. "Prawat Wat Khao Roop Chang" [History of the Temple of the Elephant-shaped Mountain]. Temple brochure, Songkhla Province, Thailand.

Raybeck, Douglas, and Linda.Y. C. Lim, eds. 1983. "Chinese Patterns of Adaptation in Southeast Asia." In L. A. Peter Gosling and LindaY. C. Lim, eds., *The Chinese in Southeast Asia, Vol. 2: Identity, Culture and Politics*. Singapore: Maruzen Asia.

Reader, Ian. 1987. "From Asceticism to the Package Tour: The Pilgrim's Progress in Japan." *Religion* 17 (April): 133–48.

Reichelt, Karl L. 1934. *Truth and Tradition in Chinese Buddhism: A Study of Chinese Mahayana Buddhism*. Shanghai: The Commercial Press.

Reina, Peter. 2000. "$150-Million Statue for India Designed to Last 1,000 Years." *Engineering News Record* 244, no. 13: 20–21.

Sammyboy.com. *The Complete Idiot's Guide to Cheong Hat Yai* Internet Site

Scott, Ken. 1995. "Malaysia's Road, Thailand's Gain." *Bangkok Post*, 7 September.

A Shi'ite Encyclopedia. 1995. Chapter 6A Version 2.0, Internet Edition. Gale Publishing.

Tambiah, Stanley. 1984. *The Buddhist Saints of the Forest and the Cult of Amulets*. Cambridge: Cambridge University Press.

TAT (Tourism Authority of Thailand). 1990. *Thailand Tourism Statistical Report 1990*. Bangkok: Tourism Authority of Thailand.

———. 2000. *Thailand Tourism Statistical Report 2000*. Bangkok: Tourism Authority of Thailand.

Tadao Sakai. 1981. "Some Aspects of Chinese Religious Practices and Customs in Singapore and Malaysia." *Journal of Southeast Asian Studies* 12, no. 1: 133–41.

Theh Chongkhadikij. 1979. "Hat Yai: The Honky-Tonk Town." *Bangkok Post*, 2 September.

Tomasi, Luigi. 2002. "Homo Viator: From Pilgrimage to Religious Tourism via the Journey." In William H. Swatos Jr. and Luigi Tomasi, eds., *From Medieval Pilgrimage to Religious Tourism: The Social and Cultural Economics of Piety*. Westport, Conn.: Praeger.

Turner, Victor. 1973. "The Center Out There: Pilgrim's Goal." *History of Religion* 12, no. 3: 191–230.

Urry, John. 1995. *Consuming Places*. London: Routledge.

Vipasai Niyamabha. 2002. "Southern Goddess." *The Nation*, 20 February.

Vorasakdi Mahatdhanobol. 1998. *Chinese Women in the Thai Sex Trade*. Bangkok: Institute of Asian Studies, Chulalongkorn University.

Wathinee Boonchalaksai and Phillip Guest. 1994. *Prostitution in Thailand*. Nakhon Pathom: Institute for Population and Social Research, Mahidol University.

Wells, Katya. 1973. "Hat Yai: Fast Developing as a Tourist Paradise." *Bangkok Post*, 12 April.

Wyatt, David K., and A. Teeuw. 1970. *Hikayat Patani: The Story of Patani*. The Hague: Martinus Nijhoff.

Yü, Chun-Fang. 1992. "P'u-t'o Shan: Pilgrimage and the Creation of the Chinese Potalaka." In Susan Naquin and Chün-fang Yü, eds., *Pilgrims and Sacred Sites in China*. Berkeley: University of California Press.

Zukin, Sharon. 1991. *Landscapes of Power: From Detroit to Disney World*. Berkeley: University of California Press.

——. 1995. *The Culture of Cities*. Cambridge, Mass: Blackwell.

9

Narrating the Border: Perspectives from the Kelabit Highlands of Borneo

Matthew H. Amster

THIS CHAPTER OFFERS A DISCUSSION of local perceptions of the international border from the perspective of the Kelabit people of Sarawak, Malaysia, on the island of Borneo. My main purpose is to explore the moral geography of the border region and the shifting social, political, economic, and military implications of the border in the everyday life of the Kelabit. I begin with a brief overview of the Kelabit people and outline the changing meanings of the political boundary line in this part of highland Borneo over the last century. The existence of the international boundary in the Kelabit Highlands has had a profound and lasting effect on Kelabit life. Throughout this chapter, I highlight the ways the border has been and continues to be utilized, as well as represented, by differently positioned actors, with Kelabit themselves featuring prominently.[1]

This account is presented largely in chronological order, starting from early accounts of the border by colonial-era government administrators that illustrate the beginning stages of the creation of a local consciousness in terms of awareness of the border and belonging to the state. I go on to show, in detail, the process by which some Kelabit became more deeply connected to the state and nation, a history marked by military campaigns, missionary activity, migration, and economic change. Embedded in this account is a detailed discussion of a text by a Kelabit author (Bala 2002a) that I use as a springboard from which to consider the Malaysian-Indonesian Confrontation in the 1960s and the emergence of a contemporary dependency among Kelabit on seasonal migrant labor and wives imported from across the border with Indonesia. My overarching aim is to highlight the contradictions and complexities of this current relationship between Kelabit and their closely related neigh-

Endnotes for this chapter begin on page 227.

bors from the other side of the border, and to document how the role of border control in the Kelabit Highlands has gone through a number of important shifts over the past century.

The Kelabit Community in Its Contemporary Context

The Kelabit have traditionally been rice farmers who have lived in large multifamily longhouses in the upland areas of the northeastern part of the state of Sarawak, Malaysia. Prior to their conversion to Christianity in the years following World War II, their society was stratified and they recognized a number of distinct classes. Each longhouse was relatively autonomous, marked by a great deal of cooperative labor, and led by a traditional headman. Today, these rural longhouse-based communities are slowly transforming into village-like clusters with increasing individual autonomy (Amster 2000). A steady process of out-migration from the highlands began in the 1960s (Lee and Bahrin 1993), and today approximately three quarters of the total Kelabit population now live in town areas (Amster 1998).

The Kelabit Highlands has the largest remaining rural concentration of Kelabit, with roughly one thousand people scattered among approximately a dozen distinct communities, each with its own headman, in which wet rice agriculture remains the main focus of daily life. The majority of these people are located within a day's walk of Bario, the regional center of commerce and education, home to such government services as a medical clinic, and, most critically, the location of an airstrip. Recently, Bario received Internet and telephone connections, using solar-powered and satellite-based technology as part of an effort to bridge the digital divide in Malaysia.

The Kelabit Highlands is a plateau or tableland region, bordered on both the east and west sides by mountain ranges (Figure 9.1). There are two principle ways people typically travel in and out of the region, the main one being daily flights on 17-seat Dehaviland Twin Otter aircraft operated by Malaysian Airlines System as part of a government-subsidized rural air service. These flights connect the Kelabit Highlands to the coastal towns of Miri and Marudi, where the majority of Kelabit now live. The other main route in and out of the highlands is by foot across the international frontier with Kalimantan, Indonesia along small tracks that traverse an uninhabited jungle and mountain region. There are three main routes currently in use across the border and each involve an arduous, daylong, journey. These paths lead into neighboring, culturally and linguistically related, indigenous communities in Kalimantan, Indonesia. The population of this plateau region on the Indonesian side of this mountain border is estimated at around nine thousand people in roughly forty different villages. The main town and market center on the Kalimantan side of the border is Long Bawan, where there are regular flights to the coastal town of Tarakan, near Samarinda, on the eastern side of the island of Borneo.

Figure 9.1. The border region of the Kelabit Highlands.

Both of these routes—to town areas of Sarawak by air and across the border into Kalimantan on foot—are critical to understanding the local political economy of the Kelabit Highlands. The Kelabit out-migration to towns, and particularly to Miri along the west coast of Sarawak, south of Brunei, has been fueled largely by economic and educational opportunities related to the booming oil industry in Sarawak. Kelabit who have been empowered economically by employment in town often send remittances and other forms of support back to their home communities. Economic advancement in town and the strength of the Malaysian economy in relation to that of Indonesia has also enabled Kelabit to attract migrant labor, as well as wives, from across the border to work in the Kelabit Highlands. If not for the close proximity to the border and the substantial population on the other side, it is unlikely that Bario and the Kelabit Highlands would be the places they are today. As such, the two different routes in and out of the highlands—one linking Kelabit to economic opportunity in town and the other leading to a source of cheap labor—help explain why Bario is a center of commerce today. Both routes in and out of the Kelabit Highlands connect this seemingly remote, "out-of-the way place" (Tsing 1993) to different socioeconomic conditions and economies and underlie the current options and possibilities for individual agency in the lives of these borderland residents.

Before turning to a more detailed discussion of the contemporary context of the Kelabit Highlands, it is valuable to sketch the history of the border in this region and the nature of relationships between Kelabit and their neighbors across the international frontier.

Early Sources on the Kelabit Frontier

There is very little information from which to reconstruct local perceptions of the border prior to World War II. Most of it is found in accounts from Brooke government officials who made occasional journeys into the interior, and these offer superficial views of Kelabit life at the time. A number of these sources, particularly those of Douglas (1908, 1909a, 1909b) and Owen (1913, 1918, 1919) during the early part of the 1900s, explicitly comment on considerable tension and conflict existing between residents of Sarawak, under the control of the Brooke government, and the Dutch-controlled side of the border. While there are reasons to suspect that these accounts may have exaggerated the extent to which these tensions corresponded with the international frontier, they do show that regional conflicts were a source of local concern.

A report by R. S. Douglas, Resident of the Baram, is one of the earliest sources referring specifically to the Kelabit Highlands in relation to the border between Sarawak and what was then Dutch Borneo. Douglas wrote that he "received a letter from the Kalabit chiefs...requesting the Government to build a Fort at Lio Mato" (Douglas 1908: 156), located at the headwaters of the Baram fishery near the border, approximately a five day walk south of Bario and more than a week's journey by boat from the government station at Claudetown (present day Marudi). The fort was to be placed along a key trade route Kelabit used to travel downriver. The ostensible purpose of the fort, from the government's view, was to protect the area's natives from the threat of "raiding," which Douglas described as "prevalent" (1908: 156) at the time, including raiding from across the border with the Dutch territories to the east.

In the final months of 1908, Douglas mounted an expedition into the interior lasting fifty-five days, from which we have one of the earliest descriptions of the Kelabit Highlands.[2] During his journey, Douglas was warned of impending attacks by the people of the Berian, and he made note of the continued hostilities between peoples in the area. In response, he reports gathering together leaders in the region for a peace conference in which he secured their allegiance to the government of Sarawak and extracted the promise that they would cease raiding. In the course of his brief account, Douglas mentions that the people of the Kerayan river, on the Dutch side, "had been attacked by the Government Expedition in 1905" (Douglas 1909a: 30). He then describes how "these people then made peace with the Baram Kayans, Kenyahs, and Kalabits with me, and swore not to break the peace again" (Douglas 1909: 30). Douglas's report seems to suggest that the boundary line established in the Anglo-Dutch treaty of 1891, at least in an approximate sense, corresponded to existing boundaries of hostility between culturally related peoples in the region, who still engaged in or at least feared traditional forms of headhunting and raiding despite government efforts at intervention.

A more detailed account of the border region comes from another Brooke government officer, Donald Owen, who spent a month at the end of 1912 traveling into the interior. Owen began his journey in Lawas—near the coast in the northern part of Sarawak—and traveled up the Trusan Valley into the interior highlands of Dutch-controlled Borneo before circling back into Sarawak in the Kelabit Highlands and returning to the coast along the Baram River.[3] From Owen's account, it is clear that there was substantial tension between people on both sides of the border as well as people in neighboring communities on the Dutch side. As does Douglas, he makes oblique reference to past government expeditions that had destroyed villages in efforts to suppress headhunting.

Owen describes how the so called "Bah Muruts" (the present day Lun Bawang of northeast Sarawak) had called upon him asking permission to attack their neighbors, the Bawan people across the border in Dutch territory. The ostensible purpose of Owen's journey was to investigate and resolve the source of this local conflict. Owen's account details how he helped broker peace between these neighboring peoples as he proceeded into Dutch territory, by easing tensions between the Bah and Bawan people (corresponding to the present-day communities of Ba Kelalan and Long Bawan), and then between both these groups and the Berian, Belawit, and other "people about whom numerous complaints have been made by the Bahs" (Owen 1913: 42). "I was assured they were bitterly hostile to the Government and would certainly resent any attempt on my part to settle matters and really required to be attacked in force. Every argument was used to prevent a meeting, the Bahs—who possessed some 400 guns—wishing to attack the Brians who had none, but finding that I intended to visit the Brian with my party in any case and not allow any attack to be made they eventually took my message which they had up to now refused to do, talking a lot of nonsense about the messenger probably being killed on arrival" (Owen 1913: 42).

Owen goes on to describe how his efforts led to lengthy negotiations between former enemies, among them neighboring communities on the Dutch side of the border. Having brought together various headmen, he describes their holding of rituals that extended "half the night" and included "an exchange of blood between the chief on either side" (1913: 42). "The chiefs assured me that no further ill-feeling now existed and that the Bahs proved it to me by going without escort through the Brian country in which they had never dared set foot before, and which was quite strange to them, though only a day's walk from their own doors" (Owen 1913: 42).

As the expedition continued, Owen's party traveled south through Dutch territory from the Berian into the Kerayan region before crossing back into Sarawak along the Kelabit frontier. A close reading of this account makes it clear that Owen first came upon what he calls "Kelabit" houses while still on the Dutch side of the border. (Only later, during Confrontation in the 1960s, as discussed below, was this community, Pa' Bengar, relocated across the border to the Bario area.) In Sarawak, he arrived at a longhouse on the southern end of the Kelabit Highlands where he found that the headman, "having obtained news of our arrival in the Brian country, had called his men together and had set out fully armed to extricate me, being certain that there would be trouble in the Brian owing to my arrival as it was known that the Brian were an evilly disposed and treacherous tribe" (Owen 1919: 143). He goes on to report that when the men returned, they were "rather disappointed at having been deprived" of a chance to fight their enemies, the Berian (Owen 1919: 144). As this account indicates, while the actual borderline between Sarawak and Dutch territory may not have been locally meaningful in precisely the same way as it was to these government officials, there is already evidence of loyalty to the Brooke regime and an association of Berian enemies with Dutch territory, though there still were Kelabit houses located on the Dutch side of the border.

The Border and World War II

It was not until nearly three decades after Owen's journey that the next detailed account of the border region is available, this from Tom Harrisson's (1959a) famous memoir, *World Within: A Borneo Story*, about the time of World War II. Harrisson arrived by parachute in the Kelabit Highlands on the Plain of Bah, as he called it, in 1944 as part of Allied efforts to challenge the Japanese occupation of Borneo. His account, as well as a lengthy biography of Harrisson (Heimann 1997), documents Harrisson's relationship with the Kelabit during and after the war and includes some insight into the nature of existing hostilities between Kelabit and their neighbors in Dutch territory (Figure 9.2).

Harrisson confirms that people in Bario, a name he coined, feared their neighbors to the east, and that the locally salient borders between the Kelabit and their Berian and Kerayan neighbors essentially matched the line that marked the division between Dutch and Brooke territory. After Harrisson and his men made a base in Bario, people began to arrive from surrounding areas, even from across the border in Dutch territory, to volunteer their services. Harrisson was viewed, and seems to have encouraged himself to be viewed, as a "Rajah" who had come to liberate the island from the Japanese:

> Very soon, people began to come in who had never been here before. Some, in the past, had been at war with the Kelabits. Many held exaggerated or fantastic views of who and what the Kelabit were; thought they would be poisoned, beheaded or swallowed up by long-legged monsters of the uplands. Such people much preferred to come and see me direct and not to go to the long-house until sanctioned by 'the Rajah' [i.e., Harrisson] and accompanied by his men. Included in this group were many of the Bawang people who had been falsely and fiercely treated by a Brooke Punitive Expedition years before. (Harrisson 1959a: 213)

Figure 9.2. Tom Harrisson during World War II, Kelabit Highlands. Photo courtesy of Sarawak Museum.

Harrisson describes how the local Kelabit leadership, with whom he developed close bonds of friendship and mutual respect, strongly "urged that we should not make our base to the east but stay in Sarawak which, through its loyalty to the Brookes, now pledged itself utterly to us" (Harrisson 1959a: 206). Ignoring these local concerns, as well as his commanders' expectation that he avoid occupying Dutch territory, Harrisson crossed the border to investigate what he was told was the easiest route to Brunei and the coast, where the Japanese were concentrated. Harrisson claims that this route, roughly the same one Owen used, "had been closed to the Kelabits for decades past" (1959a: 214). In discussing his negotiations with representatives from both sides of the border, Harrisson explains that their consent was eventually secured "(a)fter a good deal of trouble sorting out temporarily the aged disagreements between Bawang and Bario," which he "insisted must be dropped in the present emergency" (1959a: 216). It is unclear whether Harrisson's representation of the conflict across this border is entirely accurate. First, one can assume that the Kelabit were eager to keep Harrisson's base of operations in their community as a source of prestige and goods which may have colored their effort to protect it. Second, as firsthand accounts of Kelabit elders suggest, movement across this border was probably not as tenuous as Harrisson implies, though past headhunting was certainly a part of local memory at the time.

Harrisson, however, quickly saw that the region across the border made better strategic sense for receiving airdrops and for an airstrip, as the valley was much wider. The Dutch side also had a much larger population from which to recruit fighters to supplement the Kelabit who had already joined him. Harrisson notes that the Long Bawan area of 1945 was far more developed than the Kelabit Highlands, and that the Dutch side had "embryo educational services, crude medical facilities, even iron-wire bridges over rivers and chasms, undreamed of to the west" as well as "a police and native officer depot at Long Bawang" (1959a: 218).

What was perhaps most important to Harrisson, who was eager to be a war hero, was that relocating to the Dutch side offered him his best chance of meeting an anticipated Japanese retreat, once an attack was mounted along the coast near Brunei, up the Trusan Valley. In relocating to the Dutch side of the border, and bringing many Kelabit along with him, Harrisson played a significant role in creating more peaceful contacts and easing tensions between people on both sides of the border, who he noted were "at the fringes of different dialects of the same language" and already shared many cultural features. He also united the Kelabit with their Berian neighbors in a common fight against the Japanese, who were eventually ambushed by Harrisson and his native army as they retreated up the Trusan Valley near the end of the war (Harrisson 1959a).

After the war was over, relationships became much more open between Kelabit and their immediate neighbors to the east. Accounts of Kelabit elders suggest that contact across the border flourished in the postwar era, particularly in terms of religious gatherings and weddings between prominent Kelabit and Lun Berian (Berian People). However, a number of elders I spoke with asserted that such contracts were not entirely uncommon prior to Harrisson's arrival, as headhunting had already ceased to be a major problem long before World War II and alliances were frequently formed between neighboring people in the region. It is thus valuable to remember that Harrison's account may have been biased by the fact that Kelabit leaders did not want him to relocate from Bario.

One Kelabit elder, Edtoh Mengadih, recalls personally visiting the Long Bawan area prior to the war.[4] Now in his eighties, he described how as a youth ("before being married") he traveled to Belawit in Dutch Borneo to attend bible school, initially alone and eventually joined by three other young Kelabit men. These men stayed in Belawit for more than a year, learning to read and write and becoming the first Kelabit Christians. According to Edtoh Mengadih, Christianity had already been accepted by the entire population of the Berian at that time, and he recalled being impressed by how clean it was there—in contrast to the view today, in which Kelabit now consider the Indonesian side unclean, as discussed below. More specifically, he referred to the then new practices being adopted at the instigation of the missionaries, such as moving pigsties out from under longhouses and the discouraging of drinking. He said that when he returned home to Pa' Terap, he told the headman, Tama Bulan, about Christianity but could not convince him or others to convert until after the war.

Consistent with Edtoh Mengadih's story, a memoir by an Australian missionary, C. Hudson Southwell, describes two trips by foot into the Kelabit Highlands. On the first trip, in 1939, Southwell walked into the highlands from the west, staying entirely within Sarawak territory. His second visit, in 1947 after the war, was by way of the less difficult but longer route, walking up the Trusan Valley through Dutch territory. On both visits he stayed at the former Kelabit longhouse of Pa' Terap near the border (Southwell 1999: 190–91).[5] In discussing both journeys, Southwell makes no mention of hostilities between people in the region.[6] The accounts of Southwell and Edtoh Mengadih both offer evidence that Kelabit were in contact with people on the Dutch side of the border prior to the war and offer a considerably different perspective from what one gets out of reading only Harrisson, who implies ongoing hostilities. Indeed, despite Harrisson's efforts to encourage the preservation of traditional rituals and belief, Christian conversion took hold of the Kelabit Highlands after the war, and the airstrip he helped build at Bario facilitated access by missionaries using light aircraft.

After the war, Harrisson remained in Sarawak and went on to become the director of the Sarawak Museum, making a second home at Bario and marrying a Kelabit woman there (whom he eventually divorced). He was responsible for helping the Kelabit in innumerable ways, including establishing the first school in the Kelabit Highlands, at Pa' Mein, for which he brought from across the border a teacher who spoke some English—a man known as Guru Paul who had taught at the Belawit bible school in Dutch Borneo prior to the war (Figure 9.3). The Kelabit and their neighbors to the east became increasingly engaged in a range of cross-border activities and relationships in the postwar era, including common participation in large gatherings, such as Easter celebrations and weddings, which continue to draw people together from both sides of the border each year (Amster 2003). During this period, Harrisson also was instrumental in helping Kelabit migrate to town and acquire education, and is credited with assisting Kelabit in their successful transition to town life. It is understood in the Kelabit community that Harrisson's arrival during the war was a key event in their history, and that his personal interest in the Kelabit people played a pivotal role in transforming this once isolated location into a center of settlement and commerce in the interior of Sarawak.[7]

The Malaysian-Indonesian Confrontation

One of the main themes of Poline Bala's 2002 book, *Changing Borders and Identities in the Kelabit Highlands: Anthropological Reflections on Growing Up in a Kelabit Village Near the International Border,* is how the Malaysian-Indonesian Confrontation of the 1960s was a pivotal event that shaped local attitudes toward the border. The Confrontation (*Konfrontasi*) was an undeclared border war between Indonesia and the newly formed nation of Malaysia

Figure 9.3. Guru Paul (far left) with Kelabit Bamboo Band, Pa' Mein school, circa 1950. Photo courtesy of the Sarawak Museum.

that spanned the years from 1963 to 1966. During Confrontation, British SAS set up a base of operations in Bario and recruited local Kelabit in the war effort, in what must have been locally reminiscent of Tom Harrisson's command during World War II less than twenty years earlier (James and Sheil-Small 1971; Mackie 1974; Shaw 1964). One of the major impacts of Confrontation was that the SAS using helicopters, relocated a number of Kelabit longhouse communities away from the border area and closer in to Bario. This had the effect of concentrating the Kelabit population and creating an uninhabited frontier region between the two nations.

As the preceding sections have shown, Confrontation was neither the first moment in history when Kelabit became aware of this border, nor the only time in recent history when a military campaign played a critical role in reshaping local perceptions of the border. However, as Bala argues, Confrontation represents a critical turning point in local consciousness in relation to attitudes toward the border. Bala's account offers a range of insights on the border, synthesizing Kelabit narratives and her own personal views. She relates the story of her own father's involvement in guarding the border during Confrontation and explains how this was critical in shaping her own and others' perceptions of the international frontier. One of Bala's key points is that local notions of territory and the concept of an "enemy" (*munu'*) shifted during the Confrontation in such a way that "Kelabit were able to name their *munu'* based on a distinctive national identity—the Indonesian—which gave new meaning to their idea of *munu'*" (Bala 2002a: 79). She argues that this shift in thinking took place, first and foremost, among Kelabit border scouts—including her own father—who gained new understandings of the physical boundary as part of their engagement in defending the newly formed nation of Malaysia. For other villagers, she argues the concept of the boundary continued to remain abstract.

During this time, she emphasizes, "Kelabit found themselves in opposition to their relatives in the Berian area, since their relatives were in Indonesian territory" (2002: 79). While conflicts between Kelabit and Berian people were not entirely new, the difference during Confrontation, she contends, is that for the first time conflict was being structured in terms of fixed geography and the space of sovereign nations. Whereas her father experienced the border mainly in terms of military conflict, her own impressions of the border—particularly as she traveled abroad—were linked more to perceptions about the government's ability to require official documents (such as passports, ID card, and border passes).[8]

Using Confrontation as a starting point, Bala (2002a, 2002b) explains how the Kelabit have gradually come to view people from across the border as outsiders rather than relatives (*lun ruyung*). In noting this, she expresses concern over how neighboring Lun Berian have come to be marginalized by the political, economic, and social effects of the international boundary line, in particular how Kelabit have used the inequality of the border to their own advantage. "The boundary," she writes, "was not so much a concrete boundary as it was a mental image with political significance, which largely influenced the way they looked at each other across the border" (2002a: 80). She expresses frustration that "Indonesians," including her own relatives, were stigmatized simply because they came from the side of the border with a weaker national economy, and even admits looking at her "relatives from the Berian area more as Indonesians than as my *lun ruyung*" (Bala 2002a: 95).

The drive to understand this process by which Lun Berian "relatives" (*lun ruyung*) came to be seen as outsiders appears to be a factor motivating Bala to write the social history of the frontier. Through these stories, she not only illustrates how the international border, in her own mind and that of other Kelabit, has become something meaningful where it had not been meaningful in the same way before, but also takes the opportunity to narrate the border from a local perspective, which she does in part by including the texts of traditional Kelabit songs that comment on social change. Her concern is to show how the artificially imposed boundary line became naturalized in local imagination, including her own imagination, and how people began to think of the border in relation to the nation-state and territorial sovereignty during the time of Confrontation. To be sure, Confrontation was not the first time shifts in local consciousness occurred in response to events along the border, as the discussion of Harrisson's activities during World War II shows. However, whereas Harrisson organized people on both sides of the border in a fight against a common enemy, thereby lessening the significance of the border, Confrontation appears to have reversed and revitalized primordial sentiments between people across this frontier.

A Contemporary Perspective of the Frontier in the Highlands

"Life is hard in Indonesia: There are too many people there and not enough jobs. The economy is good here in Malaysia." These are the words of a young Lun Berian woman from Kalimantan, Indonesia, who, when we spoke in 2003, had already been married for eight years to a young Kelabit man. The couple had three young children and were struggling to start their own rice farm while living with relatives in Bario. The woman who came from a vil-lage directly across the border in the Berian, was capable of doing the labori-ous work of wet rice agriculture. Many women from her home village had also married into the same longhouse-based community of her husband's family on the Malaysian side of the border. Most recently, her husband had been doing paid work in Bario, building a house for a cousin, and they hoped to build their own house one day. As with most of the young men in Bario today, the cousin too was married to a woman from the Indonesian side of the border—from the Kerayan, further south across border in Kalimantan.

The cousin and his wife run a small shop in Bario that sells mainly fuel for motorbikes and generators, as well as tinned foods, sugar, and beer. Often, his wife's relatives from Indonesia visit and do work for them. As a shopkeeper in Bario, he primarily makes his living by chartering light aircraft from Miri to bring goods into the highlands, to be resold at a sub-stantial markup. His profits have enabled him to hire labor and buy build-ing materials for a new house, and his workers include both Indonesian and Kelabit men. The customers in his shop too are both local Kelabit and seasonal migrant laborers from across the border—without whose busi-ness his shop would not be successful.

Often when visiting his shop, one meets small groups of men from the Indonesian side who drink beer to relax in the late afternoons. Some come to work in the Kelabit Highlands for weeks or even months at a time; oth-ers have begun to stay longer, to the shopkeeper's dismay. Most buy goods for their return home in Bario, from this and about a dozen other small shops, spending the money they earned while performing some of the most difficult tasks on Kelabit rice farms, such as planting or harvest-ing rice or doing the heavy labor involved in maintaining wet-rice fields. When they return to their homes on the Indonesian side of the border, they load new goods onto their handmade rattan backpacks before mak-ing the day-long trek back across the border.

The preceding paragraphs weave together many threads of life in this frontier, where cross-border connections—to Indonesia as well as to town areas in Malaysia—form an intricate web of social links and interactions that entwine people from different places together into a common political economy. At one and the same time, the Kelabit Highlands are a center and periphery: a place on the fringes of the state, a permeable frontier, and a place that both draws migrants across the border and sends Kelabit away to town areas where they have opportunities as migrants themselves. Because few Kelabit, particularly women, remain in the highlands after their schooling, there is a lack of potential wives in Bario. Berian and Kerayan women who marry Kelabit men increasingly fill this void (Amster 2005a). These marriages, like the labor hired from across the border to maintain Kelabit rice farms, are largely funded by Kelabit urban migrants living in town areas, who often pay substantial bride prices (*purut*) to the families of these brides on the Indonesian side of the border. The strength of the Malaysian economy and the Kelabit urban migrants' success in town allows them to help relatives remaining in the rural highlands to hire workers and attract wives, and thereby continue rice farming and maintain the family farm.

While the Berian and Kerayan regions have provided migrant labor to Kelabit rice farms for many decades, in recent years the extent to which cross-border marriages occur has increased to the point of being the overwhelming norm. These are most often arranged marriages in which the couple has typically met only briefly. While cross-border marriages are not an entirely new phenomenon—indeed, they have a long history in the region—in the last decade their prevalence has reached extreme proportions, with nearly all marriages in the Kelabit Highlands involving Kelabit men and Berian or Kerayan women. These marriages are critical to the reproduction of the rural Kelabit household and ongoing productivity of the family farm, and provide the opportunity for young Kelabit men, many of whom are disappointed with town life, to return to the highlands to start families (Amster and Lindquist 2005). They also place Kelabit in an increasingly awkward position with regard to migrants, as family ties increase with the proliferation of such marriages.

Throughout my fieldwork over the last decade, I noted many examples of the ways in which Berian and other outsiders were treated in ways that marked them as inferior. From small comments by villagers, such as "bring your shoes inside, otherwise they might be stolen by Berian workers," to more deeply institutionalized practices of keeping Indonesia's wages low, such acts have the overall effect of marginalizing and demeaning these people as outsiders. At the same time, the position and stature of women from across the border appears to be improving as their numbers grow. Bala offers insight into her own internalization of negative stereotypes about Berian people relating how jokes about Berian influenced her view of her cousins when they visited from across the border. She also recalls how someone who did something wrong or inappropriate might be chastised with comments like: "How come you are acting like a Lun Berian?" (Bala 2002a: 88). She also mentions impressions formed in her personal crossing the border into Indonesia, where she noted poorer economic conditions ("there were no toilets or bathrooms"), an interesting reversal of Edto Mengadih's comments regarding the late 1930s, when the other side of the border struck him as much cleaner and better organized. Having myself crossed the border on a number of occasions with groups of Kelabit, I can confirm that they often have strong biases about general conditions, and particularly sanitary conditions, on the other side of the border.

During my most recent visit to the Kelabit Highlands in 2003, I heard Kelabit express concerns about controlling the movement of people into the highlands, particularly migrants coming from other parts of Indonesia, including locations as far away as Java and Suluwesi. Noting the gradual influx of such outsiders, some Kelabit sought to find ways to protect their hegemony over local resources. While virtually everyone acknowledges that a lack of close government-sponsored border control is beneficial to the Kelabit economy, there is also anxiety in terms of maintaining a dominant position in these encounters. This problem was manifested in a recent policy adopted at the Bario school, which seeks to impose higher fees on the children whose fathers are not Malaysian. In this way, Kelabit seek to act as gatekeepers, control local resources, and preserve the *status quo* (Amster 2005b).

Similarly, Bala discusses how disputes have emerged over control of local resources such as the use of village land. In such cases, Kelabit wield "their identity as a Malaysian in order to claim their dominance" (Bala 2002a: 103). "As such," she continues, "these local disputes have become a vehicle by which to construct, articulate, and express one's national identity or citizenship in the village" (2002a: 103). One case Bala discusses involved an Indonesian collecting fruit from a tree belonging to an elderly Kelabit man, which resulted in a hearing in the headman's court, where an observer commented (as translated by Bala, who adds the bracketed clarifications): "You are Indonesians that came to stay with us here in Malaysia. Because of that, you need to behave yourselves while here [they can't afford to break any of the rules and regulations, otherwise they will be in trouble with the state]. If you cannot abide by our *adet* [customary law] in this place, you may return to Indonesia. We do not want you to create problems in our country" (2002: 103).

From this we see that "Indonesian" laborers have increasingly become subject to an emotional distancing and subordination that counters a potentially alternative view of them as relatives. In large part, this is a function of economic differences. While such threats by Kelabit against outsiders may not, in fact, be an effective means of controlling their movement into the highlands, they nonetheless reflect locally dominant views that seek to assert superiority by virtue of being Malaysian, a point that is not without its contradictions. As Bala writes: "Although we are linked by cultural and historical connections and economic interdependence, more often than not, we treat the "other" differently from ourselves. I suggest this to be a result of ignorance, especially ignorance of history, whereby many fail to recognize that great-grandparents or grandparents or even parents of today's Kelabit migrated many years ago from the other side of the border to settle in the Bario area" (2002a: 107–8).

Thus, while many Kelabit will comment that without the help of Berian "our farms would be laid to waste" (Bala 2002a: 52) or without Indonesian women "our longhouses would die," as one urban Kelabit told me, this dependency does not typically translate into mutual respect.

Finally, I wish to emphasize that the current conditions of the Kelabit frontier are not static. Over time, we can expect that Berian and other Indonesian women who marry into Kelabit families will *themselves* become prominent voices in these communities. As these women, and their children, come to represent the mature face of the Kelabit community, they will likely become increasingly influential in shaping local perceptions on the border.

The State's Gone Fishing

Institutions of the state are obviously present in the Kelabit Highlands, yet, there is a clear sense that the state is seen as not interfering in local affairs regarding the border. Indeed, as pointed out above, the state is often evoked by Kelabit as a means to threaten and intimidate outsiders, to keep them in their place. With that in mind, it is worthwhile to briefly consider the role of immigration in the Kelabit Highlands and attitudes toward the state more generally.

On a number of occasions during my fieldwork in the mid–1990s when I went to look for the immigration officer stationed in Bario, I was told that he had "gone fishing" with some of the local men. This image of the lone immigration officer, the only representative of the state specifically responsible for guarding the border, having gone fishing with local men, seemed to poetically capture the relationship between Kelabit and the state—at least, their relationship to the state as agents responsible for border control. While the existence of an immigration office—the only one of its kind in the region—indicates a formal state presence, it seems to be a very casual presence. Indeed, Bario is only one of eight official overland exit/entry points in Sarawak where regional trade is permitted, though it is widely understood that the entire frontier is easily traversed (Asia Foundation 2001).

During a visit to Bario in July of 2003, I again sought out the immigration officer on duty, this time one of two men stationed in Bario. The officer I met was a young Malay man who told me about the challenges of this remote posting. Sitting on the floor of the small kitchen behind his office drinking hot Milo as his wife looked after their two small children, he noted that his diesel-powered generator was out of order and expressed frustration at being posted to Bario. As an outsider with a family, he felt isolated, particularly because he could not speak the local language and, being Muslim, did not share the local religion (evangelical Christianity). I asked him about the situation with regard to migrant workers in the area, and he spoke of the difficulty of keeping track of Indonesian workers and the futility of his job. When I asked him to estimate the percentage of Indonesian migrant workers who reported to him, he ventured a guess that perhaps 90 percent of those who arrived in the Kelabit Highlands did *not* register at his office as required. He went on to explain that his task was mainly to inform longhouse headmen about the importance of sending workers to register with him and to obtain the official border passes that, under an agreement between Malaysia and Indonesia, are available to residents of the border region, though most local residents are largely ignorant about them.

The officer did not seem optimistic that the situation would change and, making light of the regular flow of Indonesians into the highlands, he pointed out that "unless people make trouble we [i.e., Immigration] do not worry about it." I asked if any Indonesians had ever made trouble and he answered: "No, so far this has not happened." From this it is apparent that the immigration office does not play a significant role in controlling the movement of people on the Kelabit frontier, nor could it easily do so, given the rugged geography of the border region. Thus, the role of Immigration remains minimal, while a seemingly "subversive economy" of the border zone flourishes (Donnan and Wilson 1999: 105). Of course, the state is active in other aspects of life in the Kelabit Highlands, and in ways that are locally viewed as beneficial, such as maintaining the schools, clinic, airport, airborne doctor service, and staffing government departments that deal with water management, aviation, forestry and agriculture, to list only the obvious. In addition, there is a small army base located in Bario, though the military tends to keep out of local affairs.

Finally, it is worth mentioning that the government is viewed as a source of funds for virtually all forms of development, including the recent installation of Internet and phone service in Bario. Such development-oriented projects are seen as a benefit of being part of the state and locally are perceived as positive aspects of incorporation into the broader processes of development that characterize life in Malaysia (as opposed to Indonesia—marked, at least recently, by economic turmoil and political problems). As such, from the Kelabit perspective, there are many visible connections to the Malaysian nation and Sarawak government and, overall, a positive understanding of this relationship to the nation and state, viewed as a source of revenue for projects and a resource for improving local infrastructure. Without the state and its funding, there would be no airstrip, schools, or clinic in the Kelabit Highlands, and people are aware of the fact that the way is open for them for them to turn to the government for help with community concerns, even if such undertakings (such as a recently failed multimillion dollar hydroelectric dam) do not always succeed.[9]

Conclusion

Life in the Kelabit Highlands has been, and continues to be, tied to being located along a political frontier. In sketching the role of the border in Kelabit life, I have sought to bring Kelabit perspectives to the forefront of my discussion, showing how current views are rooted in a history that has been marked by a number of key shifts with regard to perceptions of the border and the people on the other side of it. As this chapter shows, the border today is in many ways used as an important and empowering social construction that permeates Kelabit life, not only allowing the reproduction of the Kelabit household, family, and rice farm but also turning Kelabit themselves into de facto agents of the state who guard the borders of belonging in their communities. As borderland residents, Kelabit actively use the conditions of this highly interdependent form of permeable frontier to their advantage (Martinez 1994). In doing this, Kelabit also conceive of migrant laborers in negative terms, using the frontier as a "line of exclusion" (Anderson 1996: 189), even as they depend on cross-border labor and engage extensively in cross-border marriages. All of these practices point to a kind of agency in which there is an "uncanny displacement of the rhetoric of state rule" in local practices (Tsing 1994: 280). While the existence of agents of the state, such as the Immigration department and army base at Bario, can be seen as protecting the Kelabit Highlands from outside encroachment, in fact, the border remains porous along the frontier and this is greatly advantageous to the Kelabit.

In understanding the wider sociopolitical and economic context of this particular borderland, we must take into account the emergence, from the 1960s onward, of increased Kelabit mobility and connections across a range of different spaces away from the border area. It is this movement away from the borderland region that makes possible, and even necessary, the importation of labor and wives that characterize the current situation of life in this borderland region. Remittances from town-dwelling Kelabit constitute a major means of support for the local economy in the highlands, and much of this money is used to hire Indonesian workers and fund the demands for bride price payments for cross-border marriages. The economies of Kelabit households in town are thereby linked to those of the highlands and, further still, can be seen as extending their influence across the border into Indonesia.

As a peripheral area in relation to centers of state power, the Kelabit Highlands represents a unique kind of zone of sovereignty (Ong 1999) where links to an economically powerful state serve to bolster local forms of agency and control. "In this view," as Donnan and Wilson write, "borders are conduits to the core of the nation, but also provide alternatives to the practices and discourses of the nation" (2003: 19). Thus, it is not just resources from town that empower rural Kelabit to attract and fund the movement of Indonesians into the Kelabit Highlands, but also the implicit power of the state and the more explicit power of the market that allow them to assert their dominance in the local affairs of the border zone.

However, this chapter shows, the relationship between Kelabit and their neighbors in the borderlands has gone through many phases. Although historical documentation of local perceptions of the border is somewhat limited, I have been able to trace here a series of transformations that show the genesis of current conditions of life in the border zone today. As this essay illustrates, prior to World War II the Kelabit side of the frontier was far less developed and less controlled by governmental authorities than the Dutch side. If not for the war and subsequent events, the Kelabit Highlands could well have become a peripheral area to the more densely populated region on the other side of the border. But in fact, World War II set a very different trajectory in motion, one that has placed Bario firmly on the map of Malaysia.

Harrisson's impact, however, was just the beginning. After the war, increased contact and conversion to Christianity made cross-border links increasingly common in the border region, but with Confrontation allies once again became enemies. As Bala (2002a) argues, Confrontation helped to crystallize local understandings of belonging to the Malaysian state, just as the time of World War II had helped to solidify loyalty to the then still independent state of Sarawak. It is only in the post–Confrontation era that economic advantages of life on the Malaysian side of the border have set the stage for contemporary relationships—often based, as Bala's work shows, on inequality and distrust. This current state of affairs is strangely reminiscent of where things began in the first Western visitors' accounts during the time of headhunting at the turn of the twentieth century.

Recent work in anthropology has suggested that we begin to think about states in different ways. In particular, anthropologists have begun to focus on ways that local practices embody different languages of "stateness" and forms of "governmentality" that emerge from, and articulate, local forms of agency (Perry and Maurer 2003; Trouillot 2001; Das and Poole 2004; Hansen and Stepputat 2001). Increasingly, we are coming to envision the state as something historically fluid that is constantly being co-constructed in the interplay of exogenous and local concerns (Das and Poole 2004: 9). Border areas, particularly, are obvious locations where special opportunities for local agency can arise. Rather than being seen simply as locations for restricting movement and defining the boundaries of nations, borders can generate unique economies that themselves "became incentives for additional mobility" (Lentz 2003: 285), as has certainly come to be the case in the Kelabit Highlands. Finally, the perspective from the borderlands explored here shows how shifting notions of equality and inequality, concern about local resources, gendered dimensions of power, and local mechanisms of border control are intimately intertwined in the history and present of the border zone.

Notes

1. The research upon which this paper is based was made possible, in part, by a faculty development grant from Gettysburg College, which funded my fieldwork during the summer of 2003. I am also grateful to Alexander Horstmann for organizing a Southeast Asian borders session at the Third International Convention of Asia Scholar, held in Singapore from 19 to 22 August 2003, during which I presented a somewhat different version of this work. I am also grateful to the Sarawak State Government, including the State Planning Unit, the *Majlis Adat Istiadat*, and the Sarawak Museum, for their on-going support of my research. Most importantly, I wish to thank Poline Bala and her family for their gracious hospitality and friendship in Sarawak, Michael Giak, Jerome Giak, Sina Kuta, and the rest of my adoptive Kelabit family, Tama and Sina Raben, my friend Esther Bala, and so many other Kelabit who endured my endless questions. This paper has also benefited from numerous conversations with Johan Lindquist.

2. Douglas referred to this area as a "central plain, which comprises the Bah and Mein country" (1909: 29), indicating the area now known as Bario and the former settlement of Pa' Mein (now abandoned) just to the south. Bario was then called *Lem Bah* by the local people—a name that is still sometimes used. The name Pa' Mein refers to the salt springs located there as the word mein means "sweet" in Kelabit. The entire community of Pa' Mein was relocated to Bario during the time of the Indonesian Confrontation, as discussed in the next section. Douglas notes extensive irrigated rice cultivation in the vicinity of present-day Bario and intensive salt production at Pa' Mein. The Kelabit used their salt in regional trade, and "Kalabit salt" was relied upon by down-river people who used it to supplement their diet (Douglas 1909b: 227–28).

3. This journey was first chronicled in a brief account published in 1913 in the *Sarawak Gazette* (Owen 1913) and was subsequently described in greater detail in a five-part series in the same publication (Owen 1919).

4. I interviewed Edtoh Mengadih (formerly known as Galih Balang) on many occasions between 1993 and 1995 in the Kelabit Highlands and again in 2003 in Kuching. Edtoh Mengadih who was also one of Bala's (2002a) main informants, is generally considered one of the more knowledgeable Kelabit elders.

5. The community of Pa' Terap was abandoned in 1958 when the residents made the decision to move to other communities closer to Bario, mainly the present-day longhouse-based communities of Pa' Ukat, Pa' Umor, and Pa' Lungan.

6. With regard to the purpose of the first trip—the first time a missionary entered the Kelabit Highlands—Southwell explains that it was motivated by having "heard rumours that some Kelabits in the central highlands were wanting to become Christians" (Southwell 1999: 97). Ultimately, he reports that this turned out to be false and he had little success in gaining converts on that journey. This first visit by Southwell was likely around the same time that Edto Mengadih was away in Belawit studying in the Bible school. Regarding Southwell's second visit in 1947 after the war, he describes his frustration with Tom Harrisson, who he claims encouraged the local people to hold onto their rituals, particularly those involving the drinking of large quantities of rice beer (*borak*). His main concern were the people on the Dutch side of the border, who Southwell claimed, had already fully converted and given up drinking prior to the war, unlike the Kelabit who had yet to give up drinking rice beer. He also claims in this memoir that after his first visit, in 1939, the headman of Pa' Terap, Tama Bulan, actually decided to convert and in 1943

"sent messengers to [Pastor] Aris Doemat in Belawit [Dutch Borneo], inviting Aris and others to come teach them" (Southwell 1999: 190).

7. There are surprisingly few accounts of life in the Kelabit Highlands from the 1950s. Of those that exist, such as a journey by Arnold (1959: 179–200), no mention is made of the nature of cross-border relationships. Much of Harrisson's work during this period was concerned with documenting various aspects of traditional Kelabit culture, mostly in articles in the *Sarawak Gazette* (Harrisson 1946–47, 1947, 1948, 1949, 1954, 1958, 1959b, 1960).

8. Poline Bala grew up in the Kelabit Highlands in the longhouse of Pa' Umor and attended school in Bario. As a schoolgirl in the early 1980s, she was selected to travel to England as part of a project for a Yorkshire television series made in association with UNICEF. This project brought together six children from six different ecosystems in far-ranging parts of the world for a TV show and book called *Two-Way Ticket* (Hobson 1982). The series and book feature young "Pauline" (Poline) as a representative of the rainforest. Since that prophetic first journey, she went on to study anthropology at the University of Malaysia, and later, Asian Studies at Cornell University (where she received her MA). In 2002, she published her book on the border, a revision of the Masters thesis from Cornell (Bala 2002a, 2002b), while working as a lecturer at UNIMAS (University of Malaysia, Sarawak). Most recently, Poline entered the Ph.D. program in Social Anthropology at Cambridge University in the fall of 2003.

9. Most government-sponsored projects are viewed positively, but this is not always the case as there has been a great deal of disagreement and controversy in the Kelabit community as to whether it is a good or bad idea to encourage the government to build a road into the Kelabit Highlands. Among the people's main reservations, is the possibility that a road would open up the highlands to non-Kelabit in-migrants, including Indonesians, something that many people fear would lead to erosion of Kelabit control of local resources.

References

Amster, Matthew H. 1998. *Community, Ethnicity, and Modes of Association among the Kelabit of Sarawak, East Malaysia*. Ph.D. dissertation, Brandeis University.

——. 2000. "It Takes a Village to Dismantle a Longhouse." *Thresholds* 20, 65–71.

——. 2003. "New Sacred Lands: The Making of a Christian Prayer Mountain in Highland Borneo." In R. Lukens-Bull, ed., *Sacred Places and Modern Landscapes: Sacred Geography and Social-Religious Transformations in South and Southeast Asia*. Tempe: Arizona State University, Program for Southeast Asian Studies, Monograph Series Press.

——. 2005a. "Cross-Border Marriage in the Kelabit Highlands of Borneo." Anthropoligcal Forum 15, no. 2: 131–150.

——. 2005b."The Rhetoric of the State: Dependency and Control in a Malaysian-Indonesian Borderland." Identities: Global Studies in Culture and Power 12, no. 1: 23–434.

Amster, Matthew H., and Johan Lindquist. 2005. "Frontiers, Sovereignty, and Marital Tactics: Comparisons from the Borneo Highlands and the Indonesia-Malaysia-Singapore Growth Triangle." *The Asia Pacific Journal of Anthropology* 6, no. 1, forthcoming.

Anderson, Malcolm. 1996. *Frontiers: Territory and State Formation in the Modern World.* Cambridge: Polity Press.

Arnold, Guy. 1959. *Longhouse and Jungle: An Expedition to Sarawak.* Singapore: Donald Moore Press.

Asia Foundation. 2001. *Study on the Economic Linkages between Sarawak and West Kalimantan.* Kuching, Sarawak and Jakarta, Indonesia: Sarawak Development Institute and Center for Agricultural Policy Study.

Bala, Poline. 2002a. *Changing Borders and Identities in the Kelabit Highlands: Anthropological Reflections on Growing Up in a Kelabit Village Near the International Border.* Dayak Studies Contemporary Society Series 1. Kota Samarahan, Sarawak: Institute for East Asian Studies, Universiti Malaysia Sarawak.

———. 2002b. "Interethnic Ties Along the Kalimantan-Sarawak Border: The Kelabit and Lun Berian in the Kelabit-Kerayan Highlands." *Borneo Research Bulletin* 32: 103–11.

Das, Veena, and Deborah Poole. 2004. "State and its Margins: Comparative Ethnographies." In V. Das and D. Poole, eds., *Anthropology and the Margins of the State.* Santa Fe: School of American Research Press.

Donnan, Hastings, and Thomas M. Wilson. 2003. "Territoriality, Anthropology, and the Intersital: Subversion and Support in European Borderlands." *Focaal: European Journal of Anthropology* 41: 9–20.

Douglas, R. S. 1908. "Proposed Fort at Lio Mato." *Sarawak Gazette* 38, 156.

———. 1909a "Visit to the Kalabits of Ulu Baram." *Sarawak Gazette* 39, no. 525: 29–30.

———. 1909b. "The 'Pun Mein' or Salt Springs of the Upper Baram." *Sarawak Gazette* 39, no. 527: 52–32.

Harrisson, Tom. 1946–47. "The Kelabit Peoples of Upland Borneo." *Sarawak Gazette* [in six parts] 72, nos. 1062: 6–7, 1063: 21–22, 1064: 39–40, 1065: 56, 1066: 11–12, 1067: 28–29.

———. 1947. "A Postscipt: Two Views of Kelabits." *Sarawak Gazette* 73, no. 1068: 42–43.

———. 1948. "A Trip to the Uplands." *Sarawak Gazette* 74, no. 1086: 170–71.

———. 1949. "The Upland Plateau." *Sarawak Gazette* 75, no. 1097: 190–93.

———. 1954. "Some Notes on the Uplands of Central Borneo." *Sarawak Gazette* 80, no. 1161: 234–36.

———. 1958. "The Peoples of Sarawak, VII and VIII: 'The Kelabits and Muruts.'" *Sarawak Gazette* 84, 187–91.

———. 1959a. *World Within: A Borneo Story.* London: The Cresset Press.

———. 1959b. "An Inward Journey." *Sarawak Gazette* 85, no. 1221: 267–69.

——. 1960. "A Kelabit Diary" [in four parts]. *Sarawak Gazette* 86, nos. 1223: 5–7, 1224: 19–21, 1225: 44–45, 1226: 66–71.

Hansen, Thomas Blom, and Finn Stepputat. 2001. "Introduction: States of Imagination." In Thomas Blom Hansen and Finn Stepputat, eds., *States of Imagination: Ethnographic Explorations of the Postcolonial State.* Durham: Duke University Press.

Heimann, Judith M. 1997. *The Most Offending Soul Alive: Tom Harrisson and His Remarkable Life.* Honolulu: University of Hawaii Press.

Hobson, Sarah. 1982. *Two-Way Ticket.* London: Macdonald.

James, Harold, and Denis Sheil-Small. 1971. *The Undeclared War: The Story of the Indonesian Confrontation 1962–1966.* London: Leo Cooper.

Lee, Boon Thong, and Tengku Shamsul Bahrin. 1993. "The Bario Exodus: A Conception of Sarawak Urbanisation." *Borneo Review* 4, no. 2: 113–28.

Lentz, Carola. 2003. "'This is Ghanaian Territory!': Land Conflicts on a West African Border," *American Ethnologist* 30, no. 2: 273–89.

Mackie, James A. C. 1974. *Konfrontasi: The Indonesia-Malaysia Dispute 1963–1966.* New York: Oxford University Press.

Martinez, O. J. 1994. *Border People: Life and Society in the U.S.-Mexico Borderlands.* Tucson: University of Arizona Press.

Ong, Aihwa. 1999. *Flexible Citizenship: The Cultural Logics of Transnationality.* Durham: Duke University Press.

Owen, Donald Adrian. 1913. "Report on Visit to Head Waters of Trusan River." *Sarawak Gazette* 43, no. 622: 42–43.

——. 1918. "The Muruts of the Bah Country (Central Borneo)." *Sarawak Gazette* 48, no. 746: 127–28.

——. 1919. "A Visit to Unknown Borneo" [in five parts]. *Sarawak Gazette* 49, nos. 766: 78–79, 767: 89–90, 768: 106–18; 769: 121–23; 770: 141–45.

Perry, Richard Warren, and Bill Maurer. 2003. "Globalization and Governmentality: An Introduction." In Richard Warren Perry and Bill Maurer, eds., *Globalization Under Construction: Governmentality, Law, and Identity.* Minneapolis: University of Minnesota Press.

Shaw, Lt. N. E. 1964. "Confrontation: A Green Jacket among the Kelabits." *Sarawak Gazette* 90, no. 1282: 317–21.

Southwell, C. Hudson. 1999. *Uncharted Waters.* Calgary: Astana Press.

Trouillot, Michel-Rolph. 2001. "The Anthropology of the State: Close Encounters of a Deceptive Kind." *Current Anthropology* 42, no. 1: 125–38.

Tsing, Anna Lowenhaupt. 1993. *In the Realm of the Diamond Queen: Marginality in an Out-of-the-Way Place.* Princeton: Princeton University Press.

——. 1994. "From the Margins." *Cultural Anthropology* 9, no. 3: 279–97.

NOTES ON CONTRIBUTORS

Matthew H. Amster is Assistant Professor of Anthropology in the Department of Sociology and Anthropology at Gettysburg College in Pennsylvania. He completed his Ph.D. at Brandeis University in 1998. His work focuses on changing ethnic identity among Kelabit and cross-border movements along the international frontier in Borneo. His recent articles have appeared in *The Asia Pacific Journal of Anthropology, Asian Anthropology, Anthropological Forum,* and *Identities: Global Studies in Culture and Power.*

Marc Askew is Associate Professor in the School of Social Sciences, Victoria University of Technology, Melbourne, Australia. His research focuses on mainland Southeast Asia, particularly Thailand, and encompasses the ethnographic study of urbanism, border spaces, the state and cultural representations, and, more recently, the cultural structuring of political identities. His most recent publications include *Bangkok: Place, Practice and Representation* (Routledge 2002) and articles and chapters on Lao urbanism, pilgrimage, and prostitution in South Thailand. He is currently engaged in research on political culture in South Thailand.

Cynthia Chou, an anthropologist, is Associate Professor of Southeast Asian Studies at the University of Copenhagen. She is author of *Indonesian Sea Nomads: Money, Magic and Fear of the Orang Suku Laut* (RoutledgeCurzon 2003) and has also co-edited the volumes, *Tribal Communities in the Malay World: Historical, Cultural and Social Perspectives* (ISEAS 2002) and "Riau in Transition" (*Bijdragen tot de Taal-, Land- en Volkenkunde 1997*).

William Cummings is an ethnographic historian who teaches at the University of South Florida. His specialty is early modern South Sulawesi. He is the author of *Making Blood White: Historical Transformations in Early Modern Makassar* (University of Hawaii Press, 2002), which won the 2004 Harry J. Benda Prize sponsored by the Association for Asian Studies, as well as numerous articles on the historical anthropology of Makassar.

Sara (Meg) Davis is a researcher in the Asia Divison at Human Rights Watch and a visiting scholar at Columbia University's Weatherhead East Asian Institute. Her work at Human Rights Watch has focused on HIV/AIDS, housing rights, the Internet, and the labor movement. Davis received her Ph.D. from the University of Pennsylvania in 1999. She has taught and held postdoctoral fellowships at University of Pennsylvania, Yale University, and UCLA. Davis' book on trans-border ethnic and religious revival, *Song and Silence: Ethnic Revival on China's Southwest Borders,* (Columbia University Press, 2005). Her written work has appeared in scholarly journals and newspapers, including *The International Herald Tribune, Modern China,* and *The Wall Street Journal.*

Alexander Horstmann is a social anthropologist who teaches at the Westphalian Wilhelms-University of Münster. He received his Ph.D. from the University of Bielefeld in 2000. His research concerns religion and political conflict, borderlands, and identity politics in Southern Thailand. He is author of *Class, Culture and Space: The Construction and Shaping of Communal Space in South Thailand* (Research Institute for Languages and Cultures of Asia and Africa, ILCAA, Tokyo 2002). He is currently working on a monograph on the cultural history of Buddhist-Muslim coexistence in South Thailand.

Niti Pawakapan completed his Ph.D. in Anthropology at The Australian National University and is Assistant Professor of Sociology and Anthropology, Chulalongkorn University. He has published in both English and Thai, and is completing a book manuscript on local traders and economic and cultural changes in northwestern Thailand. His new research focuses on the Burmese migrants working in the Thai fishing industry.

Guido Sprenger has studied social anthropology in Münster, Germany, and Leiden, the Netherlands, and received his Ph.D. from Münster. Among his publications are "Erotik und Kultur in Melanesien" (Erotics and Culture in Melanesia, Münster and Hamburg 1997) and "Die Männer, die den Geldbaum fällten: Konzepte von Austausch und Gesellschaft bei den Rmeet von Takheung, Laos" (The Men who cut the money tree: Concepts of exchange and society among the Rmeet of Takheung, Laos, Berlin 2005). He is currently a postdoctoral Fellow at the Institute of Ethnology, Academia Sinica, Taipei.

Riwanto Tirtosudarmo is Senior Research Associate at the Research Center for Society and Culture, Indonesian Institute of Sciences, Jakarta. Among his many publication are "Economic Development, Migration and Ethnic Conflict in Indonesia: A Preliminary Observation" (Sojourn 1997), "Population Mobility and Social Conflict: The Aftermath of Economic Crisis in Indonesia" (in *A National Project That Failed,* 2002), and "Demography and Conflict: The Failure of Indonesia's Nation-building Project?" (in Conflict in Asia-Pacific, 2004).

Reed L. Wadley is Assistant Professor of Anthropology, University of Missouri-Columbia. His research includes borderlands, warfare, colonialism, natural resource management, and historical ecology, involving Iban communities of West Kalimantan, Indonesia. He is editor of *Histories of the Borneo Environment: Economic, Political and Social Dimensions of Change and Continuity* (KITLV Press, Leiden 2005).

INDEX